YOU &
A BIKE &
A ROAD

ELEANOR DAVIS

KOYAMA PRESS

THANK YOU SO MUCH TO
THE INCOMPARABLE ANNIE KOYAMA
& ALL THE WONDERFUL FOLKS
AT KOYAMA PRESS

PUBLISHED BY
KOYAMA PRESS
KOYAMAPRESS.COM

FIRST EDITION: MAY 2017

ISBN: 978-1-927668-40-5

PRINTED IN CHINA

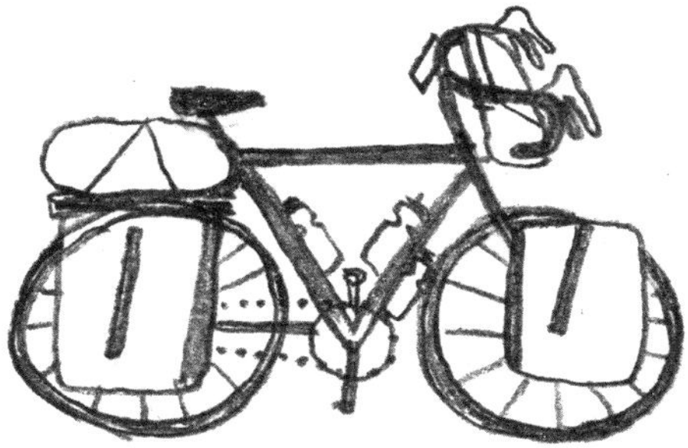

San Rafael Public Library
1100 E. Street
San Rafael, CA 94901

3.16

DAY 1 WEDNESDAY [redacted] MARCH 16TH
TUCSON TO BENSON - 54 MILES

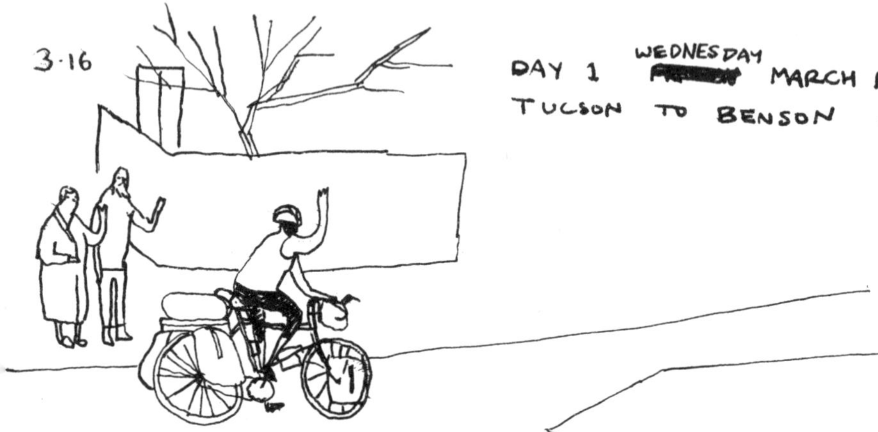

GOODBYE AT 8

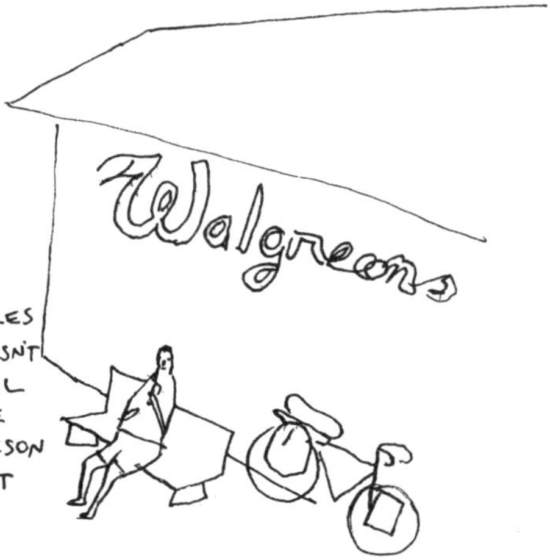
Walgreens

LUNCH AFTER 20 MILES & IT DOESN'T EVEN FEEL LIKE I'VE LEFT TUCSON YET

PLANNING [redacted] ROUTES LAST NIGHT:

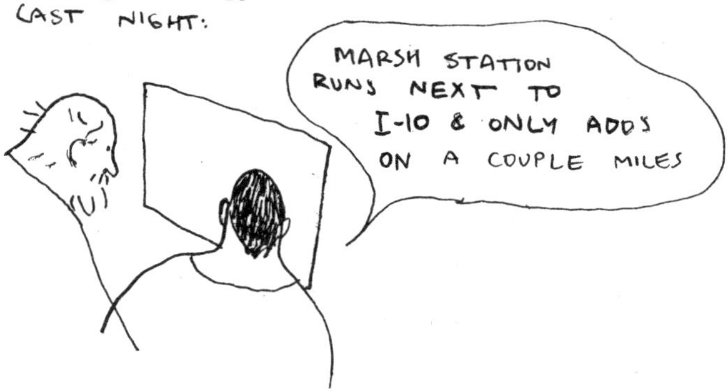
MARSH STATION RUNS NEXT TO I-10 & ONLY ADDS ON A COUPLE MILES

ON THE MAP, MARSHSTATION LOOKS LIKE THIS:

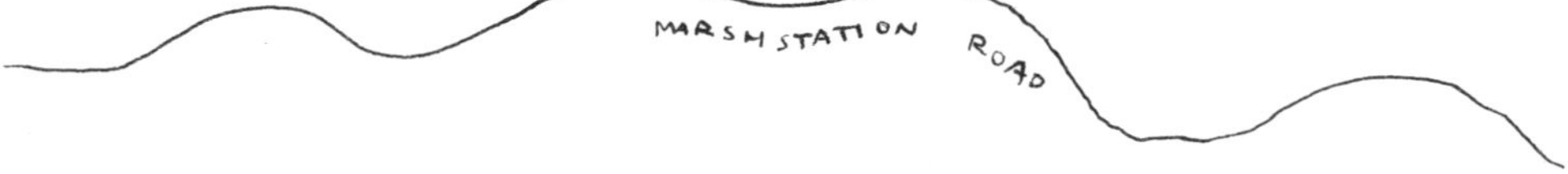
MARSHSTATION ROAD

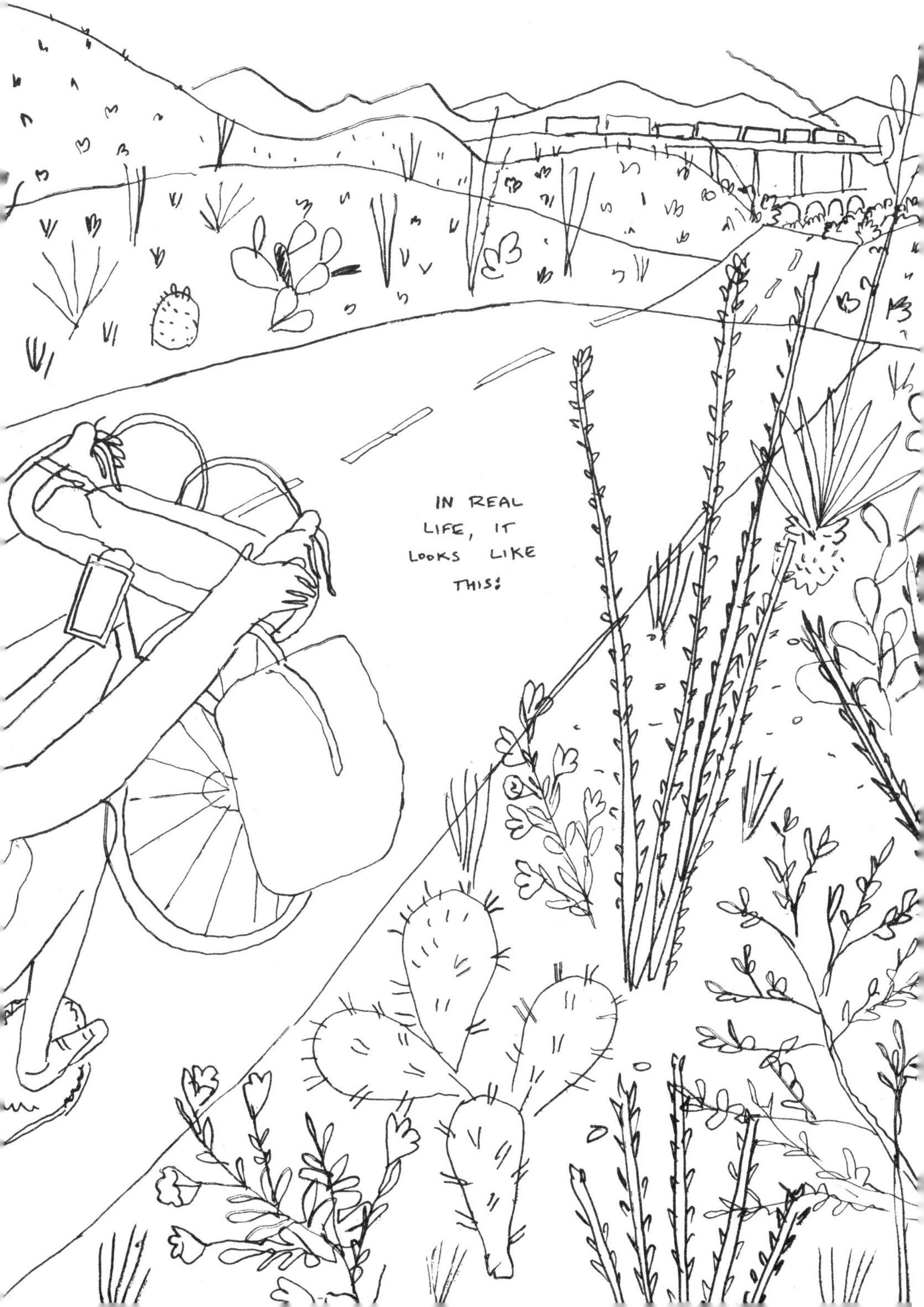
IN REAL
LIFE, IT
LOOKS LIKE
THIS:

DAY 2 THURS 3/17

BENSON TO SAN PEDRO BLM OUTSIDE SIERRA VISTA - 44 MILES

I PASSED ANOTHER PERSON BIKE TOURING GOING THE OPPOSITE DIRECTION FROM ME

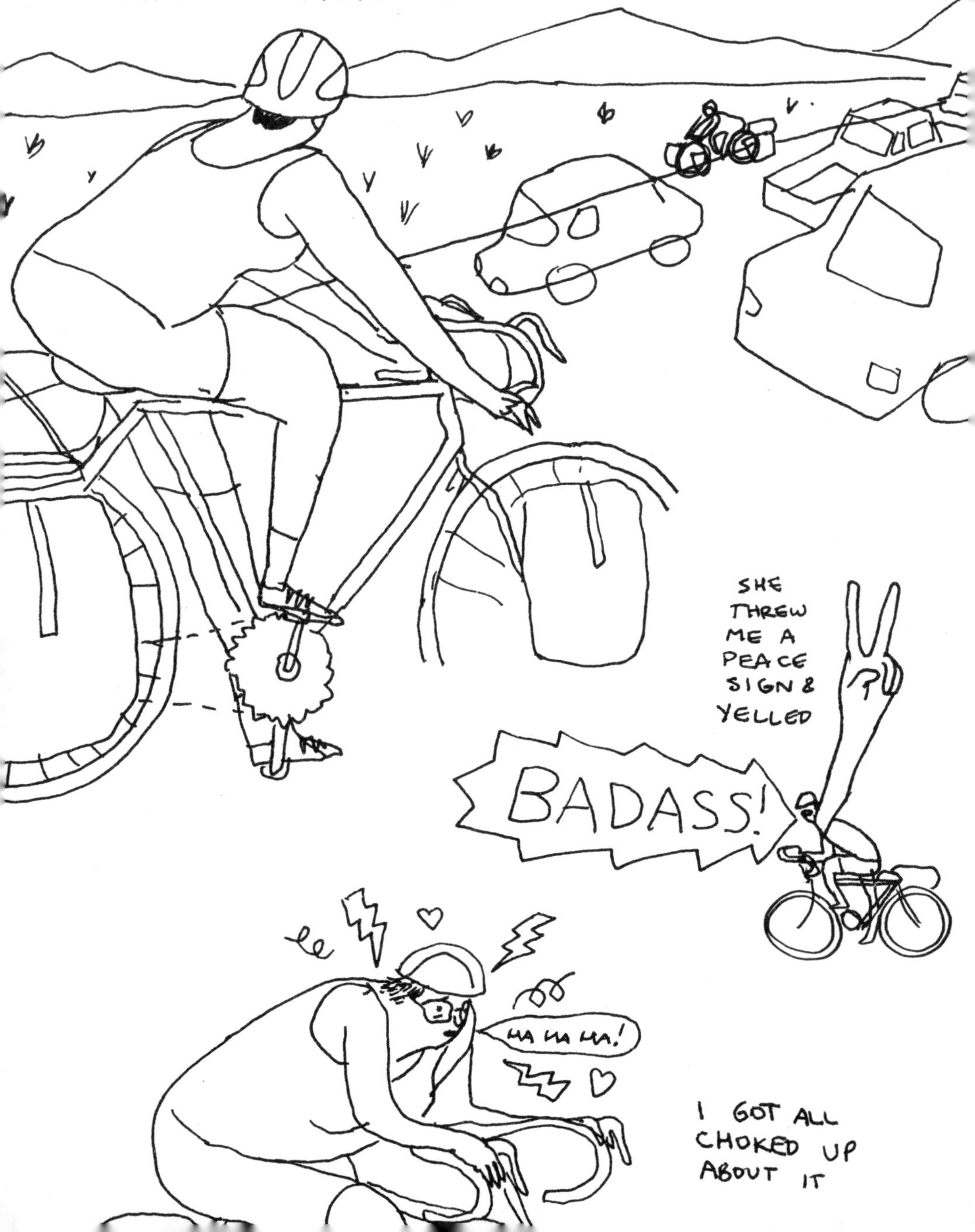
SHE THREW ME A PEACE SIGN & YELLED
BADASS!
HA HA HA!
I GOT ALL CHOKED UP ABOUT IT

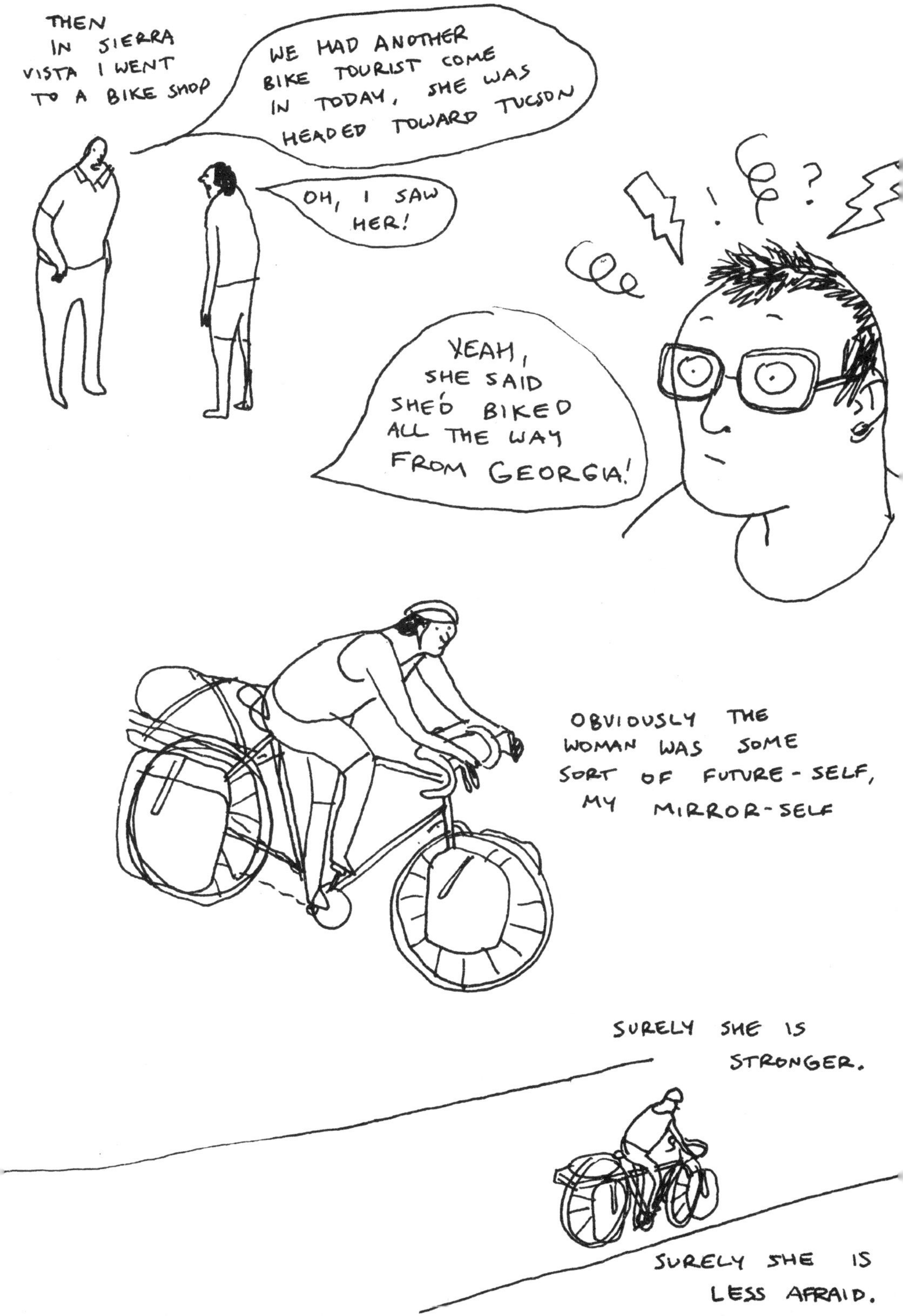
THEN IN SIERRA VISTA I WENT TO A BIKE SHOP
WE HAD ANOTHER BIKE TOURIST COME IN TODAY, SHE WAS HEADED TOWARD TUCSON
OH, I SAW HER!
YEAH, SHE SAID SHE'D BIKED ALL THE WAY FROM GEORGIA!
OBVIOUSLY THE WOMAN WAS SOME SORT OF FUTURE-SELF, MY MIRROR-SELF
SURELY SHE IS STRONGER.
SURELY SHE IS LESS AFRAID.

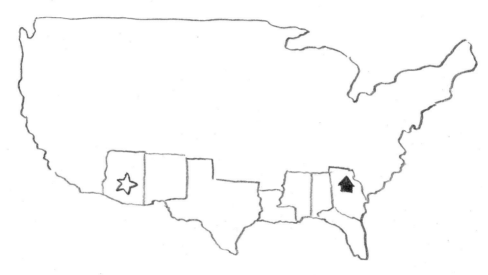

I AM HOPING TO
BIKE FROM MY PARENTS'
HOUSE IN TUCSON, ARIZONA
TO MY HOME IN
ATHENS, GEORGIA.

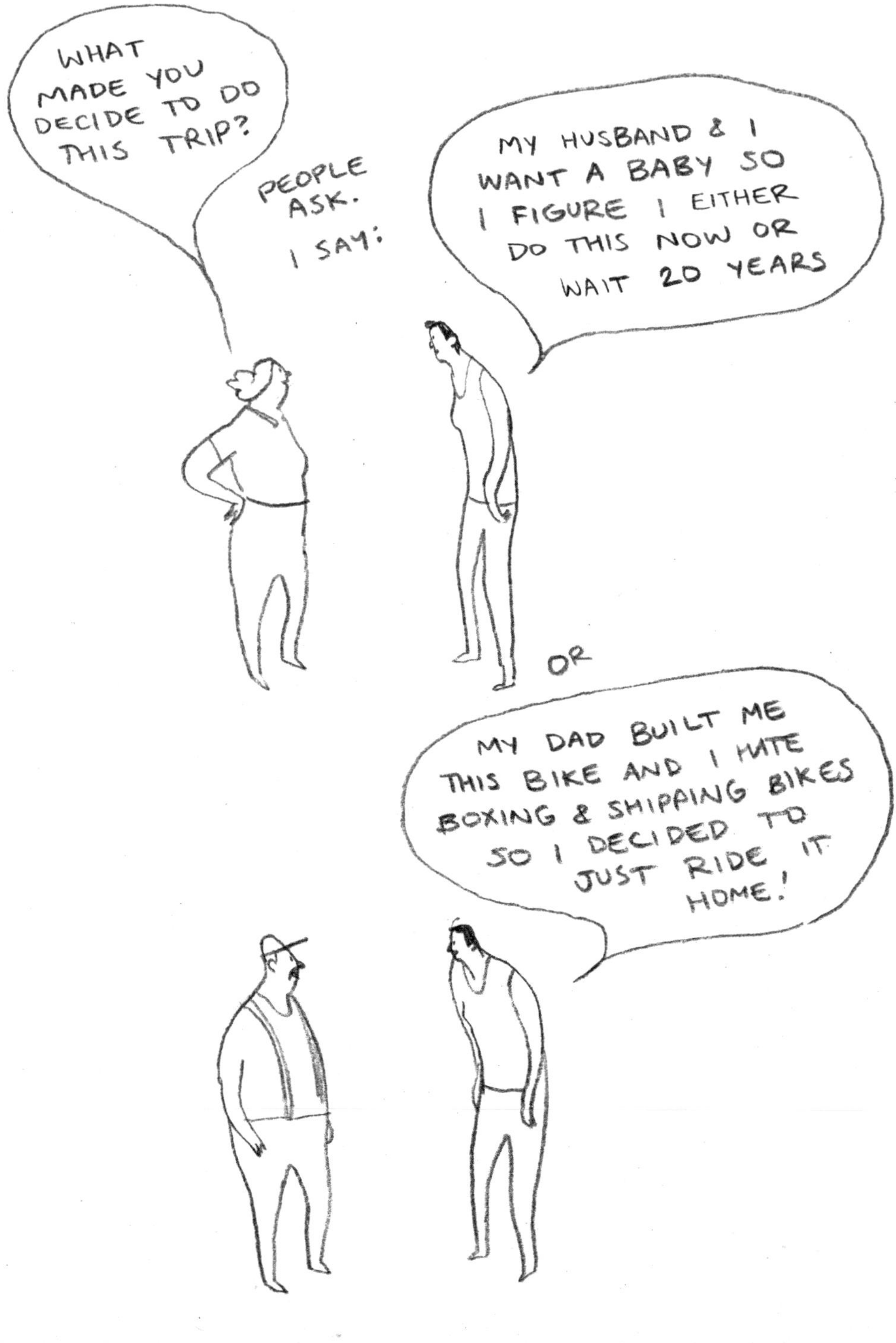
WHAT MADE YOU DECIDE TO DO THIS TRIP?
PEOPLE ASK.
I SAY:
MY HUSBAND & I WANT A BABY SO I FIGURE I EITHER DO THIS NOW OR WAIT 20 YEARS
OR
MY DAD BUILT ME THIS BIKE AND I HATE BOXING & SHIPPING BIKES SO I DECIDED TO JUST RIDE IT HOME!

I DON'T SAY:
I WAS HAVING TROUBLE WITH WANTING TO NOT BE ALIVE.
BUT I FEEL GOOD WHEN I'M BICYCLING
BUT THAT IS ALSO TRUE.

DAY 3 FRI 3/18
SAN PEDRO BLM TO BISBEE - 34 MILES

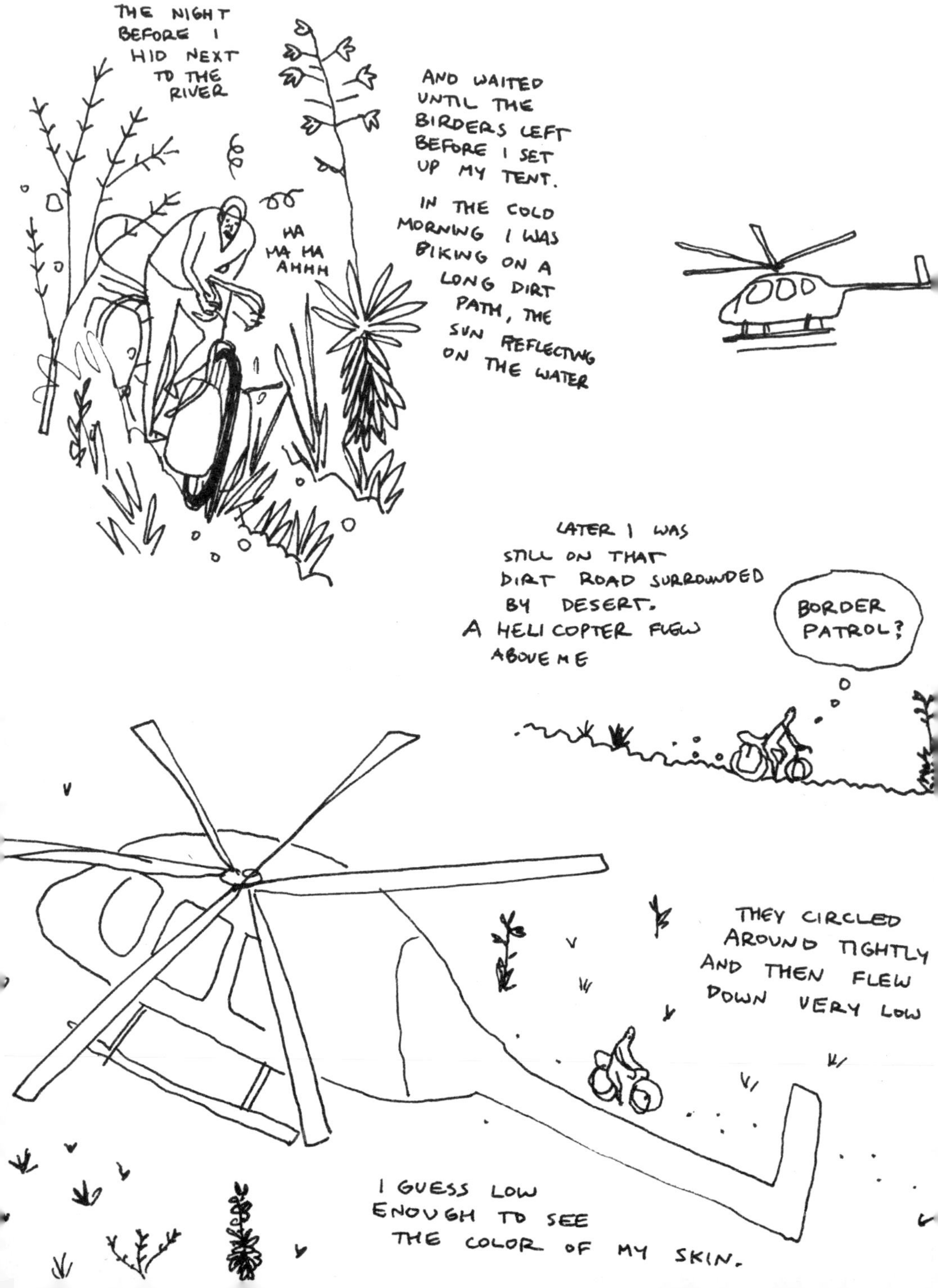
THE NIGHT BEFORE I HID NEXT TO THE RIVER
HA HA HA AHHH
AND WAITED UNTIL THE BIRDERS LEFT BEFORE I SET UP MY TENT.
IN THE COLD MORNING I WAS BIKING ON A LONG DIRT PATH, THE SUN REFLECTING ON THE WATER
LATER I WAS STILL ON THAT DIRT ROAD SURROUNDED BY DESERT. A HELICOPTER FLEW ABOVE ME
BORDER PATROL?
THEY CIRCLED AROUND TIGHTLY AND THEN FLEW DOWN VERY LOW
I GUESS LOW ENOUGH TO SEE THE COLOR OF MY SKIN.

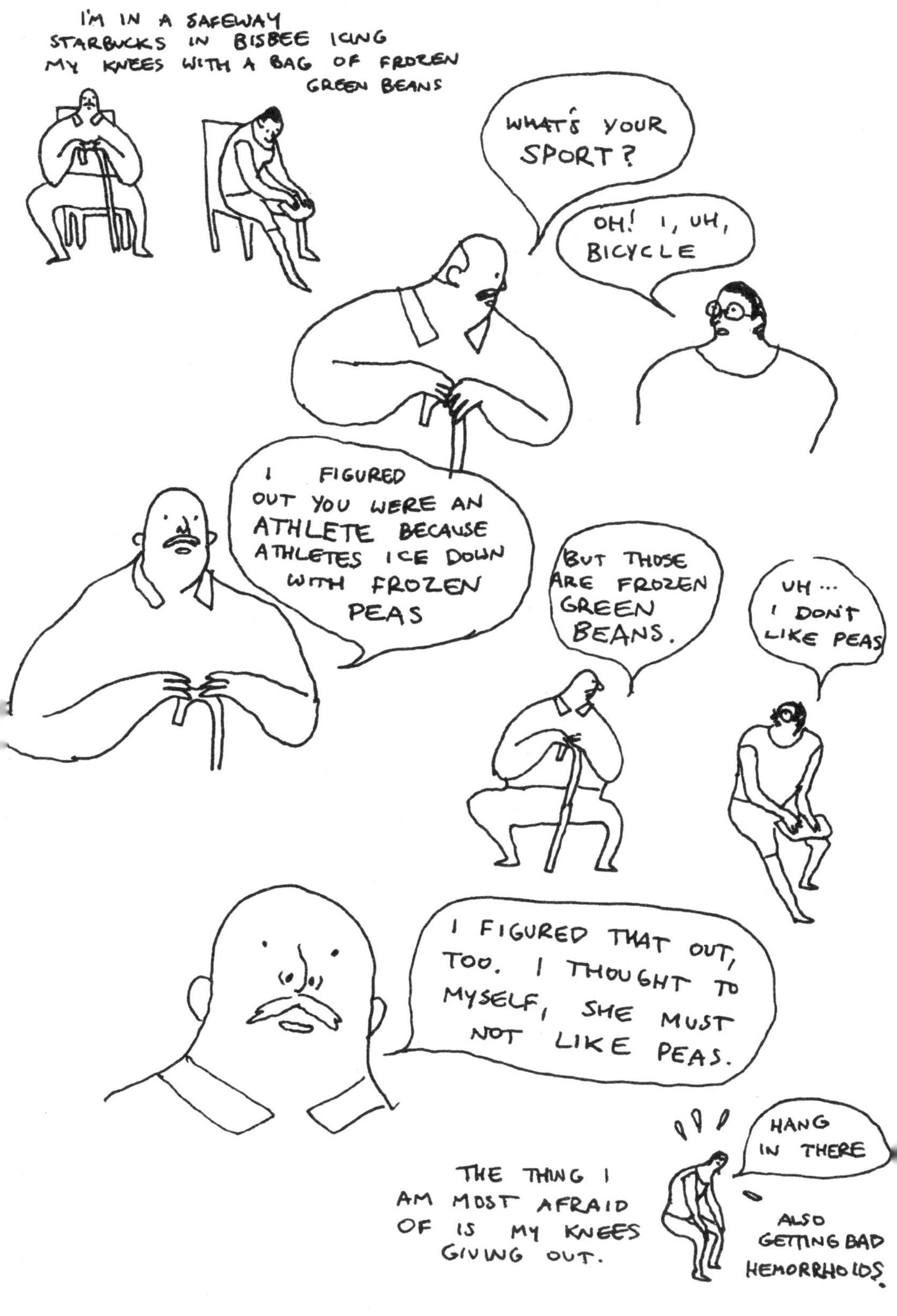
I'M IN A SAFEWAY STARBUCKS IN BISBEE ICING MY KNEES WITH A BAG OF FROZEN GREEN BEANS
WHAT'S YOUR SPORT?
OH! I, UH, BICYCLE
I FIGURED OUT YOU WERE AN ATHLETE BECAUSE ATHLETES ICE DOWN WITH FROZEN PEAS
BUT THOSE ARE FROZEN GREEN BEANS.
UH... I DON'T LIKE PEAS
I FIGURED THAT OUT, TOO. I THOUGHT TO MYSELF, SHE MUST NOT LIKE PEAS.
THE THING I AM MOST AFRAID OF IS MY KNEES GIVING OUT.
HANG IN THERE
ALSO GETTING BAD HEMORRHOIDS.

DAY 4 SATURDAY 3/19

BISBEE TO HALFWAY BETWEEN DOUGLAS & RODEO - 40 MILES

THE KIND B&B OWNER IN BISBEE DOESN'T WANT ME TO SLEEP IN THE DESERT TONIGHT BECAUSE OF "ILLEGALS"

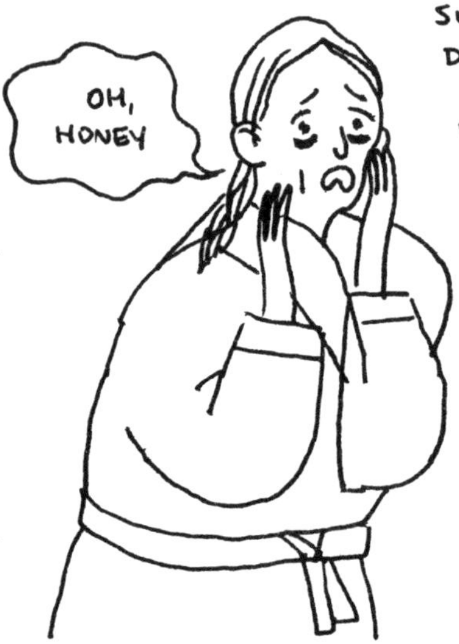
OH, HONEY

BUT I HAVE DECIDED NOT TO LISTEN TO ANYONE WHO USES THE WORD "ILLEGALS."

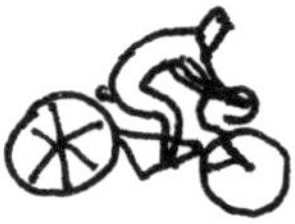

AT THE WALMART IN DOUGLAS A CASHIER IS FEEDING STRAY CATS ON HER LUNCH BREAK

20 MILES OUT OF DOUGLAS & 30 MILES TO RODEO A MAN SAYS I CAN SLEEP IN HIS GARAGE

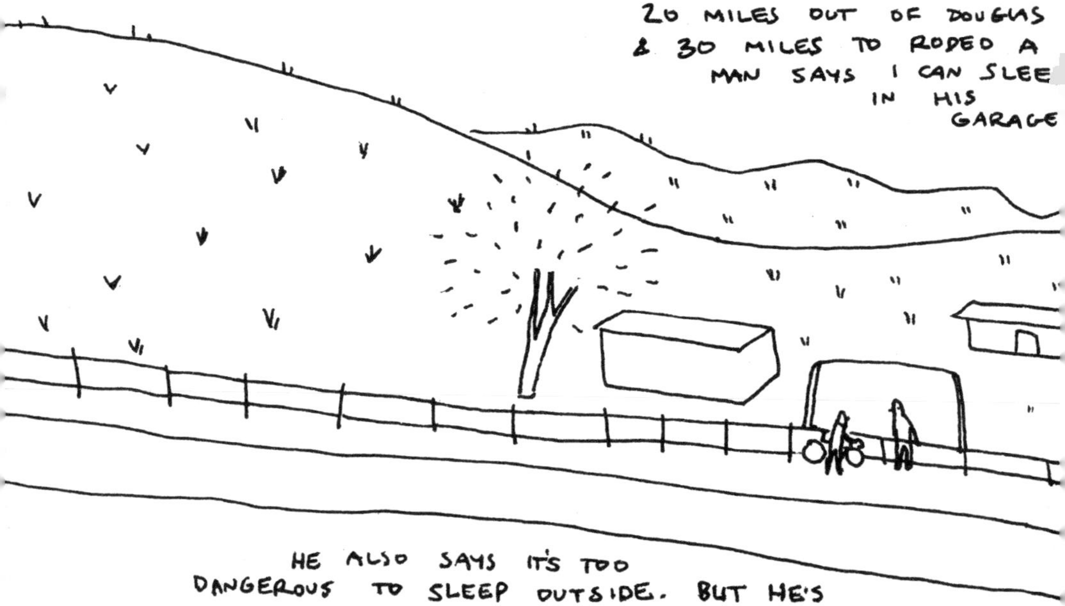

HE ALSO SAYS IT'S TOO DANGEROUS TO SLEEP OUTSIDE. BUT HE'S SCARED OF JAVELINA.

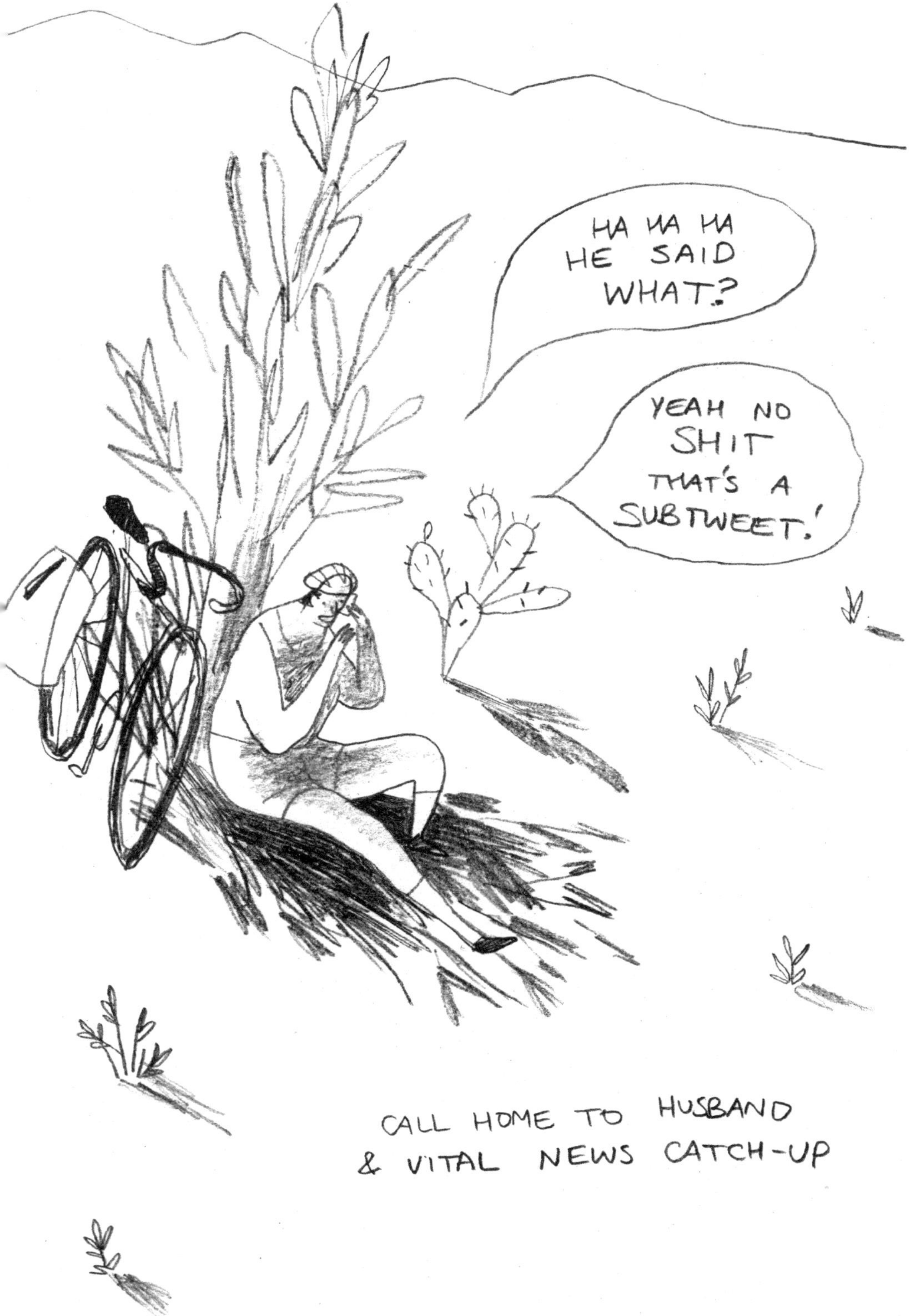
HA HA HA HE SAID WHAT?
YEAH NO SHIT THAT'S A SUBTWEET!

CALL HOME TO HUSBAND
& VITAL NEWS CATCH-UP

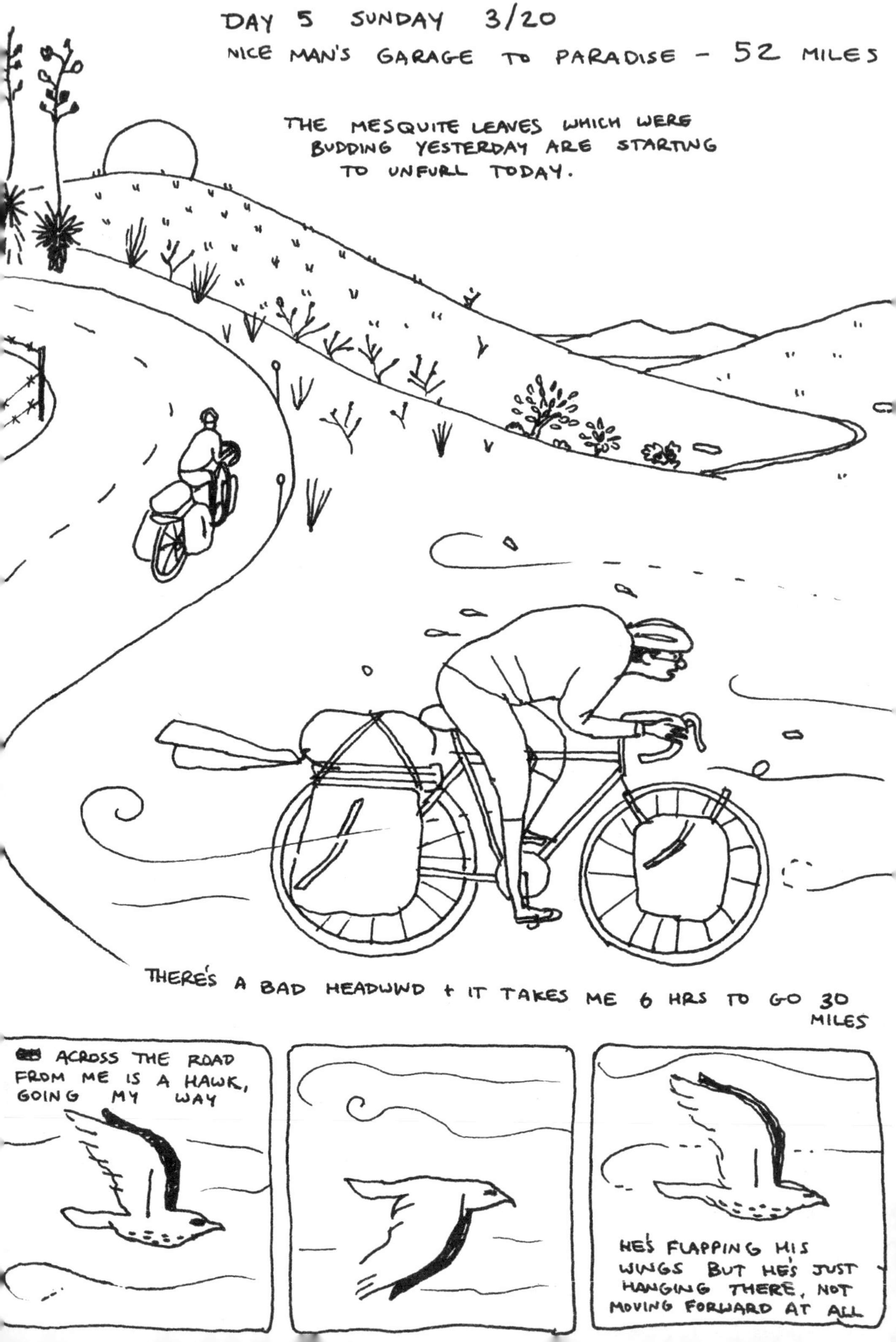
DAY 5 SUNDAY 3/20
NICE MAN'S GARAGE TO PARADISE - 52 MILES
THE MESQUITE LEAVES WHICH WERE BUDDING YESTERDAY ARE STARTING TO UNFURL TODAY.
THERE'S A BAD HEADWND + IT TAKES ME 6 HRS TO GO 30 MILES
[redacted] ACROSS THE ROAD FROM ME IS A HAWK, GOING MY WAY
HE'S FLAPPING HIS WINGS BUT HE'S JUST HANGING THERE, NOT MOVING FORWARD AT ALL

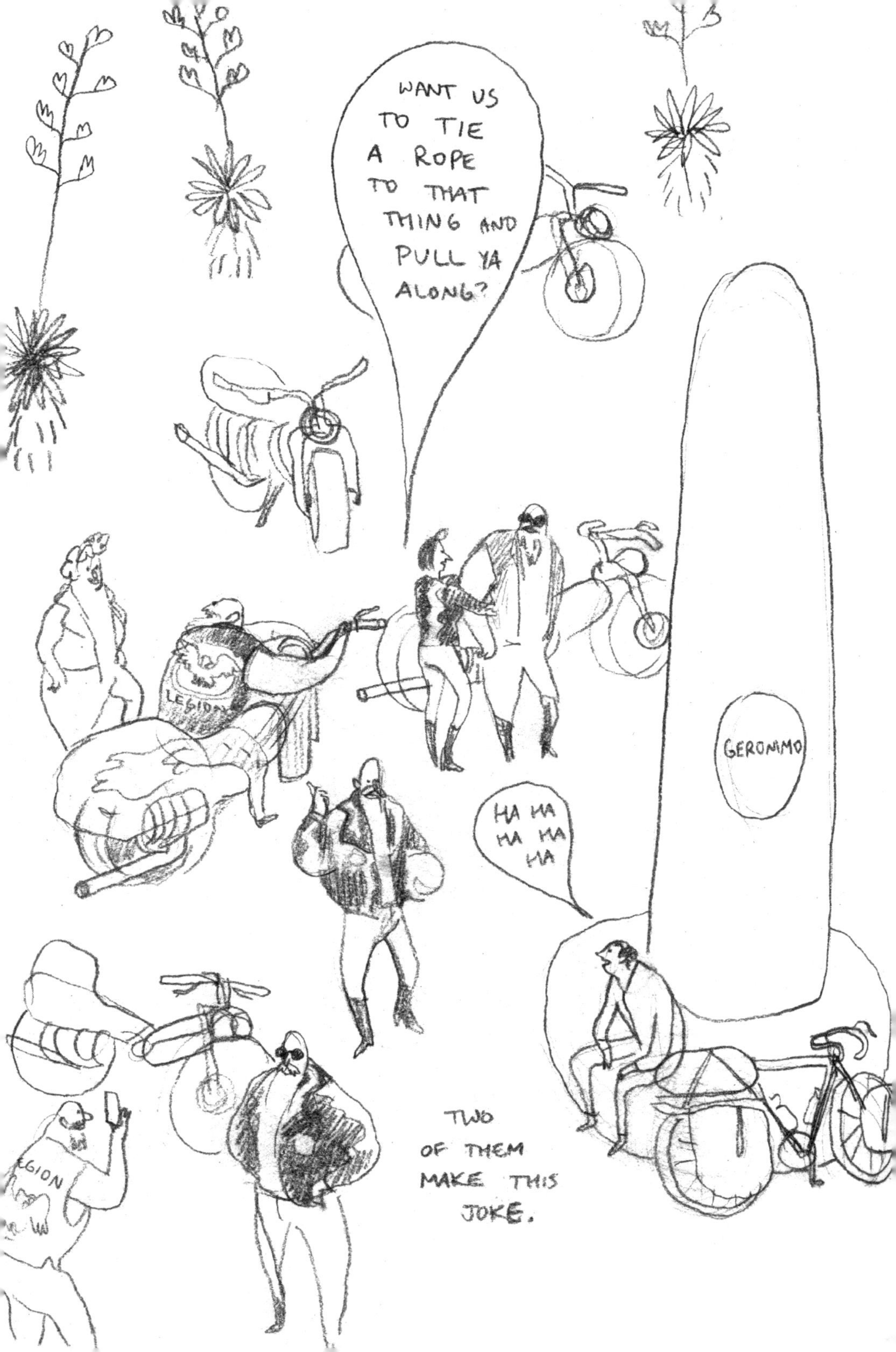
WANT US TO TIE A ROPE TO THAT THING AND PULL YA ALONG?
LEGION
GERONIMO
HA HA HA HA HA
LEGION
TWO OF THEM MAKE THIS JOKE.

DAY 6 MONDAY 3/21
BREAK DAY IN PARADISE

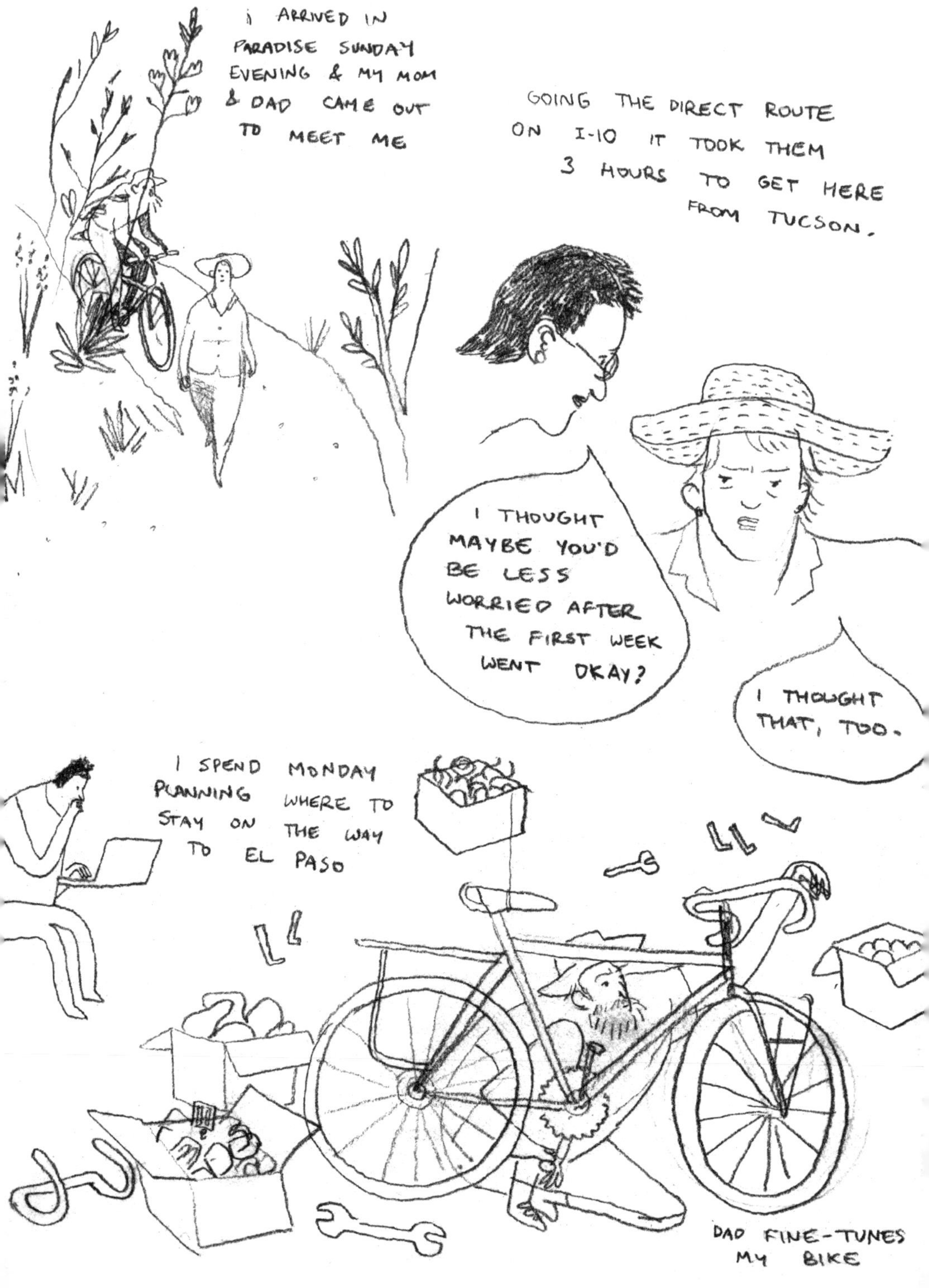
I ARRIVED IN PARADISE SUNDAY EVENING & MY MOM & DAD CAME OUT TO MEET ME
GOING THE DIRECT ROUTE ON I-10 IT TOOK THEM 3 HOURS TO GET HERE FROM TUCSON.
I THOUGHT MAYBE YOU'D BE LESS WORRIED AFTER THE FIRST WEEK WENT OKAY?
I THOUGHT THAT, TOO.
I SPEND MONDAY PLANNING WHERE TO STAY ON THE WAY TO EL PASO
DAD FINE-TUNES MY BIKE

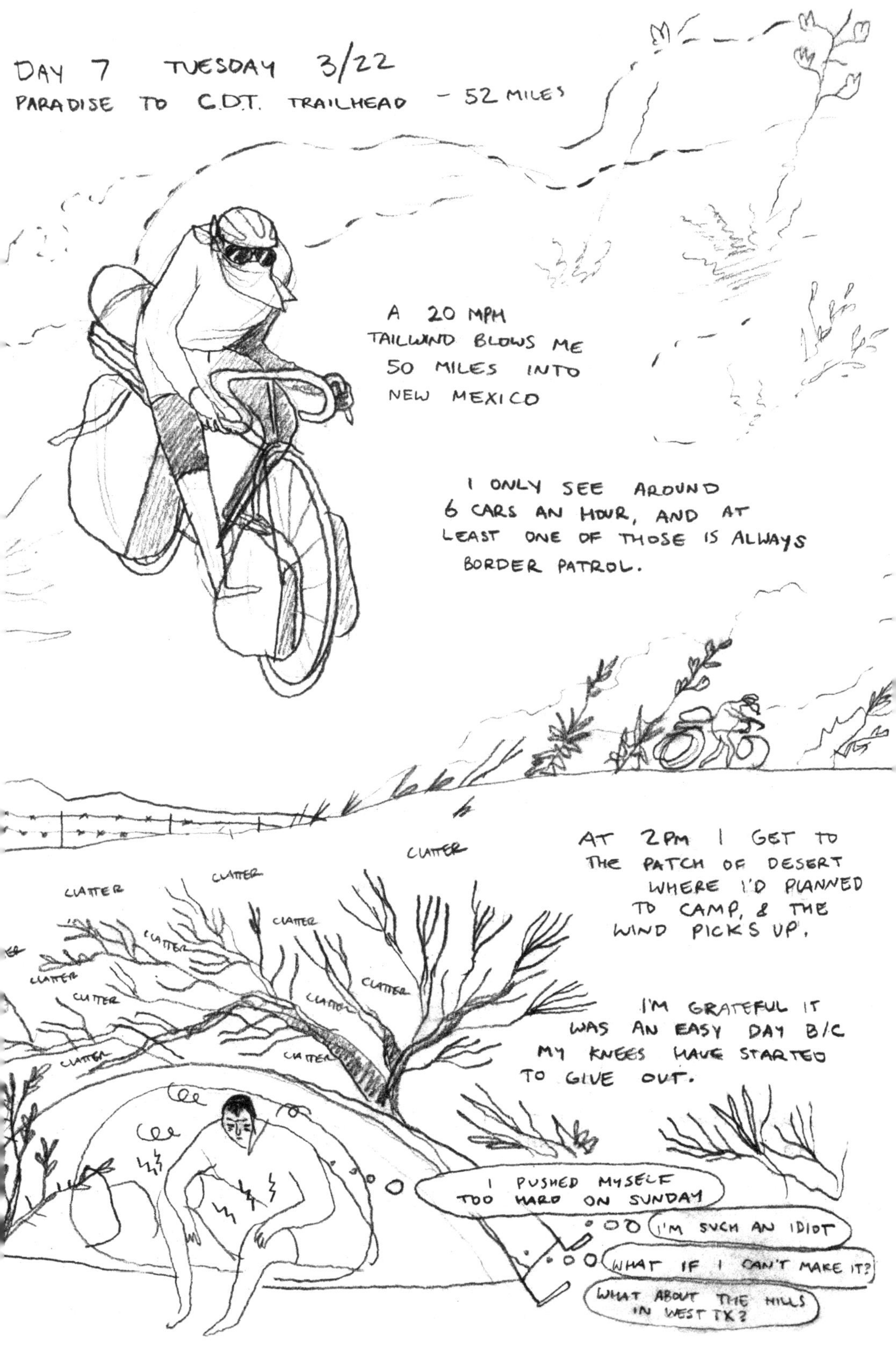
DAY 7 TUESDAY 3/22
PARADISE TO C.D.T. TRAILHEAD - 52 MILES
A 20 MPH TAILWIND BLOWS ME 50 MILES INTO NEW MEXICO
I ONLY SEE AROUND 6 CARS AN HOUR, AND AT LEAST ONE OF THOSE IS ALWAYS BORDER PATROL.
AT 2PM I GET TO THE PATCH OF DESERT WHERE I'D PLANNED TO CAMP, & THE WIND PICKS UP.
CLATTER
CLATTER
CLATTER
CLATTER
CLATTER
CLATTER
CLATTER
CLATTER
CLATTER
CLATTER
CLATTER
I'M GRATEFUL IT WAS AN EASY DAY B/C MY KNEES HAVE STARTED TO GIVE OUT.
I PUSHED MYSELF TOO HARD ON SUNDAY
I'M SUCH AN IDIOT
WHAT IF I CAN'T MAKE IT?
WHAT ABOUT THE HILLS IN WEST TX?

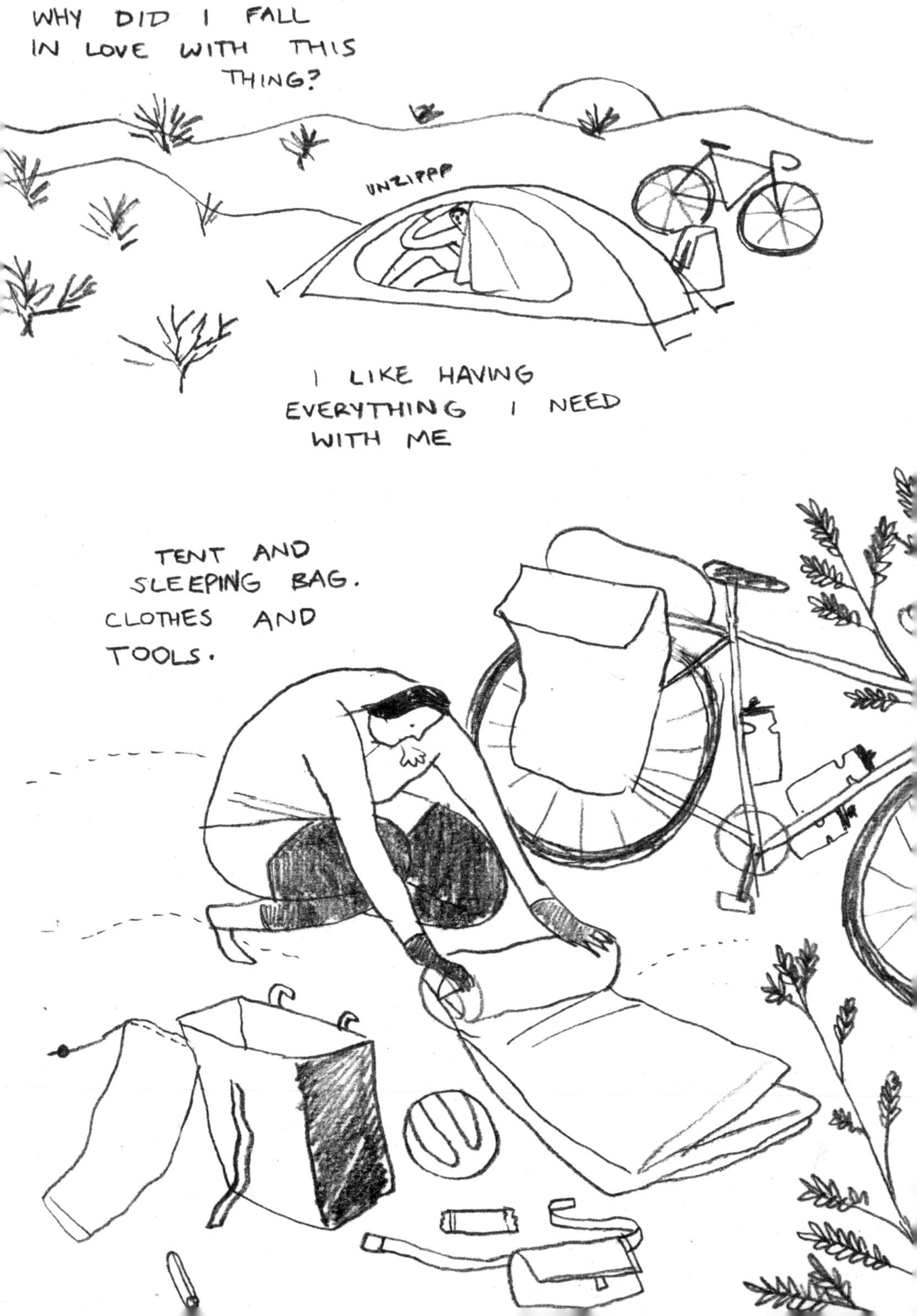
WHY DID I FALL IN LOVE WITH THIS THING?
UNZIPPP
I LIKE HAVING EVERYTHING I NEED WITH ME
TENT AND SLEEPING BAG. CLOTHES AND TOOLS.

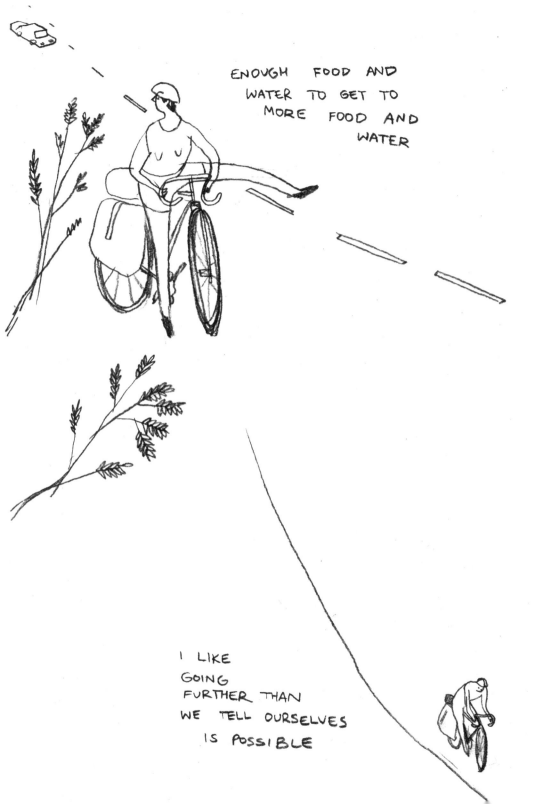

ENOUGH FOOD AND
WATER TO GET TO
MORE FOOD AND
WATER

I LIKE
GOING
FURTHER THAN
WE TELL OURSELVES
IS POSSIBLE

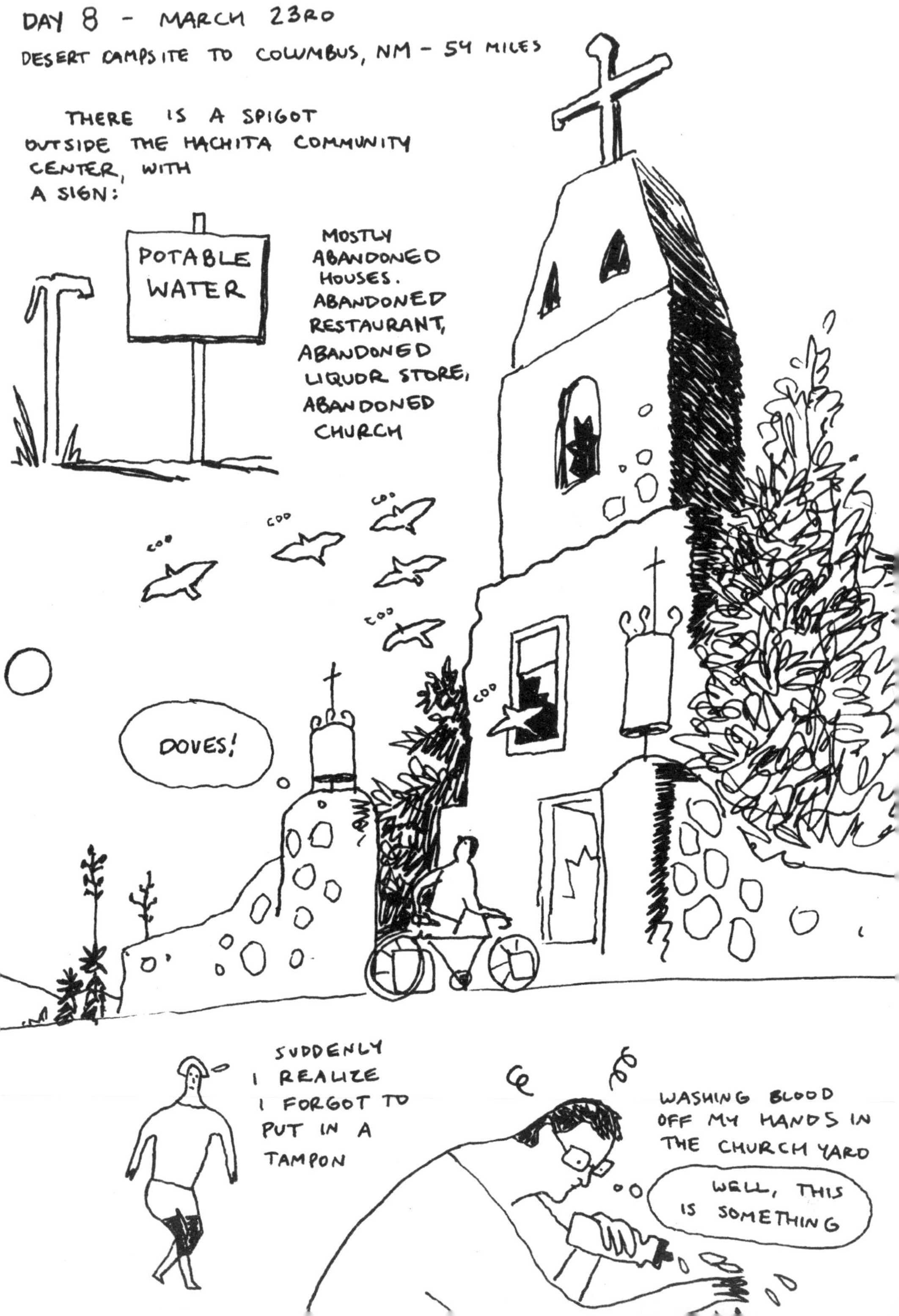
DAY 8 - MARCH 23RD
DESERT CAMPSITE TO COLUMBUS, NM - 54 MILES
THERE IS A SPIGOT OUTSIDE THE HACHITA COMMUNITY CENTER, WITH A SIGN:
POTABLE WATER
MOSTLY ABANDONED HOUSES. ABANDONED RESTAURANT, ABANDONED LIQUOR STORE, ABANDONED CHURCH
COO
COO
COO
COO
COO
DOVES!
SUDDENLY I REALIZE I FORGOT TO PUT IN A TAMPON
WASHING BLOOD OFF MY HANDS IN THE CHURCH YARD
WELL, THIS IS SOMETHING

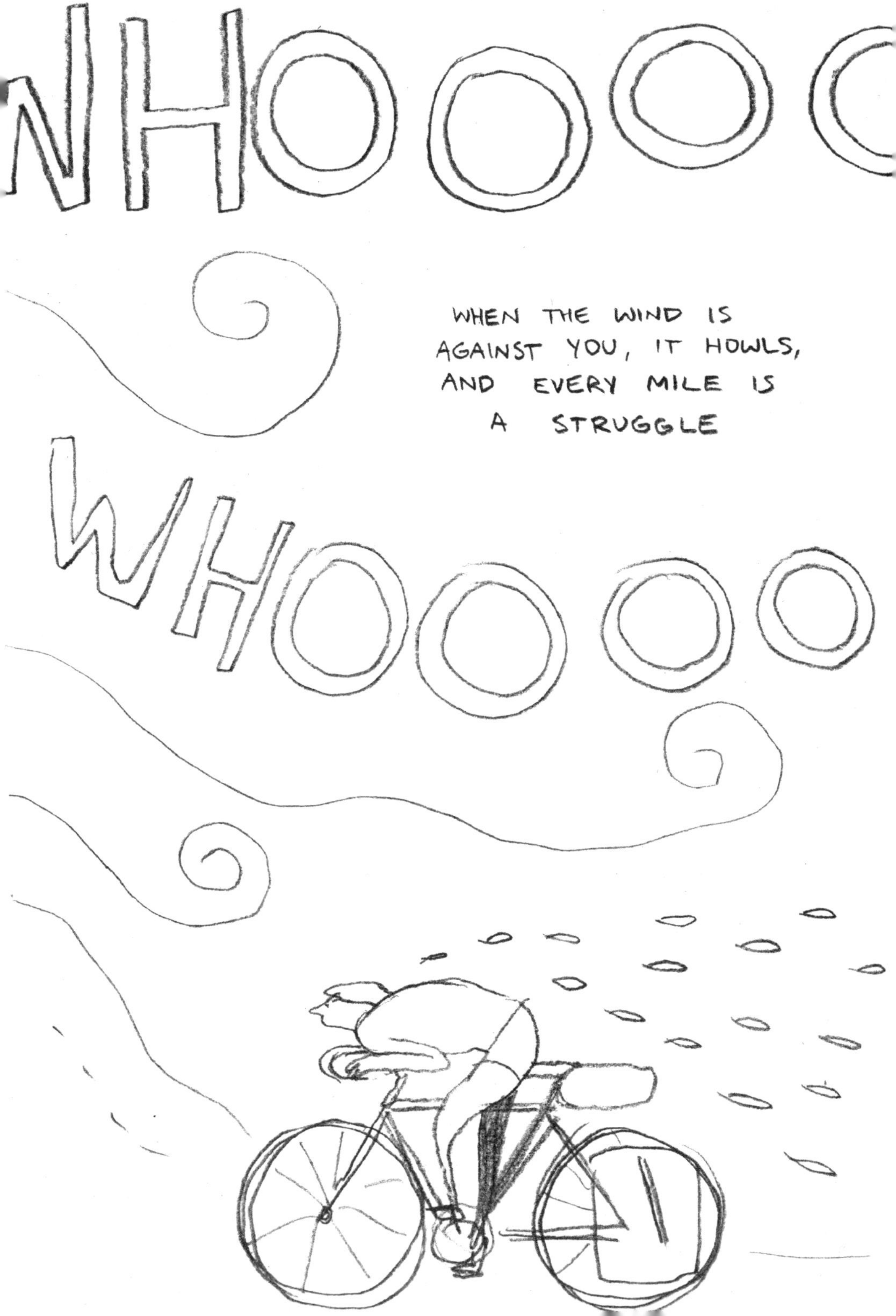
WHOOOO
WHEN THE WIND IS AGAINST YOU, IT HOWLS, AND EVERY MILE IS A STRUGGLE
WHOOOO

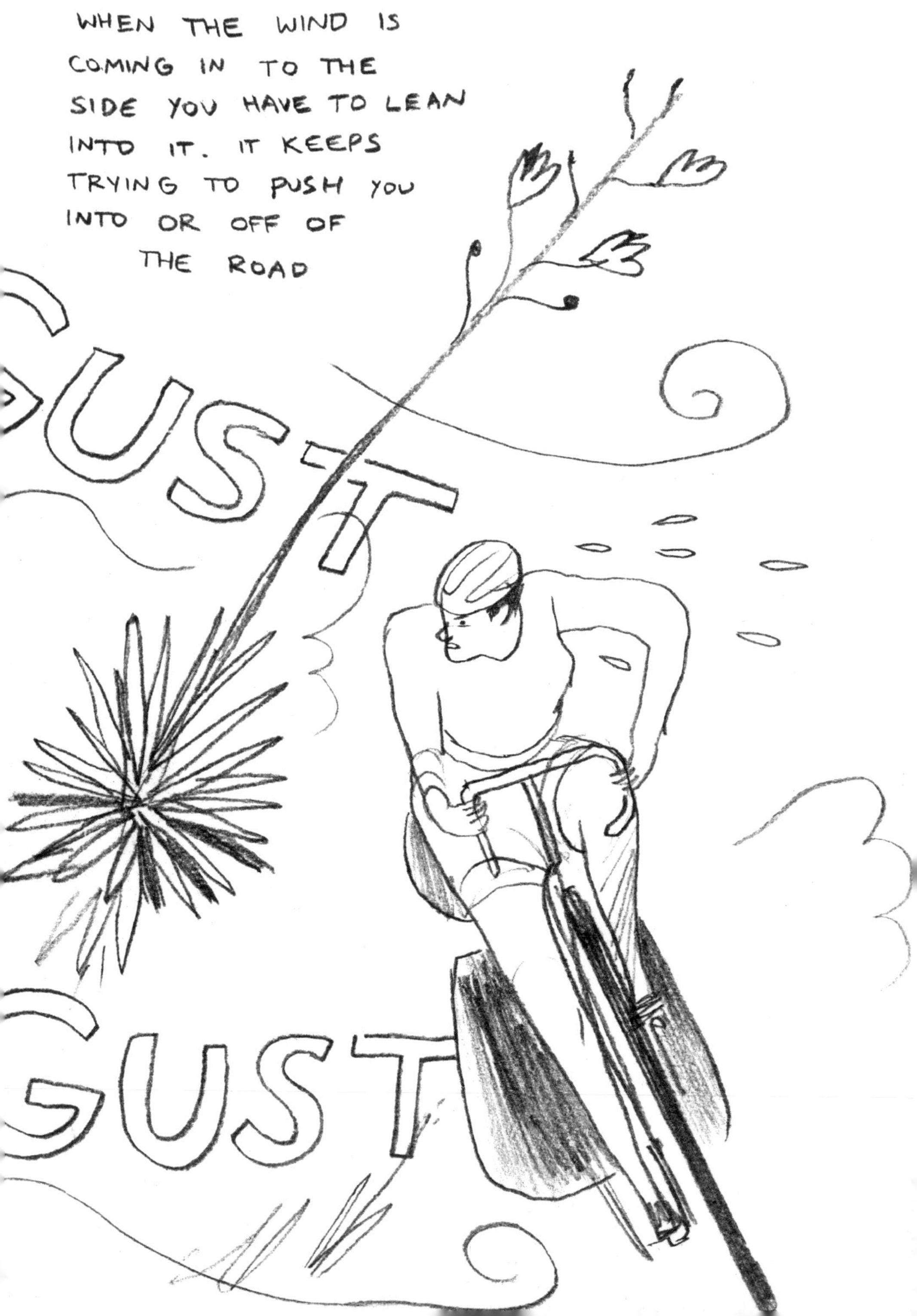
WHEN THE WIND IS COMING IN TO THE SIDE YOU HAVE TO LEAN INTO IT. IT KEEPS TRYING TO PUSH YOU INTO OR OFF OF THE ROAD
GUST
GUST

BUT WHEN THE WIND IS WITH YOU IT GOES TOTALLY SILENT. YOU STOP NOTICING IT AT ALL. YOU ONLY KNOW YOU ARE GOING VERY FAST, AND GOING FAST IS EASY.

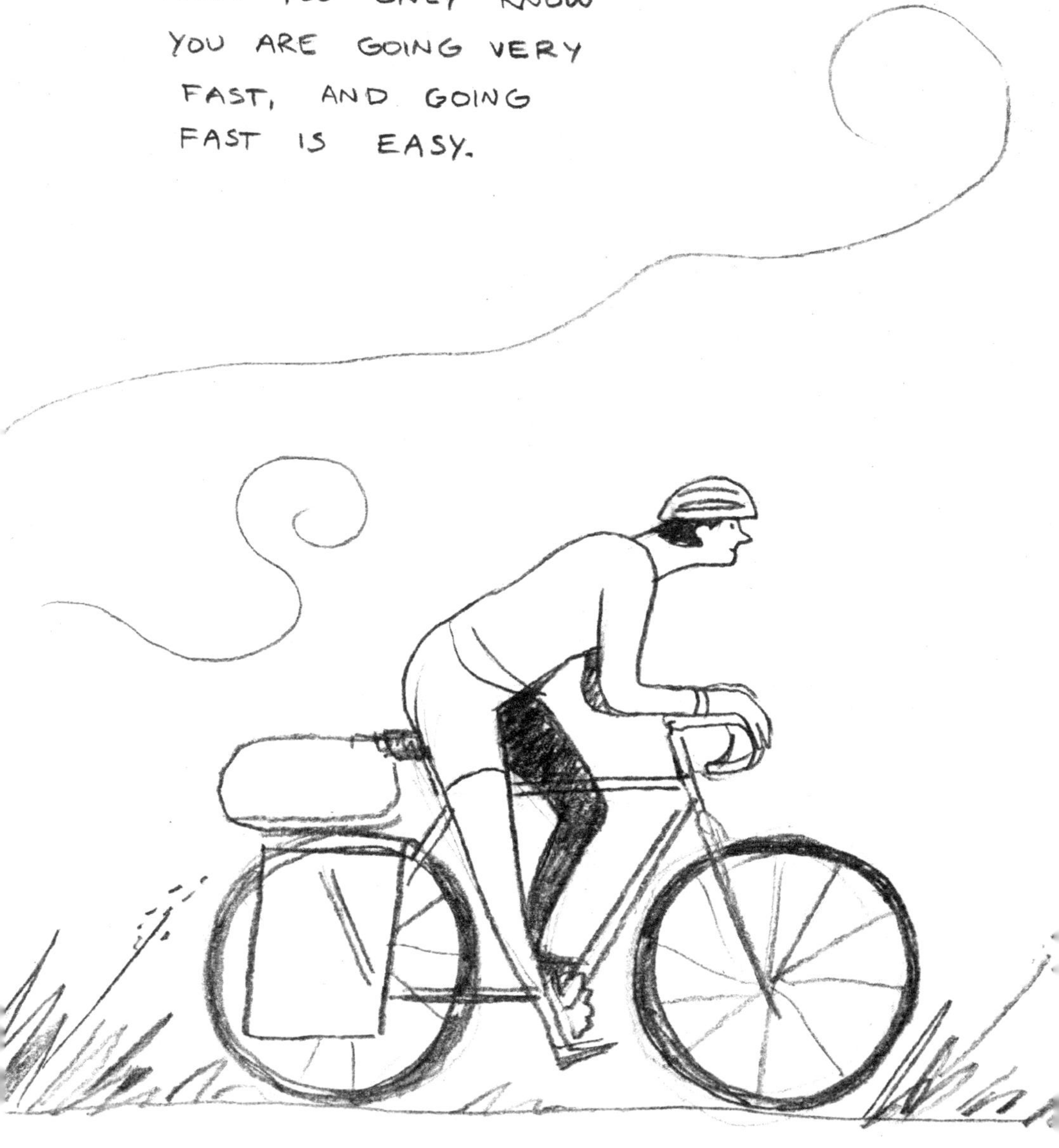

DAY 9 - MARCH 24TH
BREAK DAY
BUT I WANT TO DO THIS TRIP!!
I CAN'T QUIT NOW, I'VE ALREADY TWEETED ABOUT IT!!
POP
POP
CRACKLE
IN A BLEAK RV PARK IN AN EXTREMELY SMALL TOWN GIVING MY KNEES A BREAK AND LOSING MY MIND
TEXTING WITH PARENTS
We'll visit! You're still very close
If you want! I'm bored!
Wait, this is a bad idea
Too late haha
THEY DRIVE THE 100+ MILES IN UNDER 2 HRS, WHICH JUST MEANS SAYING GOODBYE A 3RD TIME.
YOU CAN DO THIS TRIP ANOTHER TIME
THE AMOUNT YOU'VE DONE IS ALREADY SUCH AN ACCOMPLISHMENT!
UUUUU
PAT PAT
?
SEE YOU IN A COUPLE DAYS!
I MEAN MONTHS!!
HA HA HA HA

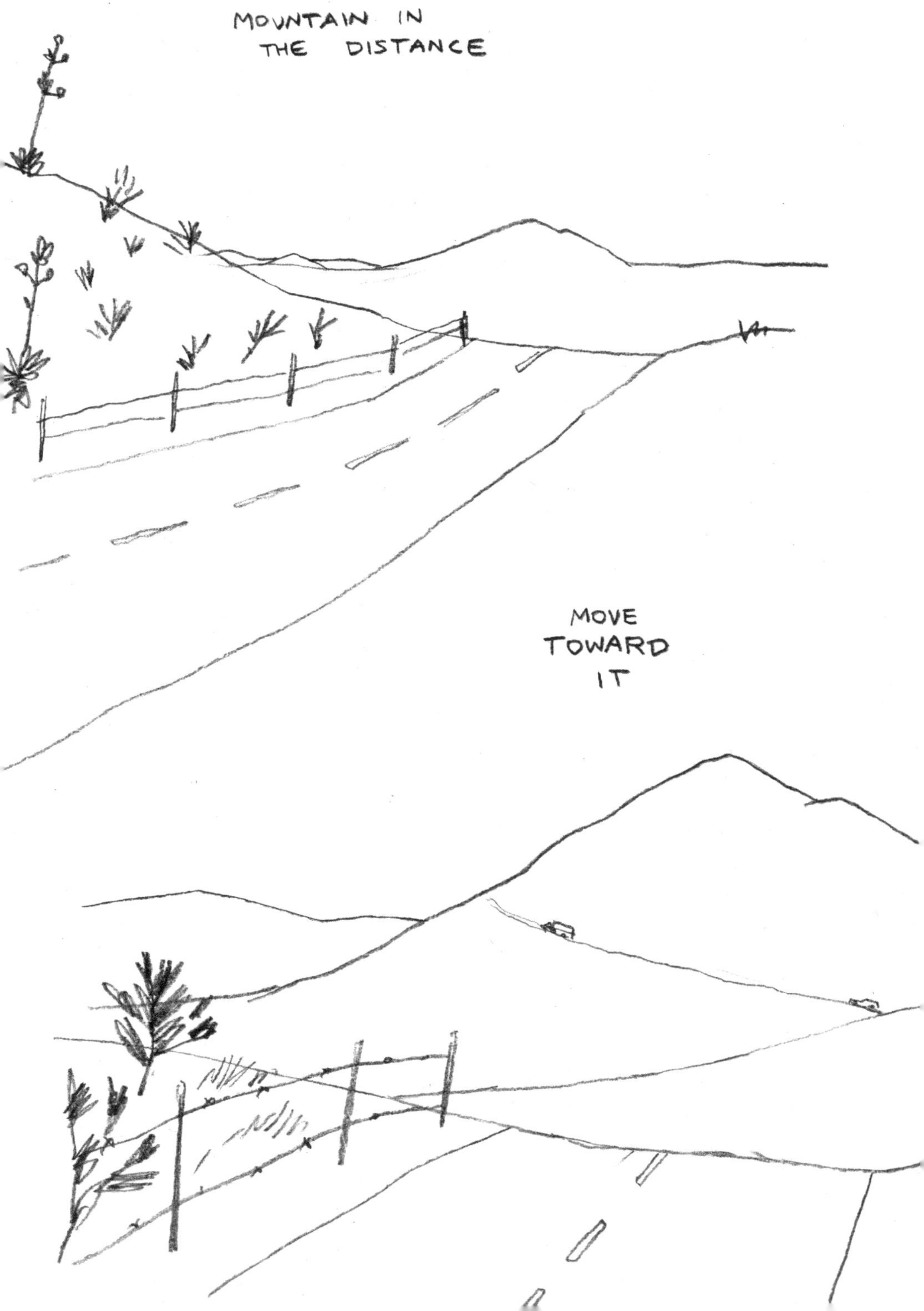
MOUNTAIN IN THE DISTANCE
MOVE TOWARD IT

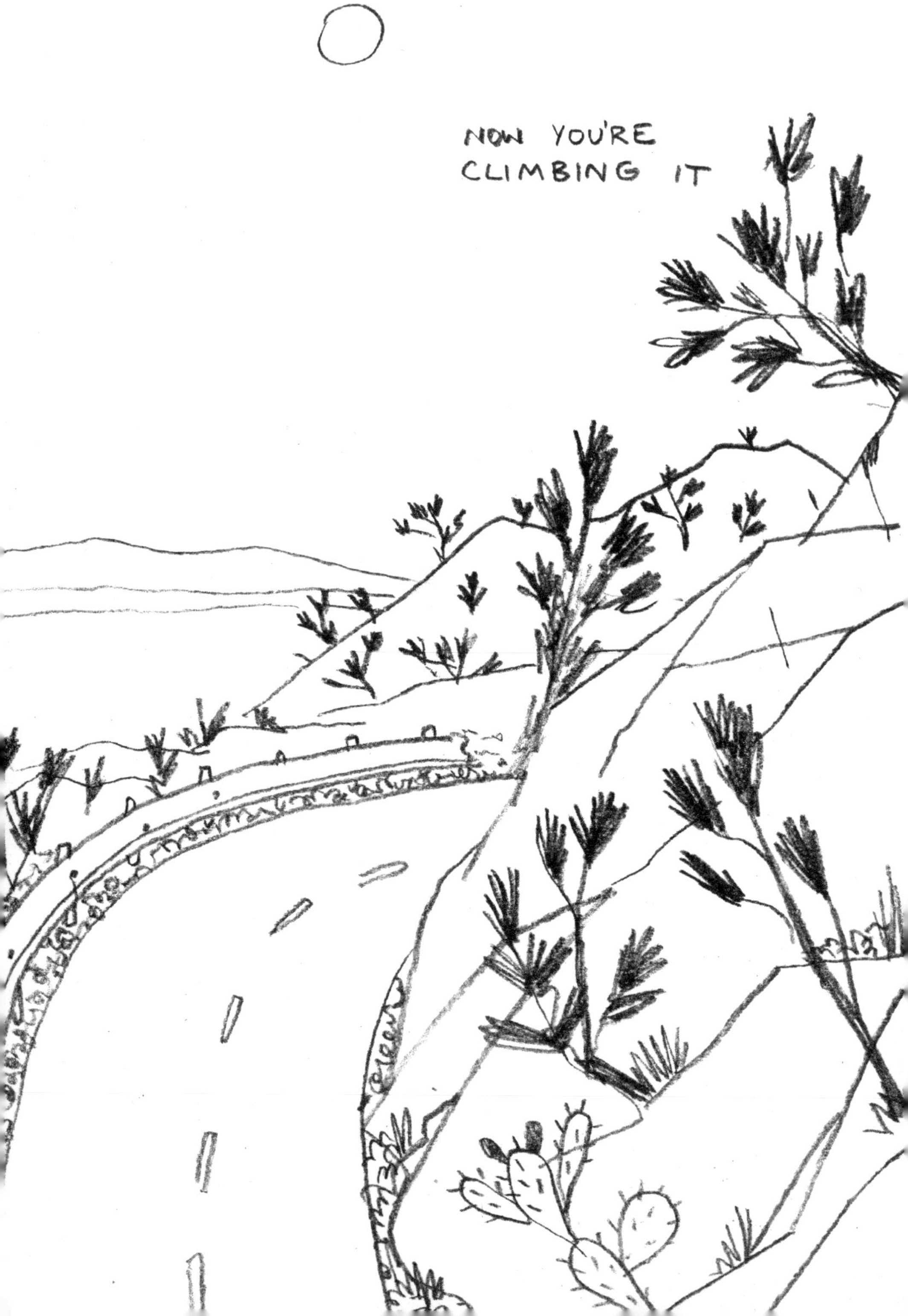
NOW YOU'RE
CLIMBING IT

NOW YOU'RE
OVER IT

NOW
IT'S
GONE.

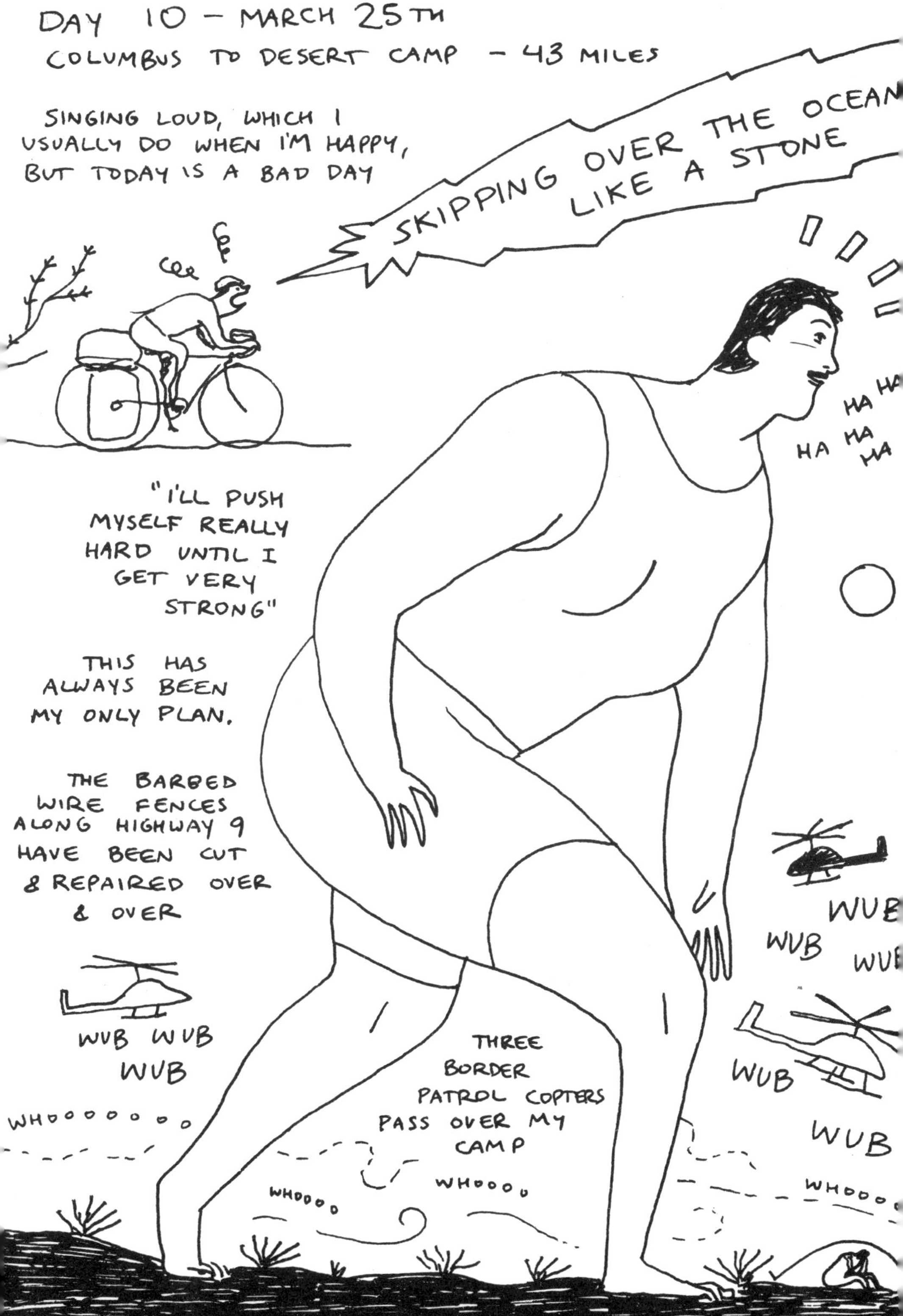
DAY 10 – MARCH 25TH
COLUMBUS TO DESERT CAMP – 43 MILES
SINGING LOUD, WHICH I USUALLY DO WHEN I'M HAPPY, BUT TODAY IS A BAD DAY
SKIPPING OVER THE OCEAN LIKE A STONE
HA HA HA HA HA HA
"I'LL PUSH MYSELF REALLY HARD UNTIL I GET VERY STRONG"
THIS HAS ALWAYS BEEN MY ONLY PLAN.
THE BARBED WIRE FENCES ALONG HIGHWAY 9 HAVE BEEN CUT & REPAIRED OVER & OVER
WUB WUB WUB
WUB WUB WUB
WUB
WUB
THREE BORDER PATROL COPTERS PASS OVER MY CAMP
WHOOOOOOOO
WHOOOO
WHOOOO
WHOOOO

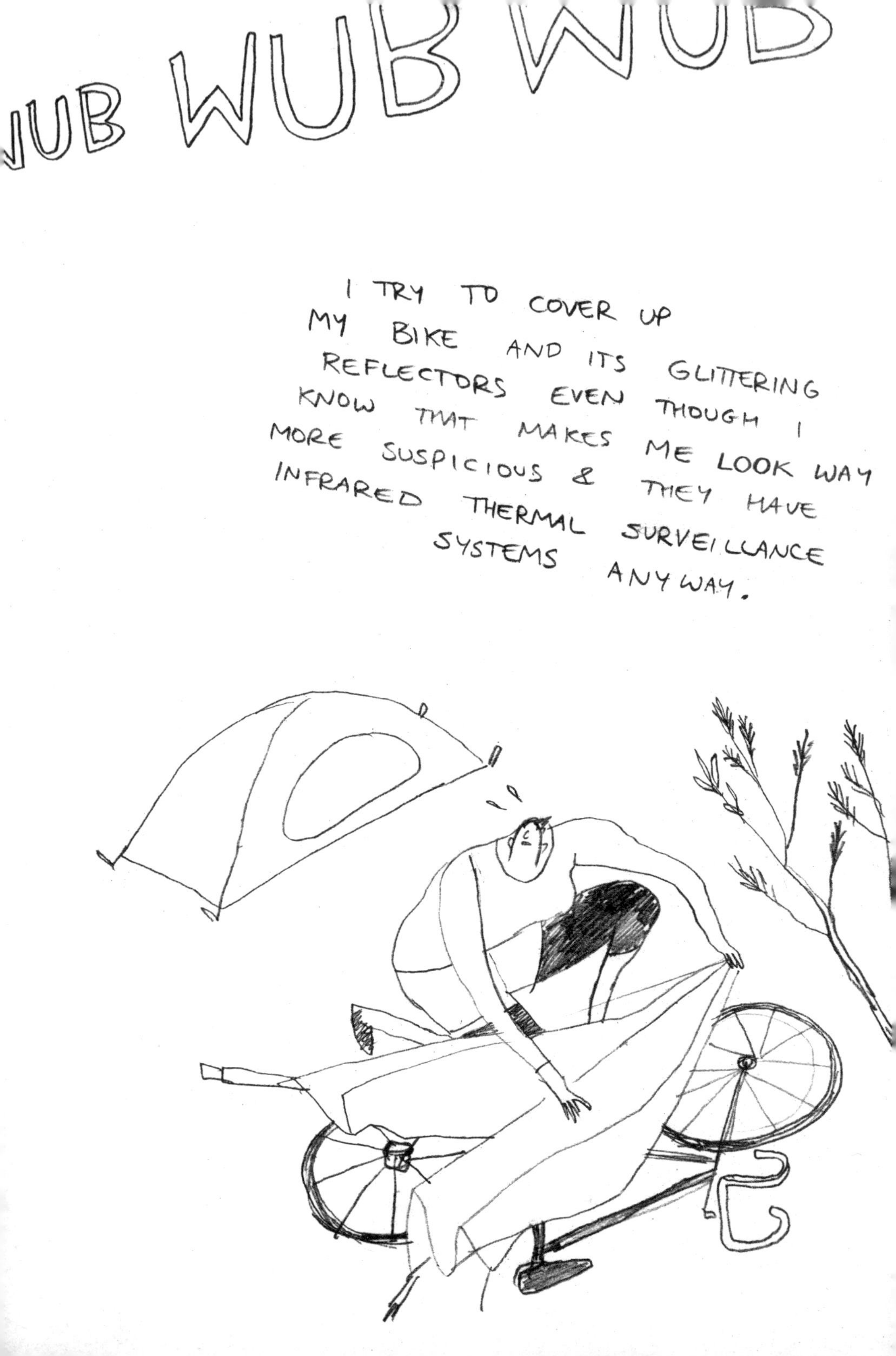
WUB WUB WUB
I TRY TO COVER UP MY BIKE AND ITS GLITTERING REFLECTORS EVEN THOUGH I KNOW THAT MAKES ME LOOK WAY MORE SUSPICIOUS & THEY HAVE INFRARED THERMAL SURVEILLANCE SYSTEMS ANYWAY.

DAY 11 - MARCH 26TH
DESERT CAMP TO EL PASO - 39 MILES

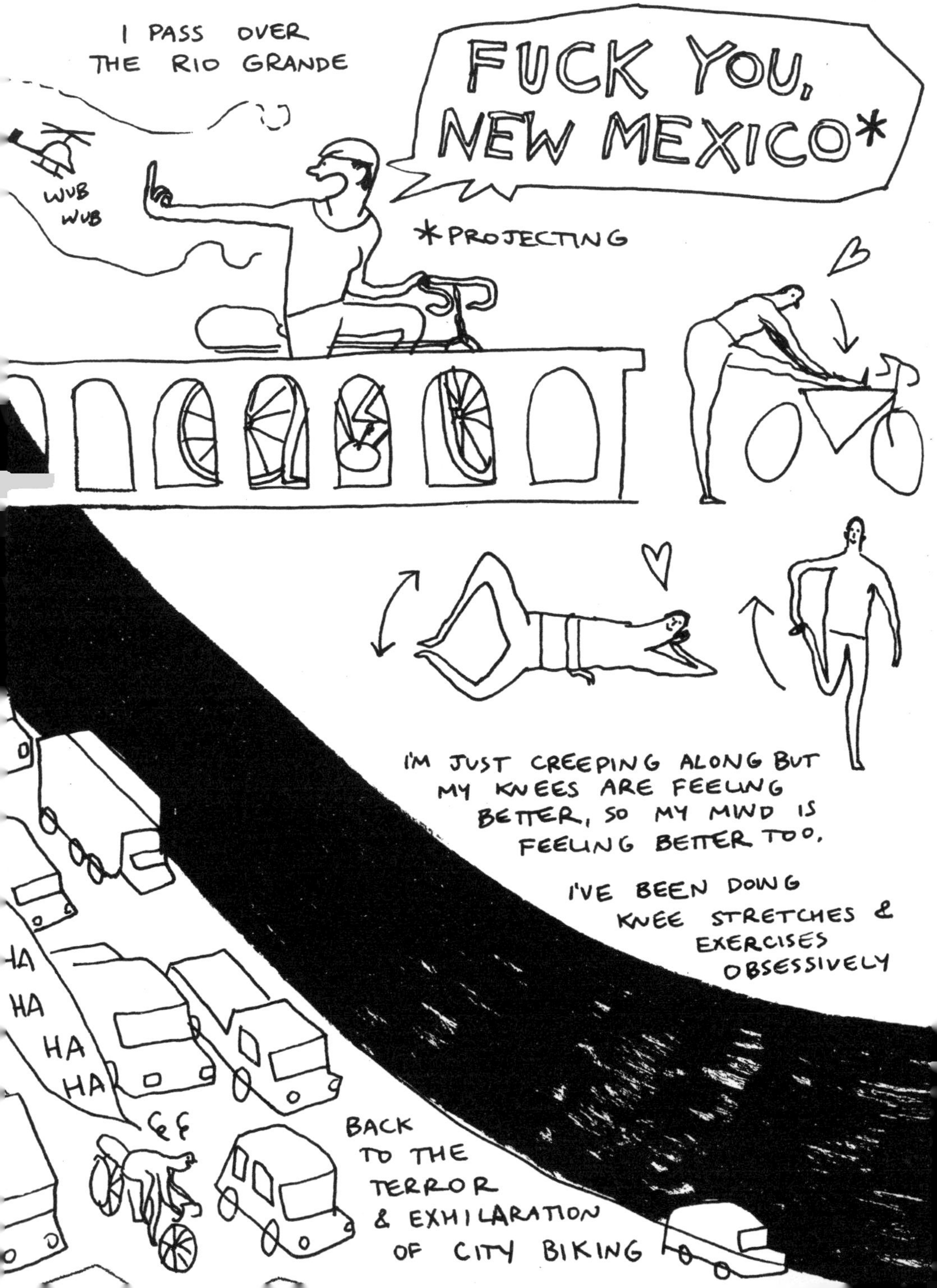

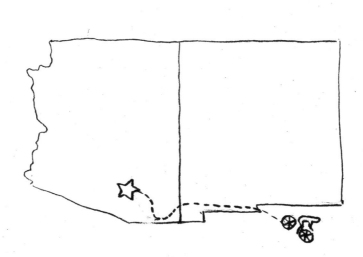

DAY 12 - MARCH 27TH
BREAK DAY

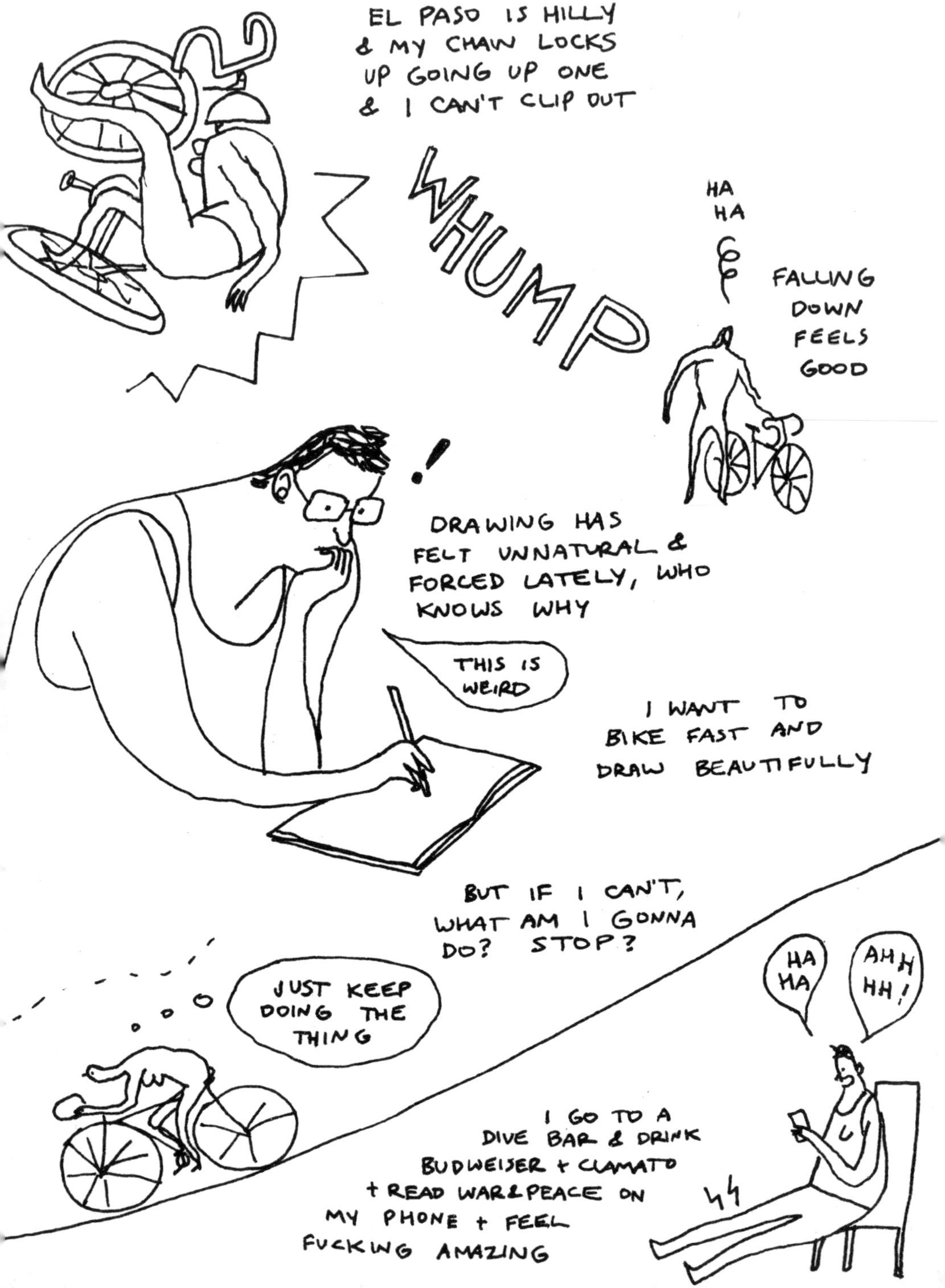

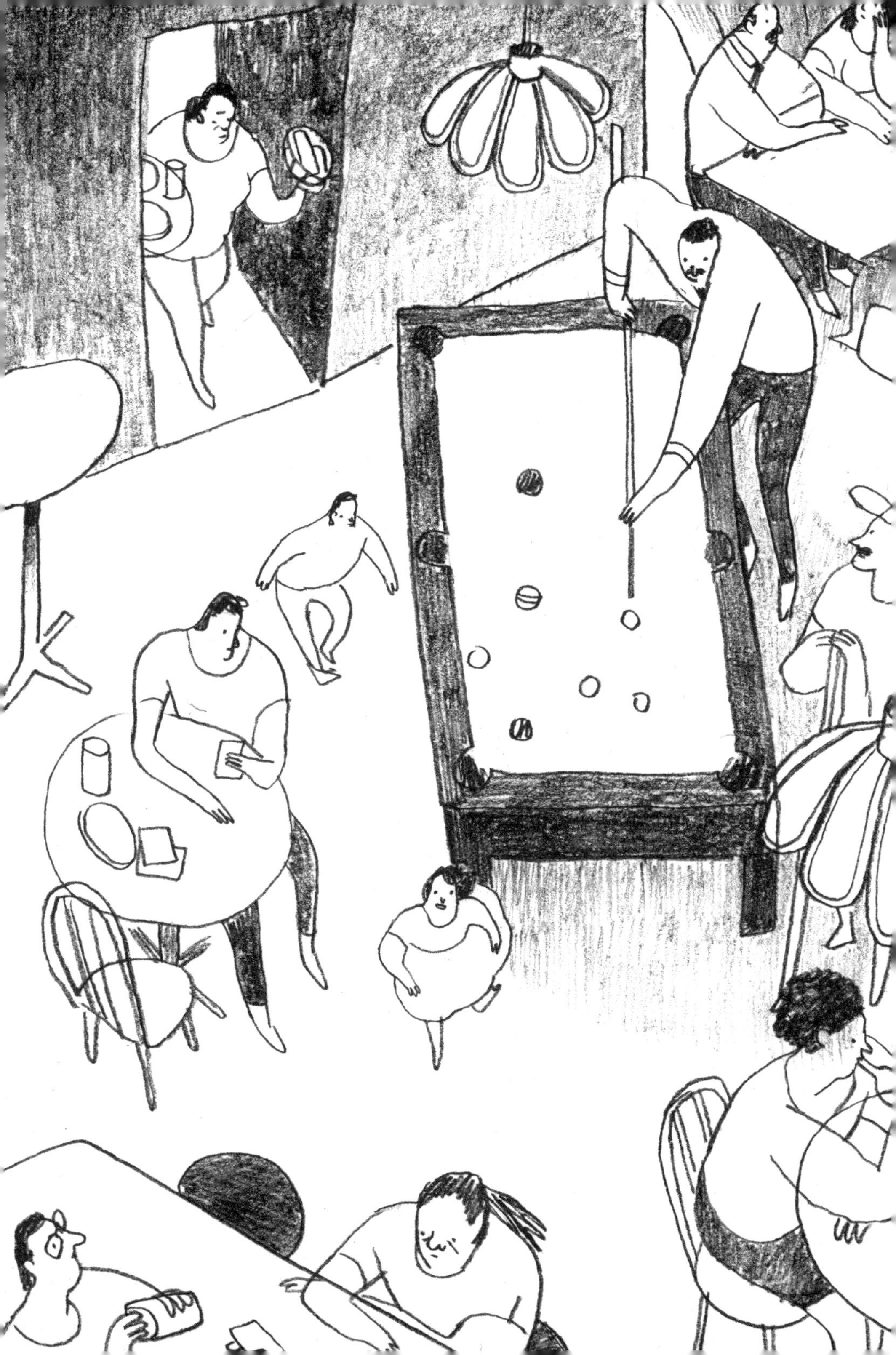

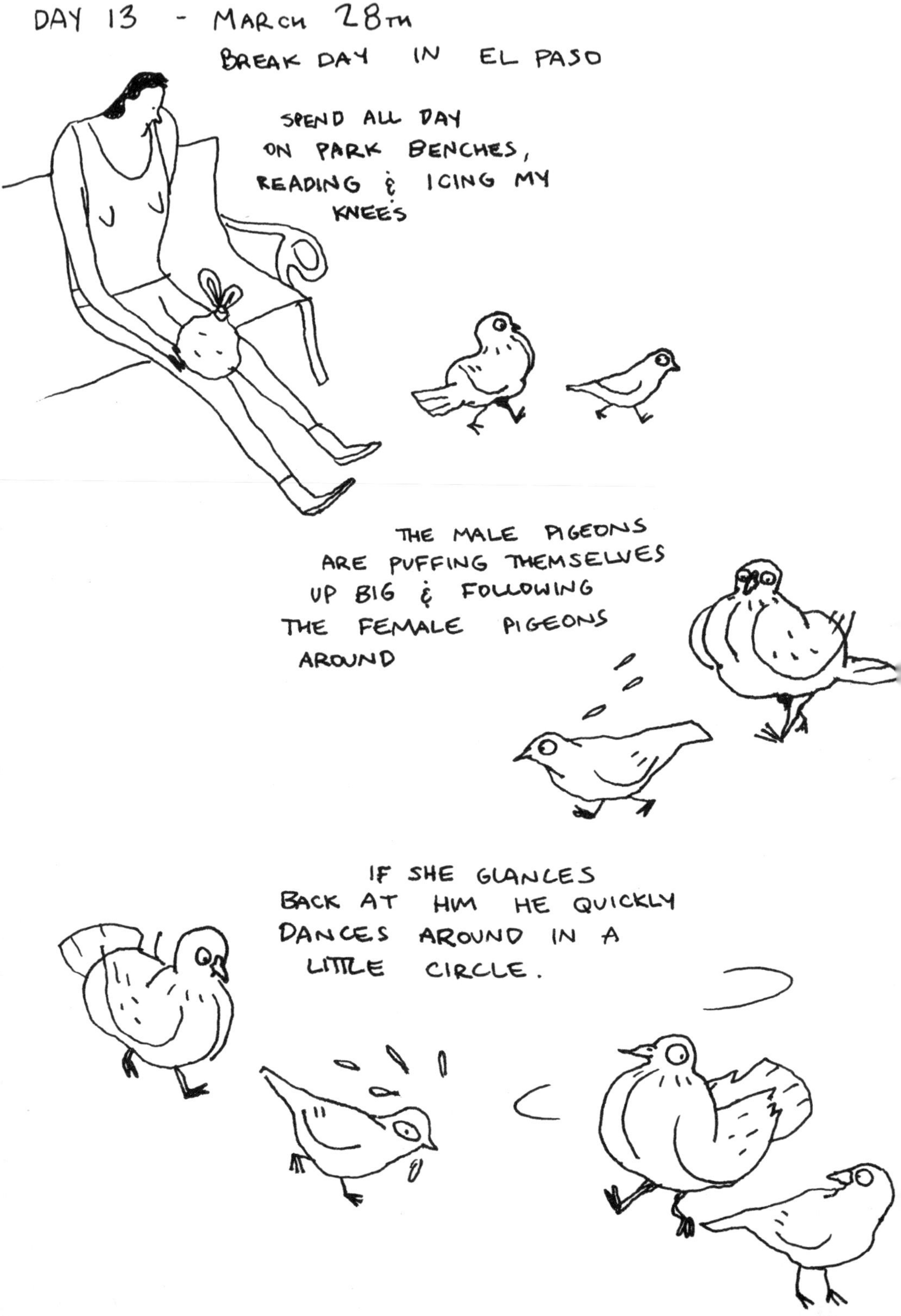
DAY 13 - MARCH 28TH
BREAK DAY IN EL PASO
SPEND ALL DAY ON PARK BENCHES, READING & ICING MY KNEES
THE MALE PIGEONS ARE PUFFING THEMSELVES UP BIG & FOLLOWING THE FEMALE PIGEONS AROUND
IF SHE GLANCES BACK AT HIM HE QUICKLY DANCES AROUND IN A LITTLE CIRCLE.

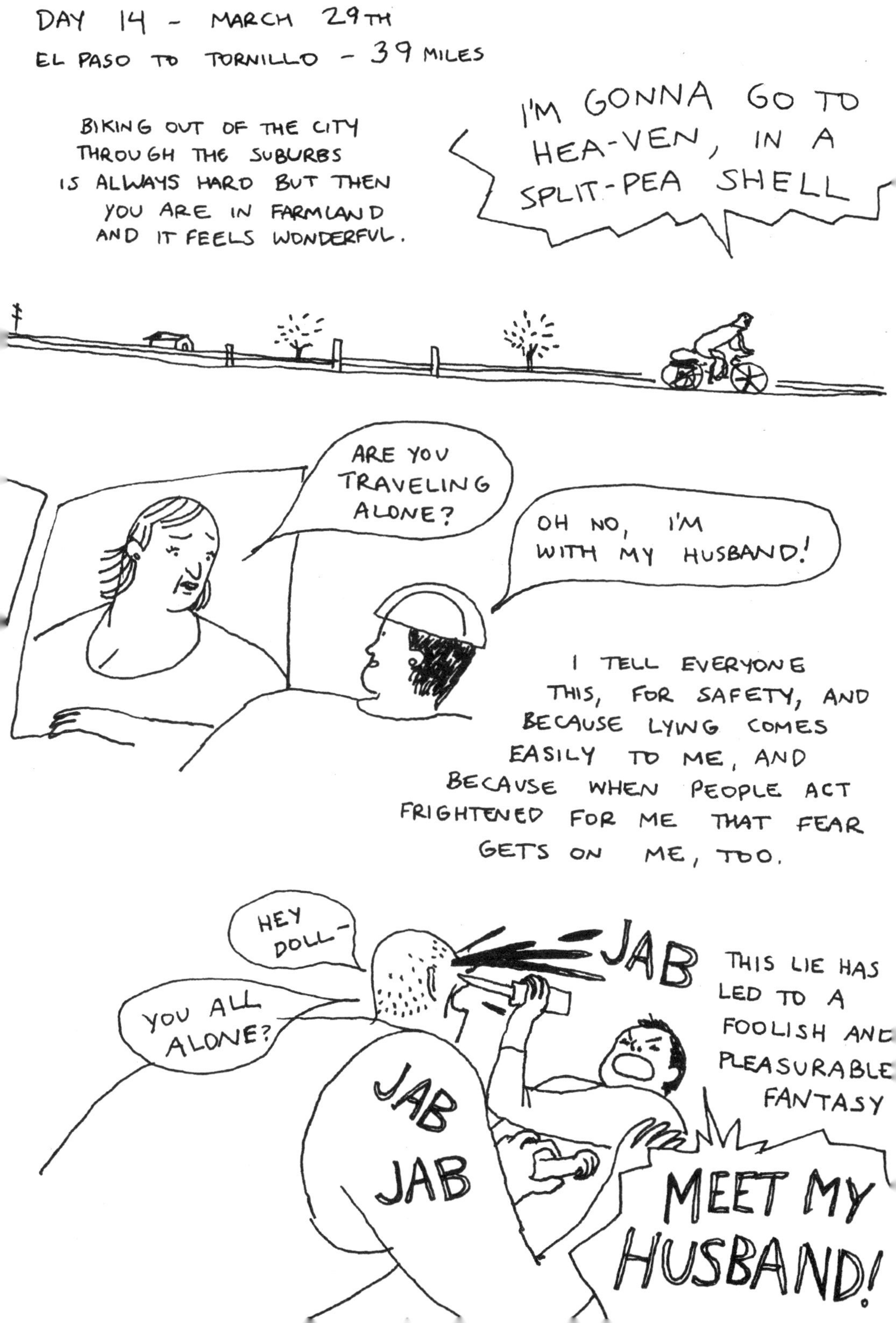
DAY 14 - MARCH 29TH
EL PASO TO TORNILLO - 39 MILES
BIKING OUT OF THE CITY THROUGH THE SUBURBS IS ALWAYS HARD BUT THEN YOU ARE IN FARMLAND AND IT FEELS WONDERFUL.
I'M GONNA GO TO HEA-VEN, IN A SPLIT-PEA SHELL
ARE YOU TRAVELING ALONE?
OH NO, I'M WITH MY HUSBAND!
I TELL EVERYONE THIS, FOR SAFETY, AND BECAUSE LYING COMES EASILY TO ME, AND BECAUSE WHEN PEOPLE ACT FRIGHTENED FOR ME THAT FEAR GETS ON ME, TOO.
HEY DOLL-
YOU ALL ALONE?
JAB
THIS LIE HAS LED TO A FOOLISH AND PLEASURABLE FANTASY
JAB
JAB
MEET MY HUSBAND!

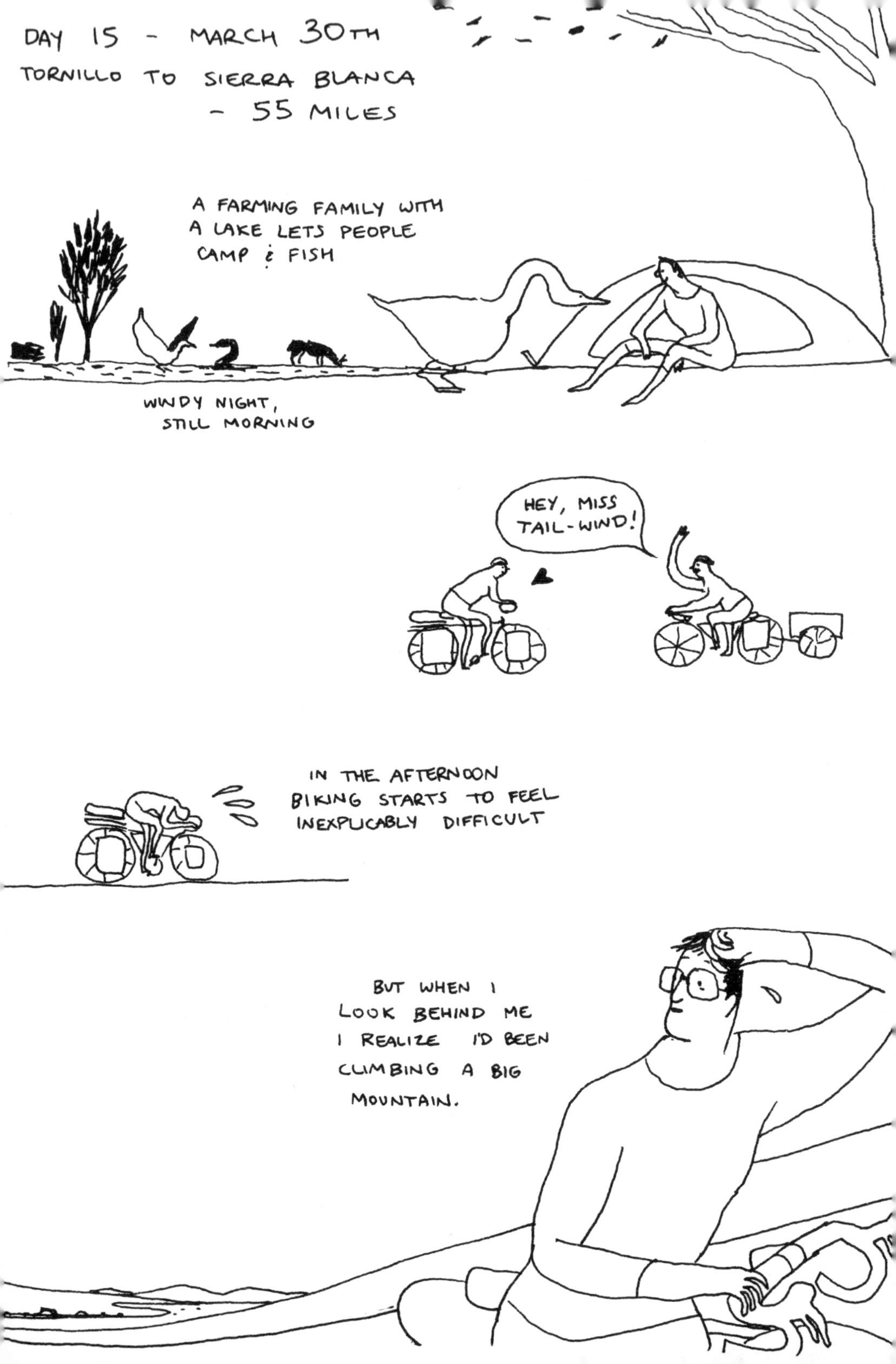
DAY 15 - MARCH 30TH
TORNILLO TO SIERRA BLANCA
- 55 MILES
A FARMING FAMILY WITH A LAKE LETS PEOPLE CAMP & FISH
WINDY NIGHT, STILL MORNING
HEY, MISS TAIL-WIND!
IN THE AFTERNOON BIKING STARTS TO FEEL INEXPLICABLY DIFFICULT
BUT WHEN I LOOK BEHIND ME I REALIZE I'D BEEN CLIMBING A BIG MOUNTAIN.

YESTERDAY IT
WAS ALL SHRUBBY
BUSHES

TODAY
THERE'S TALL
GRASS

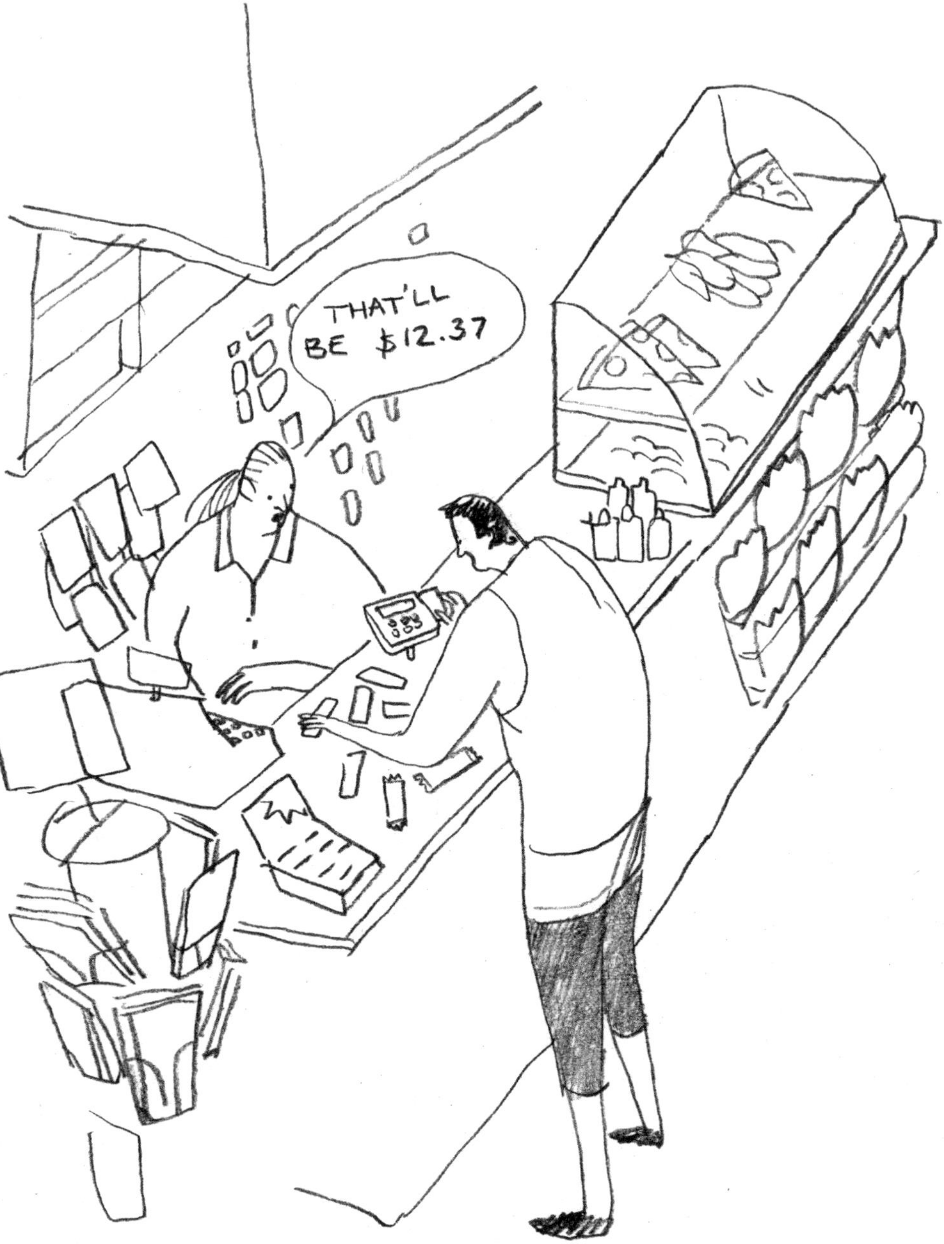
THAT'LL BE $12.37

DAY 16 - MARCH 31ST

SIERRA BLANCA TO VAN HORN - 33 MILES

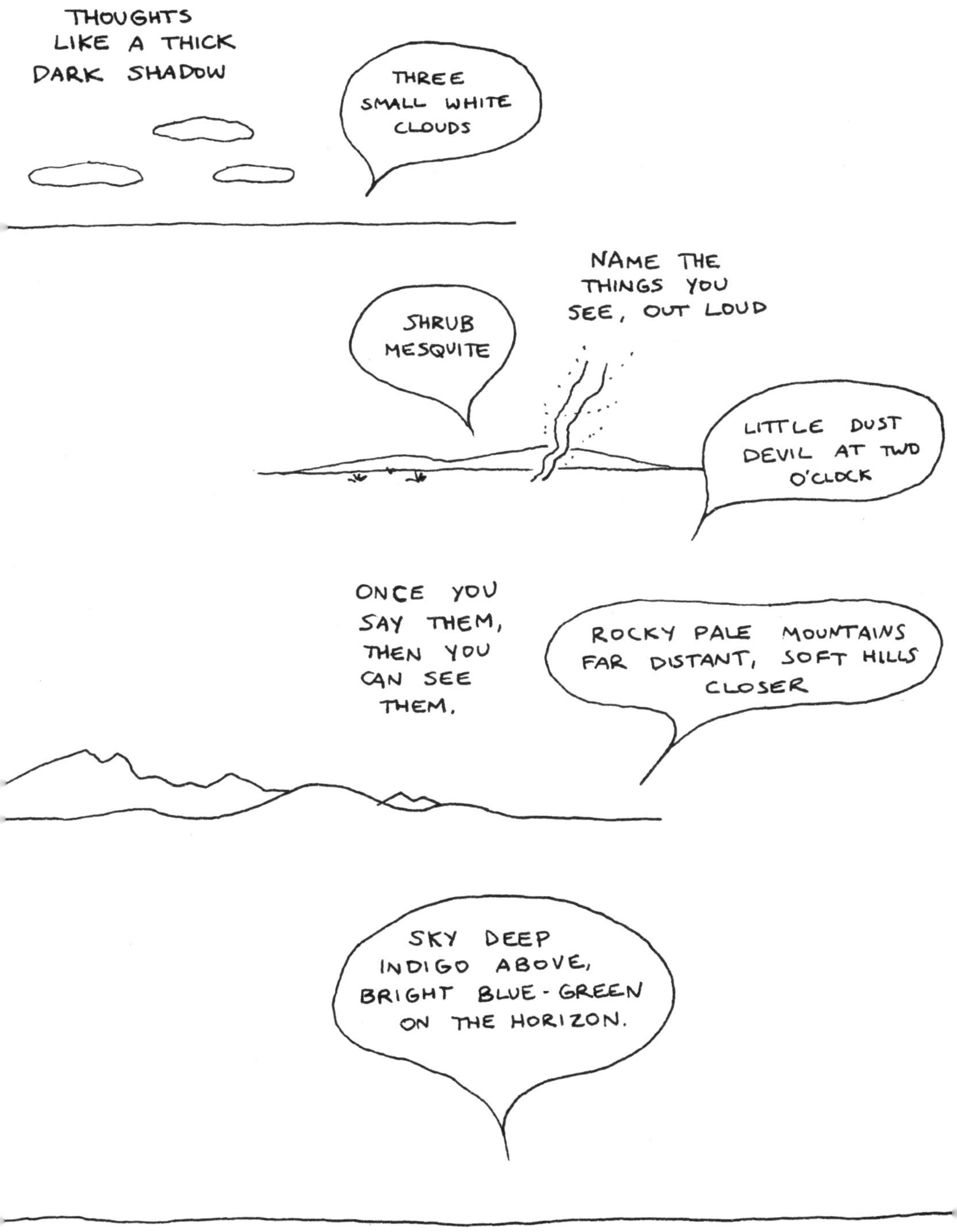
THOUGHTS LIKE A THICK DARK SHADOW
THREE SMALL WHITE CLOUDS
NAME THE THINGS YOU SEE, OUT LOUD
SHRUB MESQUITE
LITTLE DUST DEVIL AT TWO O'CLOCK
ONCE YOU SAY THEM, THEN YOU CAN SEE THEM.
ROCKY PALE MOUNTAINS FAR DISTANT, SOFT HILLS CLOSER
SKY DEEP INDIGO ABOVE, BRIGHT BLUE-GREEN ON THE HORIZON.

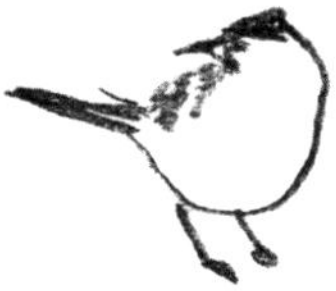

A NEW
KIND OF
BIRD

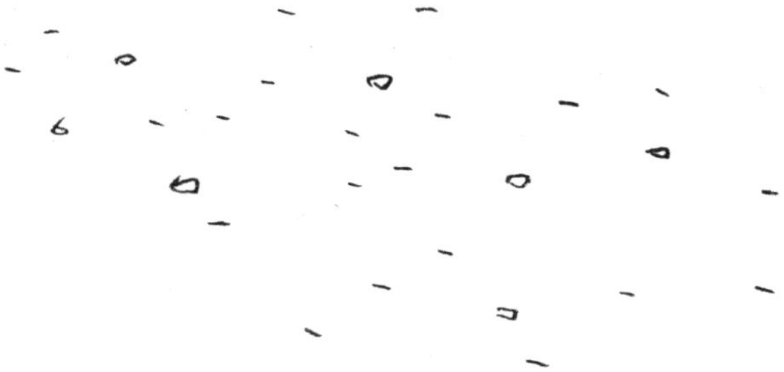

DIFFERENT
COLOR DIRT

I'M MOVING THROUGH FARMLAND
IN WEST TEXAS. THE MOUNTAINS
OF CHIHUAHUA, MEXICO ARE ON
MY RIGHT, IN THE DISTANCE,
AND BETWEEN US IS A TALL,
DARK STRIP OF FENCE.

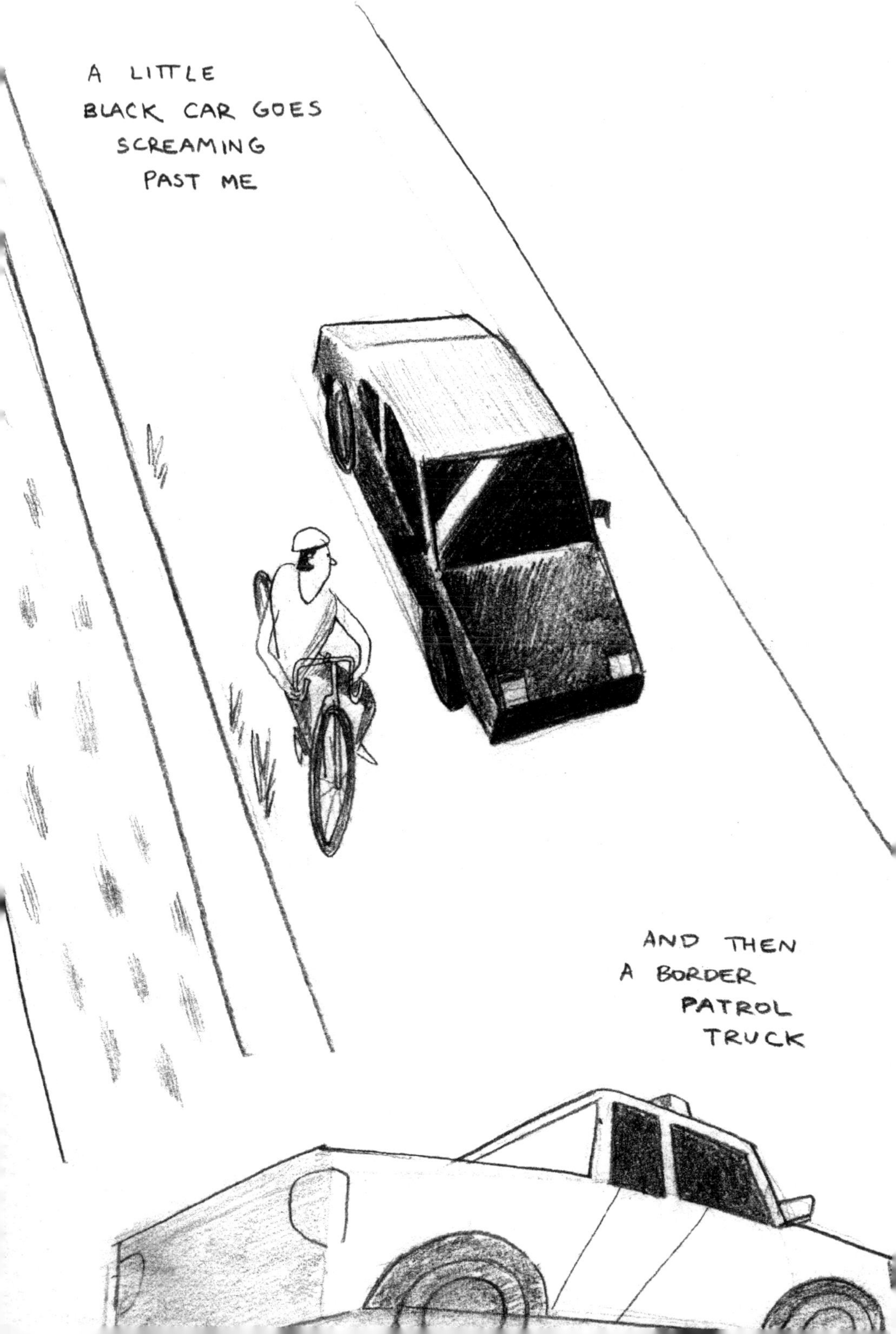
A LITTLE BLACK CAR GOES SCREAMING PAST ME
AND THEN A BORDER PATROL TRUCK

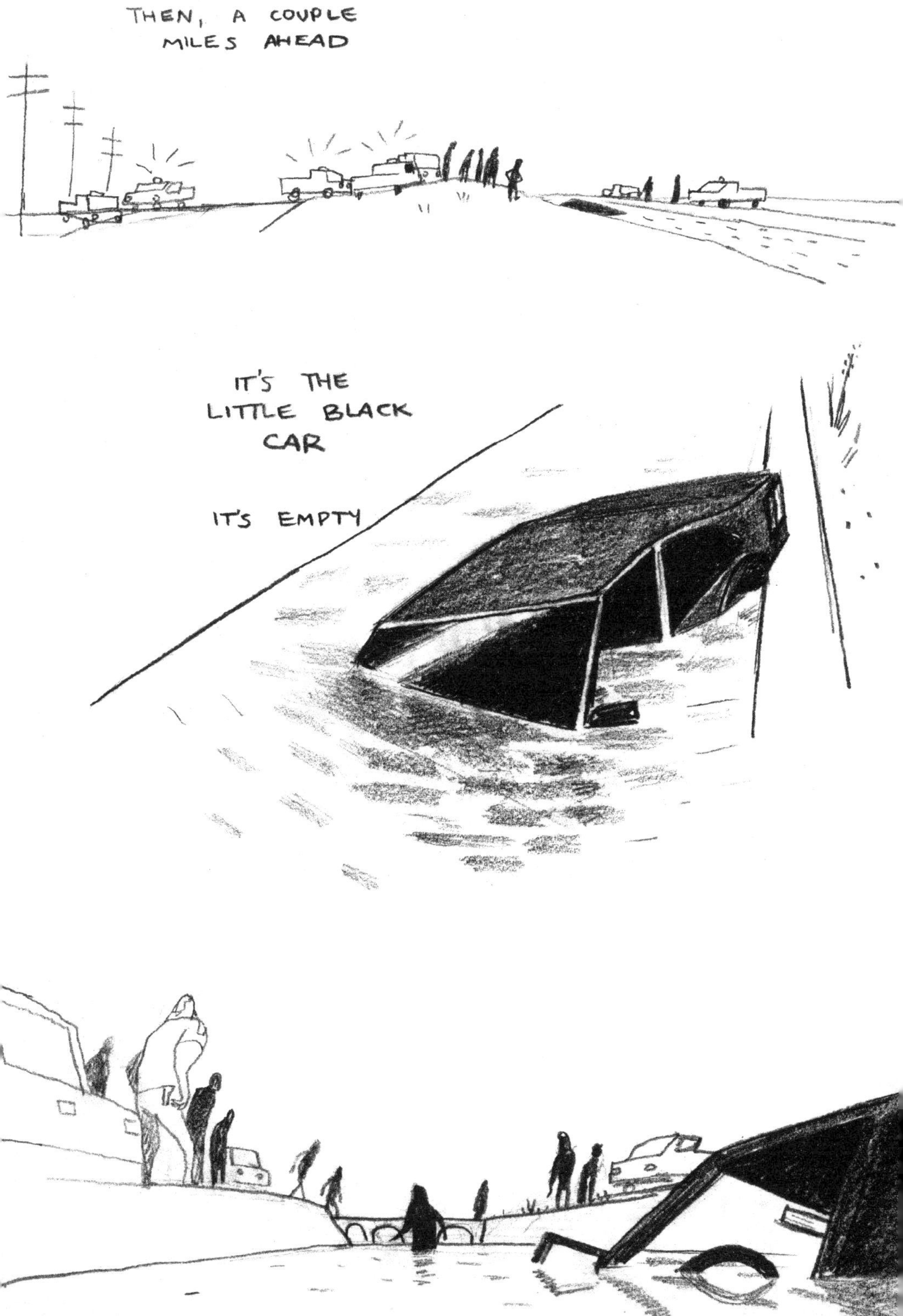
THEN, A COUPLE MILES AHEAD
IT'S THE LITTLE BLACK CAR
IT'S EMPTY

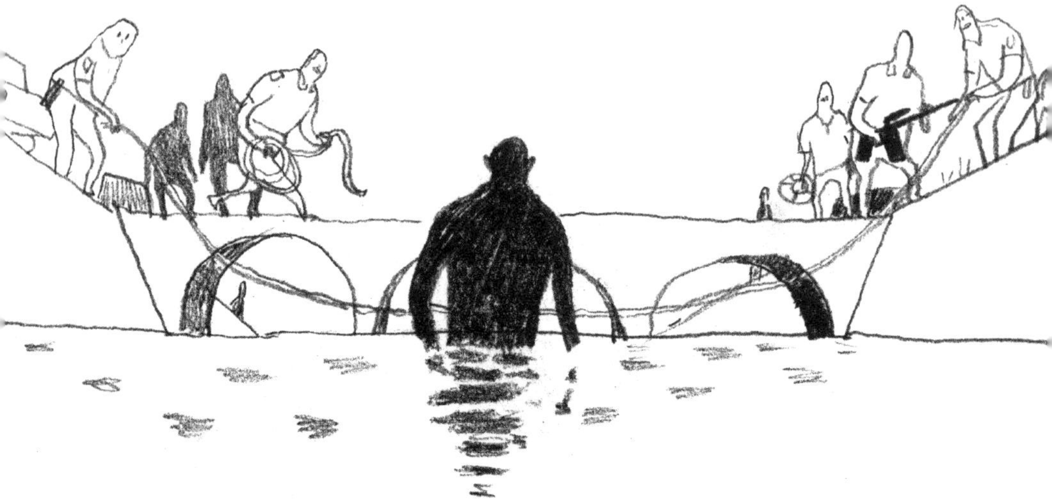

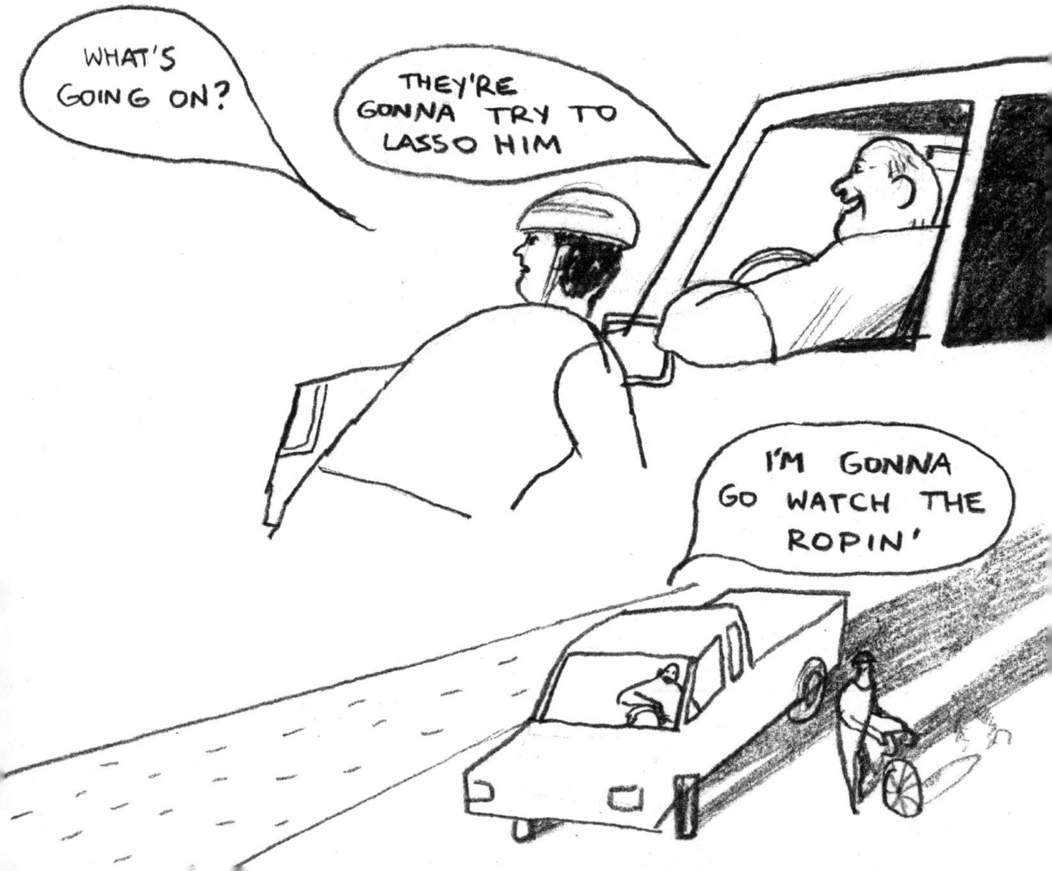
WHAT'S GOING ON?
THEY'RE GONNA TRY TO LASSO HIM
I'M GONNA GO WATCH THE ROPIN'

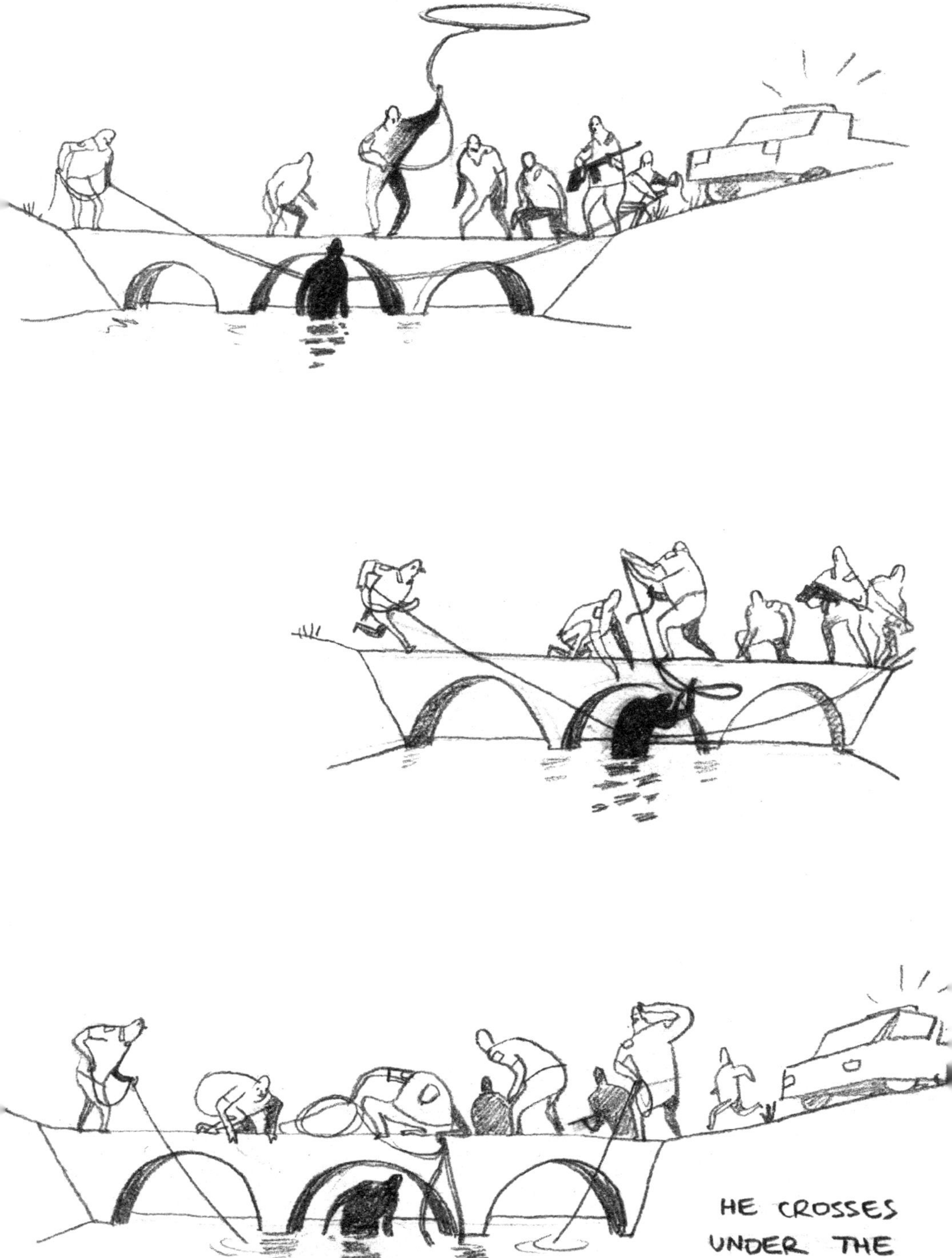
HE CROSSES UNDER THE BRIDGE

I'D THOUGHT HE WAS A BIG MAN, BUT WHEN I MOVE AROUND TO SEE HIS FACE HE'S THIN, AND YOUNG

HE'S WALKING
THROUGH THE WATER

THE BORDER PATROL,
DEPUTIES, AND EMTS WALK
BESIDE HIM ON EITHER BANK

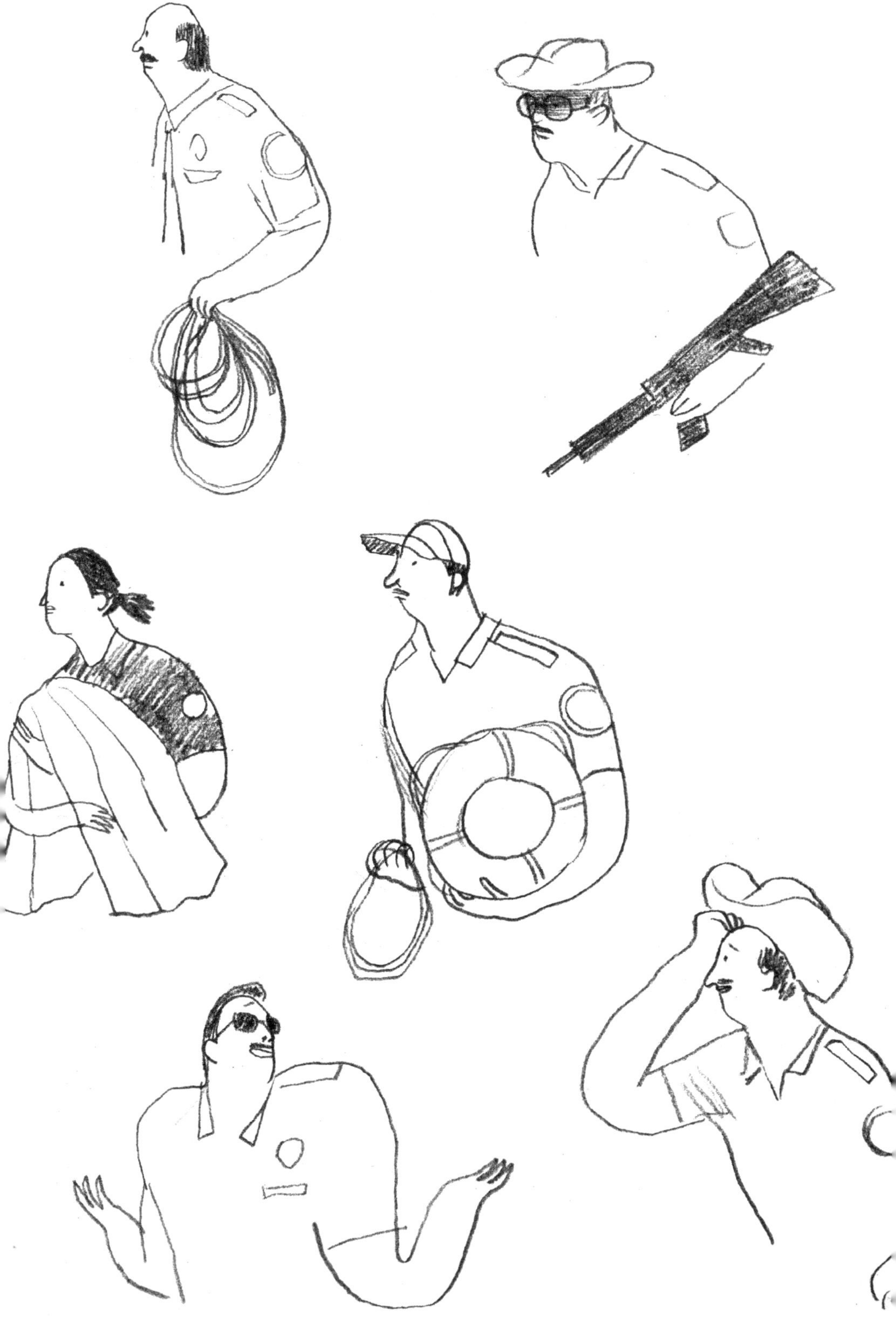

EVENTUALLY SOMEONE STARTS
SAYING "WE CAN HELP YOU, WE CAN HELP
YOU, MAN," AND HE COMES TO THE
BANK OF THE CANAL AND HE HALF
CLIMBS, HALF GETS PULLED OUT, AND
THEY PUSH HIM DOWN AND HANDCUFF
HIM AND HE'S SCREAMING HOARSELY.

THEN THE EMTS BRING A STRETCHER
AND THEY UNCUFF HIM AGAIN SO
THEY CAN TAKE HIS WET SHIRT OFF
AND THEY WRAP HIM IN BLANKETS
AND TAKE HIM AWAY.

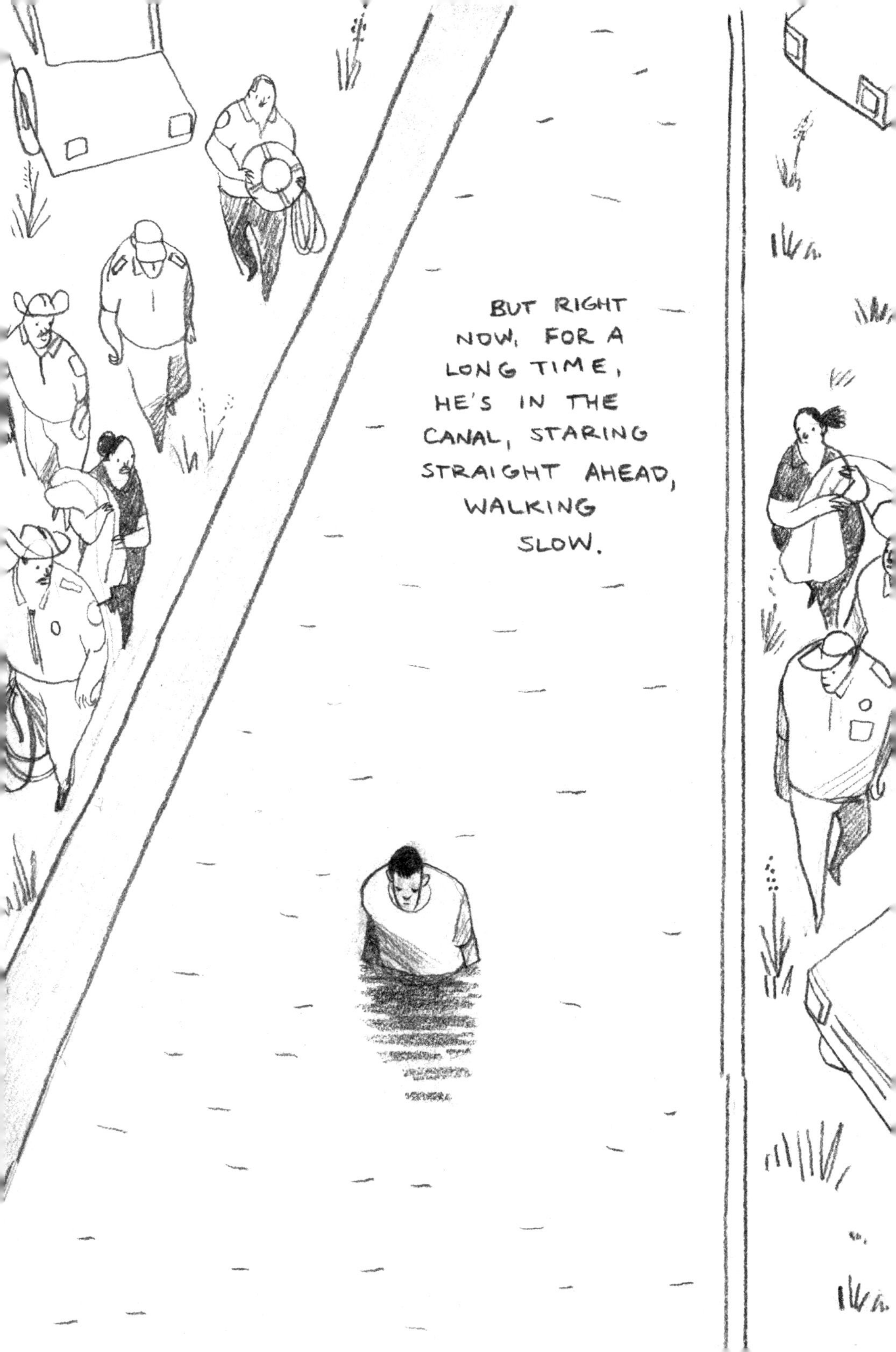
BUT RIGHT NOW, FOR A LONG TIME, HE'S IN THE CANAL, STARING STRAIGHT AHEAD, WALKING SLOW.

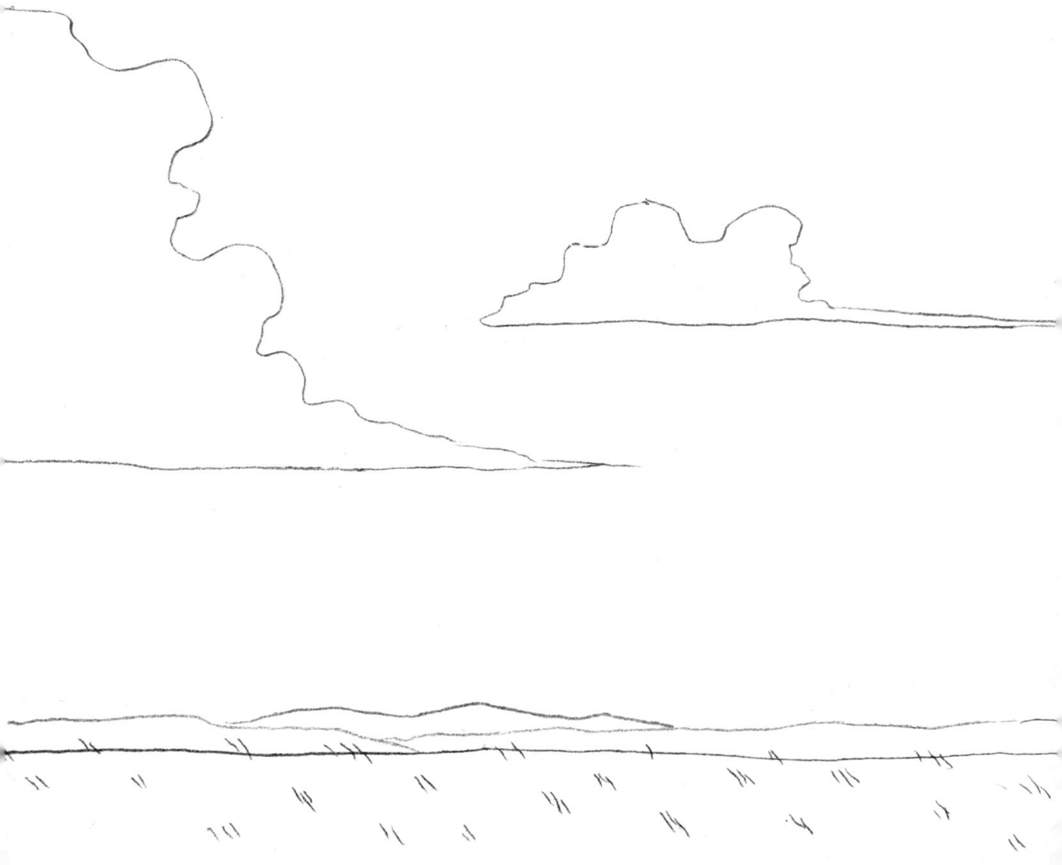

BORDER
PATROL
BLIMP

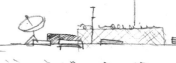

DAY 17 - APRIL 1ST

VAN HORN TO OUTSIDE OF VALENTINE - 46 M

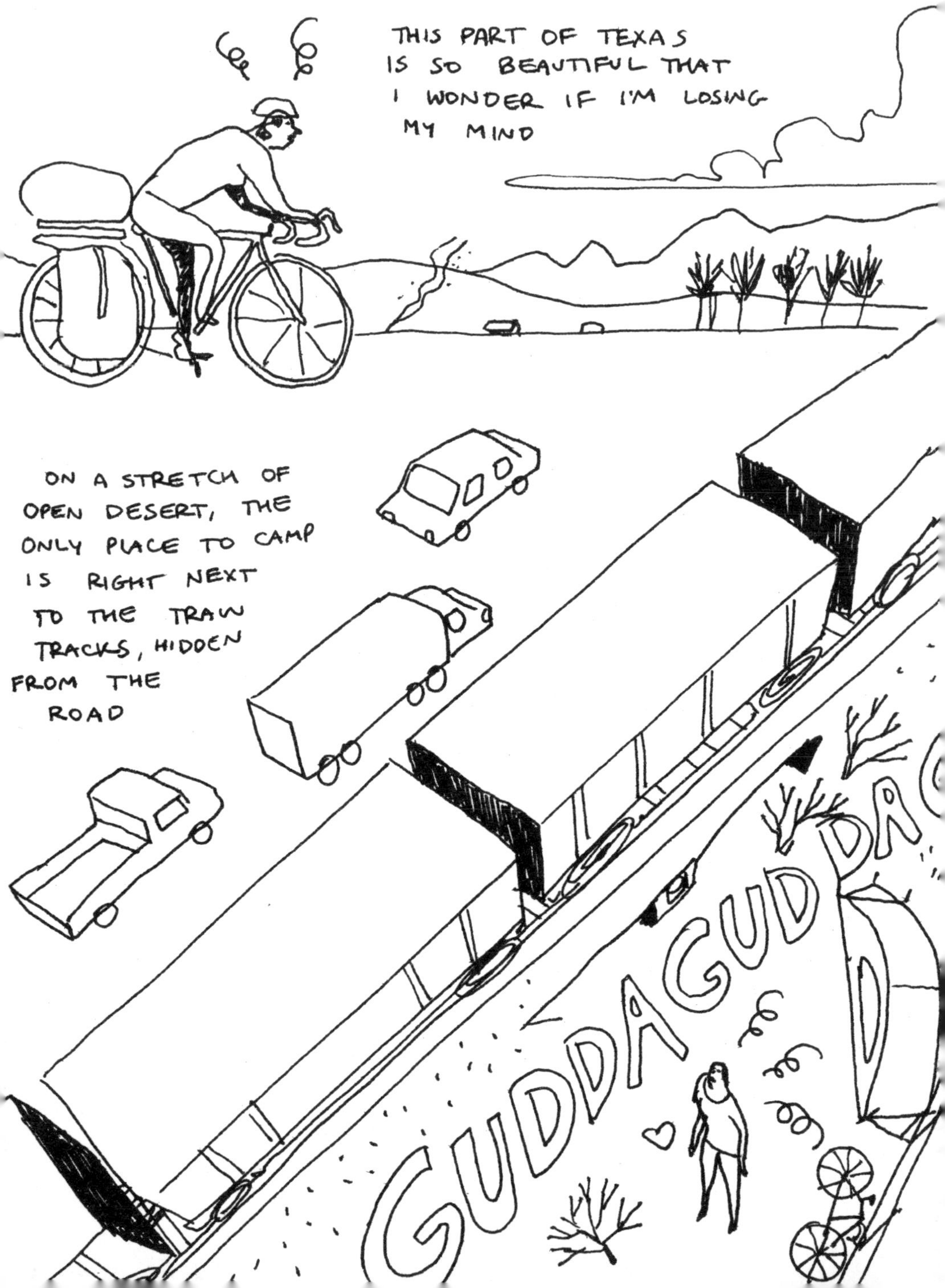
THIS PART OF TEXAS IS SO BEAUTIFUL THAT I WONDER IF I'M LOSING MY MIND
ON A STRETCH OF OPEN DESERT, THE ONLY PLACE TO CAMP IS RIGHT NEXT TO THE TRAIN TRACKS, HIDDEN FROM THE ROAD
GUDDAGUD

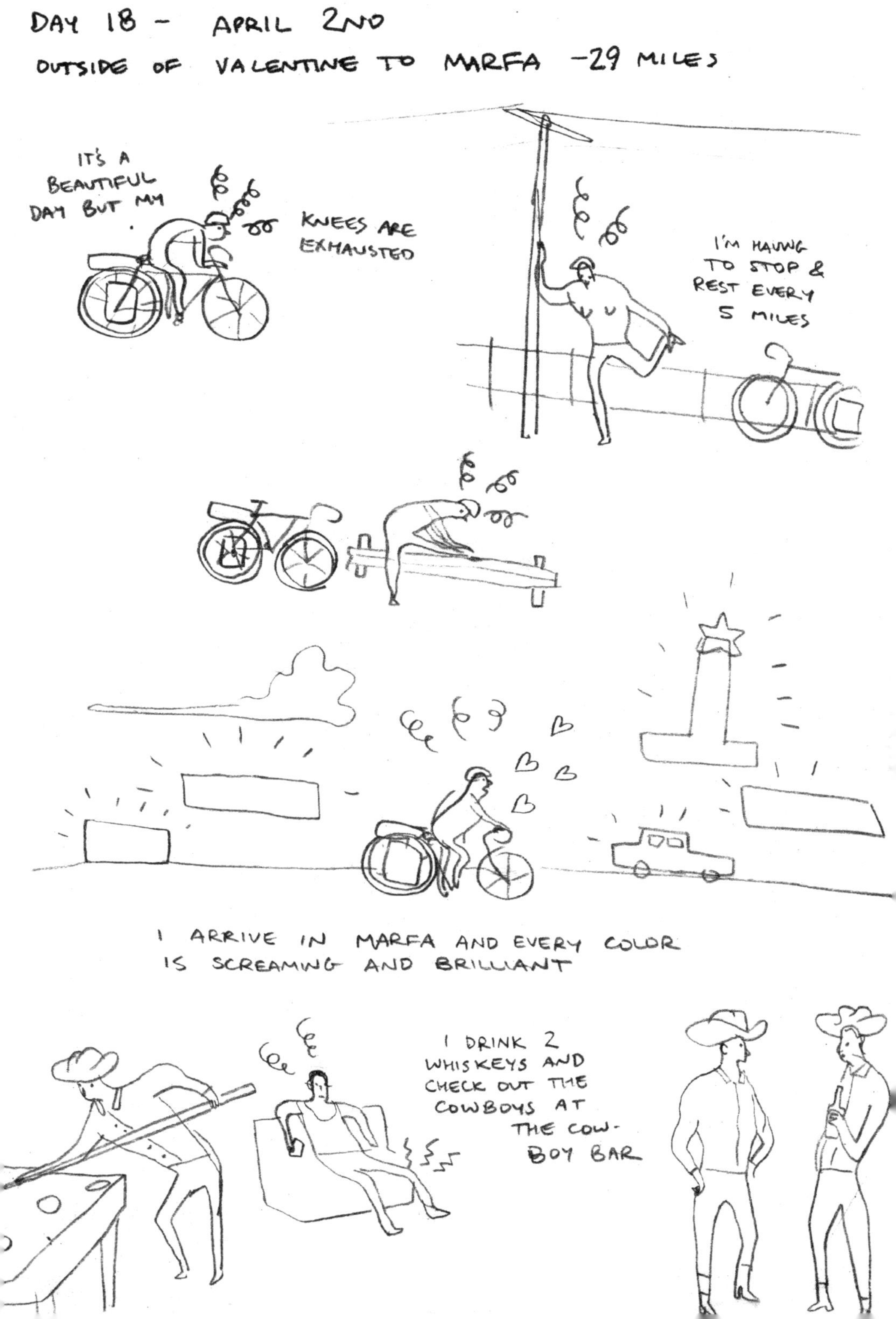
DAY 18 - APRIL 2ND
OUTSIDE OF VALENTINE TO MARFA -29 MILES
IT'S A BEAUTIFUL DAY BUT MY
KNEES ARE EXHAUSTED
I'M HAVING TO STOP & REST EVERY 5 MILES
I ARRIVE IN MARFA AND EVERY COLOR IS SCREAMING AND BRILLIANT
I DRINK 2 WHISKEYS AND CHECK OUT THE COWBOYS AT THE COW-BOY BAR

DAY 19 - APRIL 3RD

BREAK IN MARFA

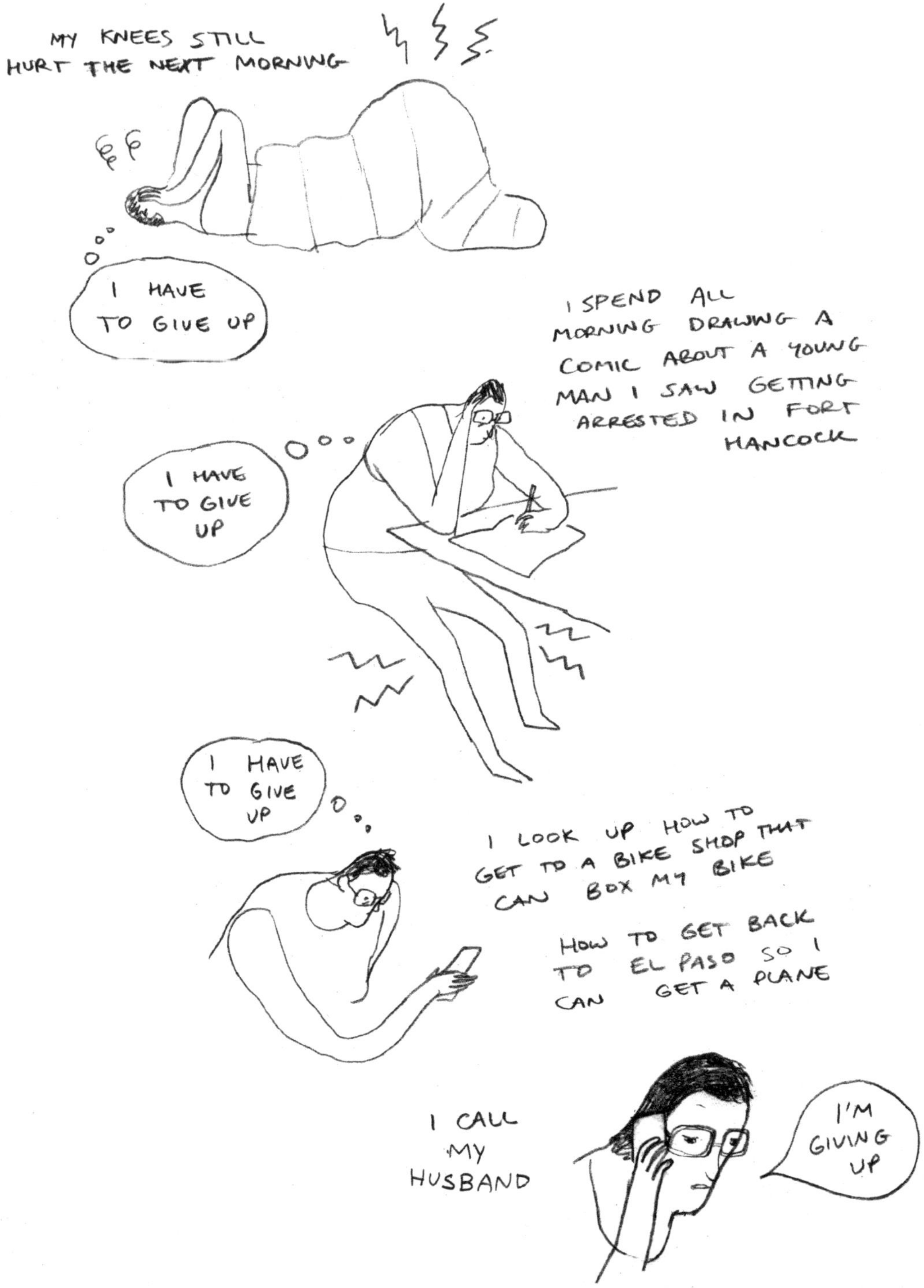
MY KNEES STILL HURT THE NEXT MORNING
I HAVE TO GIVE UP
I SPEND ALL MORNING DRAWING A COMIC ABOUT A YOUNG MAN I SAW GETTING ARRESTED IN FORT HANCOCK
I HAVE TO GIVE UP
I HAVE TO GIVE UP
I LOOK UP HOW TO GET TO A BIKE SHOP THAT CAN BOX MY BIKE
HOW TO GET BACK TO EL PASO SO I CAN GET A PLANE
I CALL MY HUSBAND
I'M GIVING UP

DAY 21 - APRIL 5TH
MARFA TO ALPINE - 25 MILES

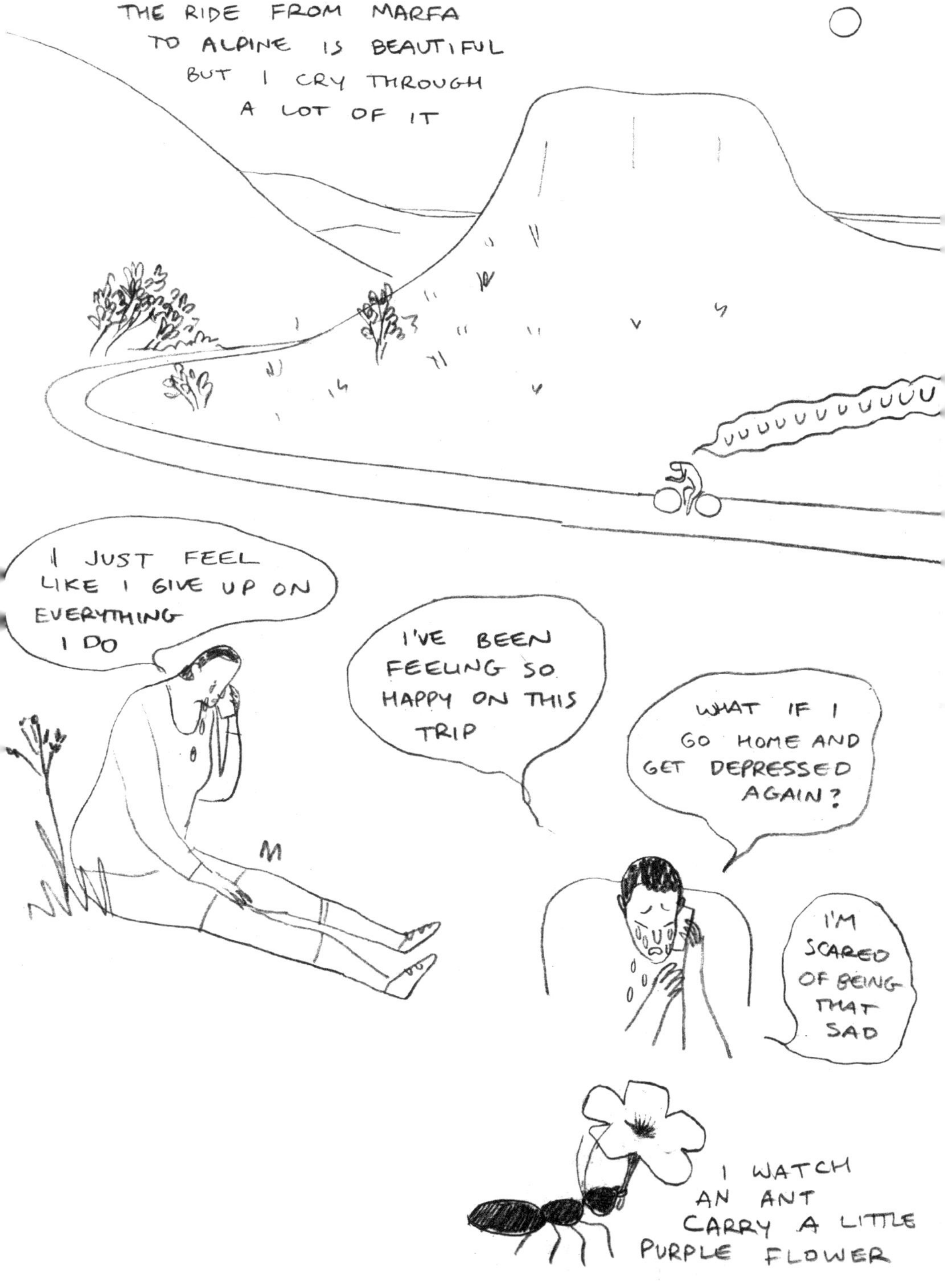

DAY 21 - APRIL 5TH (CON'T)

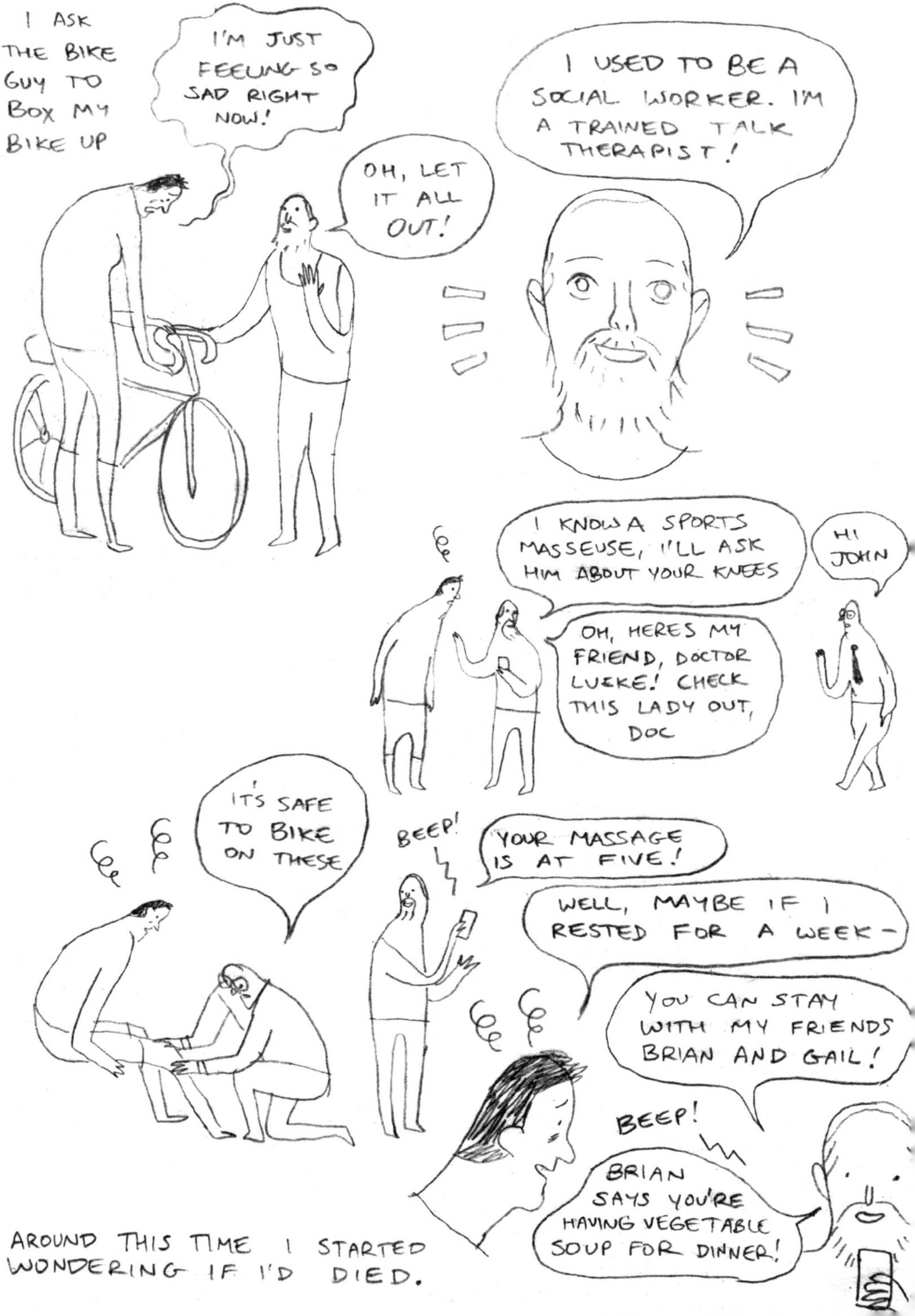

I ASK THE BIKE GUY TO BOX MY BIKE UP
I'M JUST FEELING SO SAD RIGHT NOW!
OH, LET IT ALL OUT!
I USED TO BE A SOCIAL WORKER. I'M A TRAINED TALK THERAPIST!
I KNOW A SPORTS MASSEUSE, I'LL ASK HIM ABOUT YOUR KNEES
OH, HERES MY FRIEND, DOCTOR LUEKE! CHECK THIS LADY OUT, DOC
HI JOHN
IT'S SAFE TO BIKE ON THESE
BEEP!
YOUR MASSAGE IS AT FIVE!
WELL, MAYBE IF I RESTED FOR A WEEK-
YOU CAN STAY WITH MY FRIENDS BRIAN AND GAIL!
BEEP!
BRIAN SAYS YOU'RE HAVING VEGETABLE SOUP FOR DINNER!
AROUND THIS TIME I STARTED WONDERING IF I'D DIED.

THIS IS BRIAN AND GAIL.
AND THIS IS HOBO!
BUT THERE'S BEEN NO LIVING WITH HIM SINCE THAT ARTICLE IN THE BIG BEND GAZETTE
BIG BEND GAZETTE
HOBO IS A CUTE DOG
NO PIPELINE

WE HAVE A DAUGHTER YOUR AGE!
BOY DO WE HATE REPUBLICANS!
IT'S WONDERFUL THAT YOU'RE AN ARTIST!
I MAKE GLASS ART
HAVE MORE SOUP!

TOWN MAYOR
HI BRIAN!
HI HOBO!
THERE'S BEEN NO LIVING WITH HIM SINCE THAT ARTICLE IN THE BIG BEND GAZETTE!

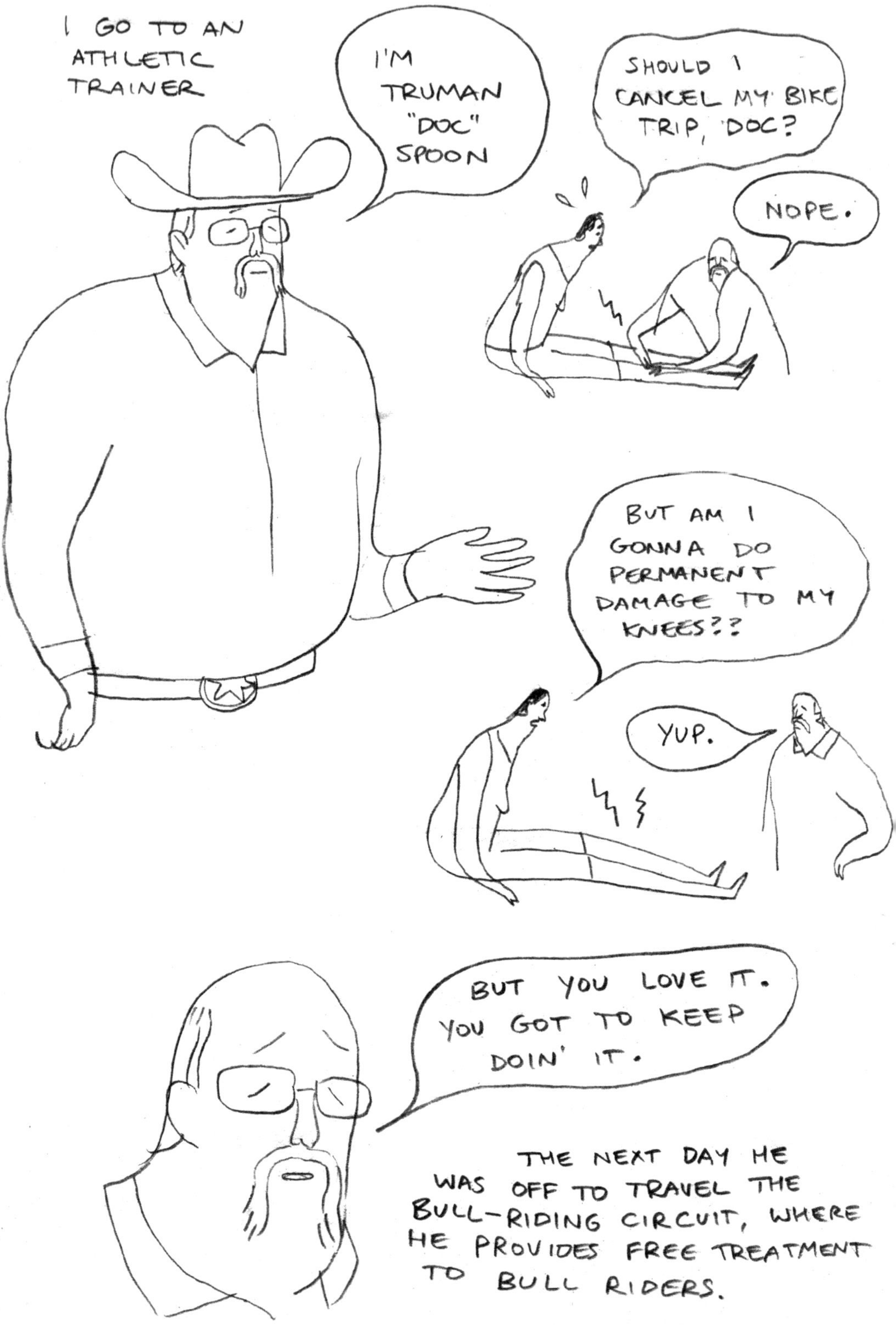
I GO TO AN ATHLETIC TRAINER
I'M TRUMAN "DOC" SPOON
SHOULD I CANCEL MY BIKE TRIP, DOC?
NOPE.
BUT AM I GONNA DO PERMANENT DAMAGE TO MY KNEES??
YUP.
BUT YOU LOVE IT. YOU GOT TO KEEP DOIN' IT.
THE NEXT DAY HE WAS OFF TO TRAVEL THE BULL-RIDING CIRCUIT, WHERE HE PROVIDES FREE TREATMENT TO BULL RIDERS.

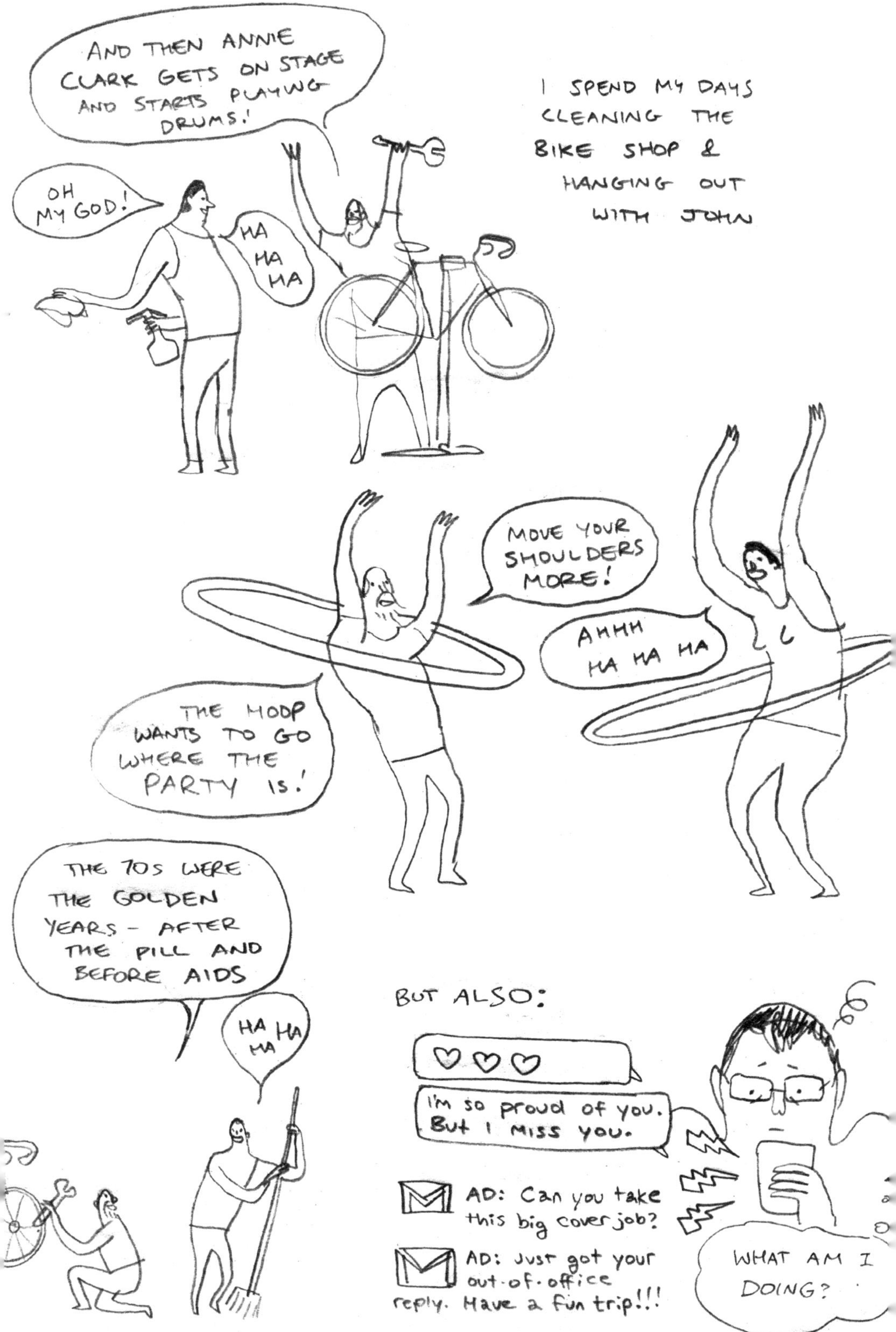
AND THEN ANNIE CLARK GETS ON STAGE AND STARTS PLAYING DRUMS!
OH MY GOD!
HA HA HA
I SPEND MY DAYS CLEANING THE BIKE SHOP & HANGING OUT WITH JOHN
MOVE YOUR SHOULDERS MORE!
AHHH HA HA HA
THE HOOP WANTS TO GO WHERE THE PARTY IS!
THE 70S WERE THE GOLDEN YEARS - AFTER THE PILL AND BEFORE AIDS
HA HA HA
BUT ALSO:
I'm so proud of you. But I miss you.
AD: Can you take this big cover job?
AD: Just got your out-of-office reply. Have a fun trip!!!
WHAT AM I DOING?

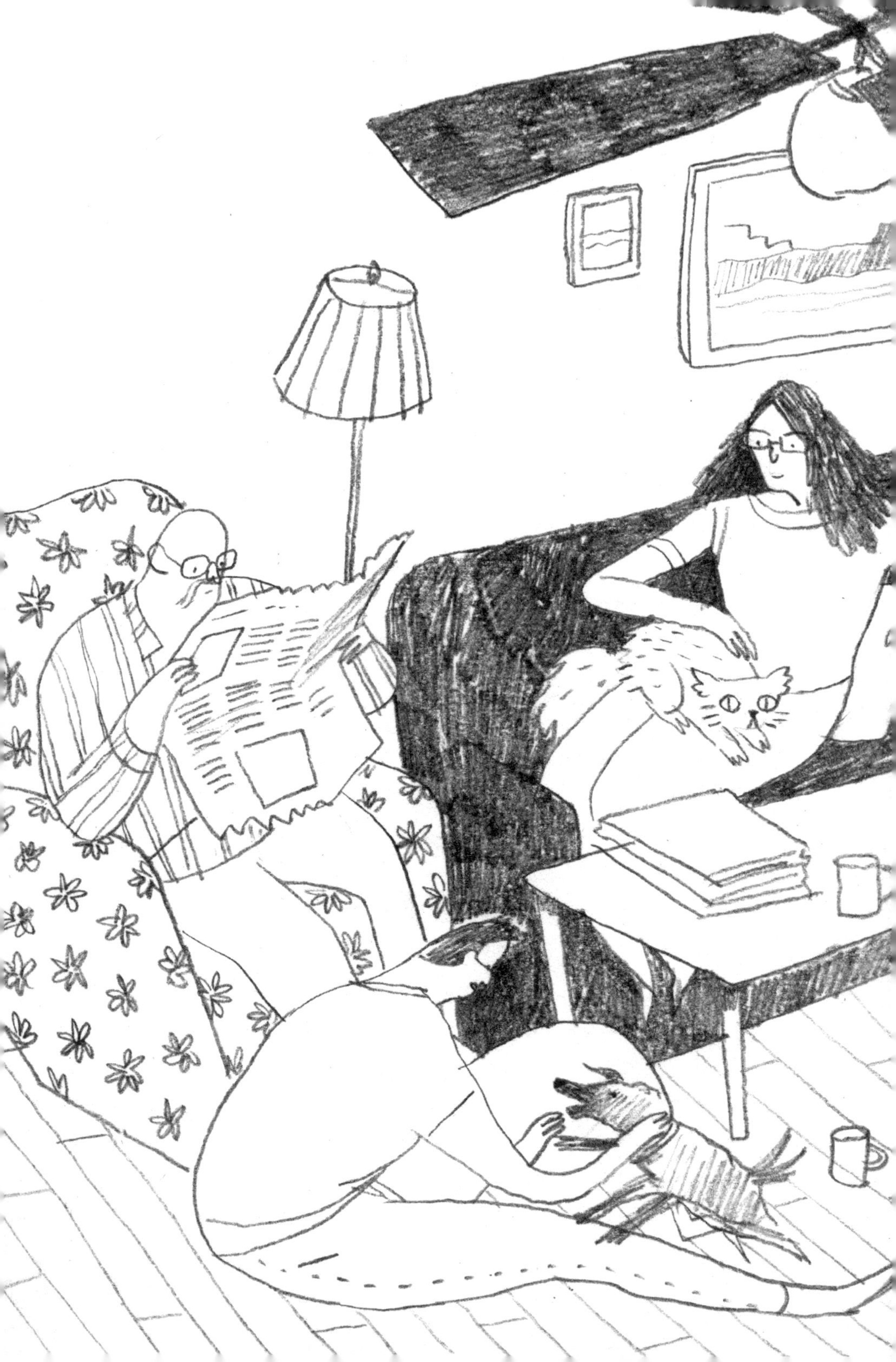

I KNEW I MIGHT FAIL AND I PROBABLY WILL FAIL
I THINK THERE'S ABOUT AN 80% CHANCE.
AND WHAT WILL I DO WITH TH EXPERIENCE?

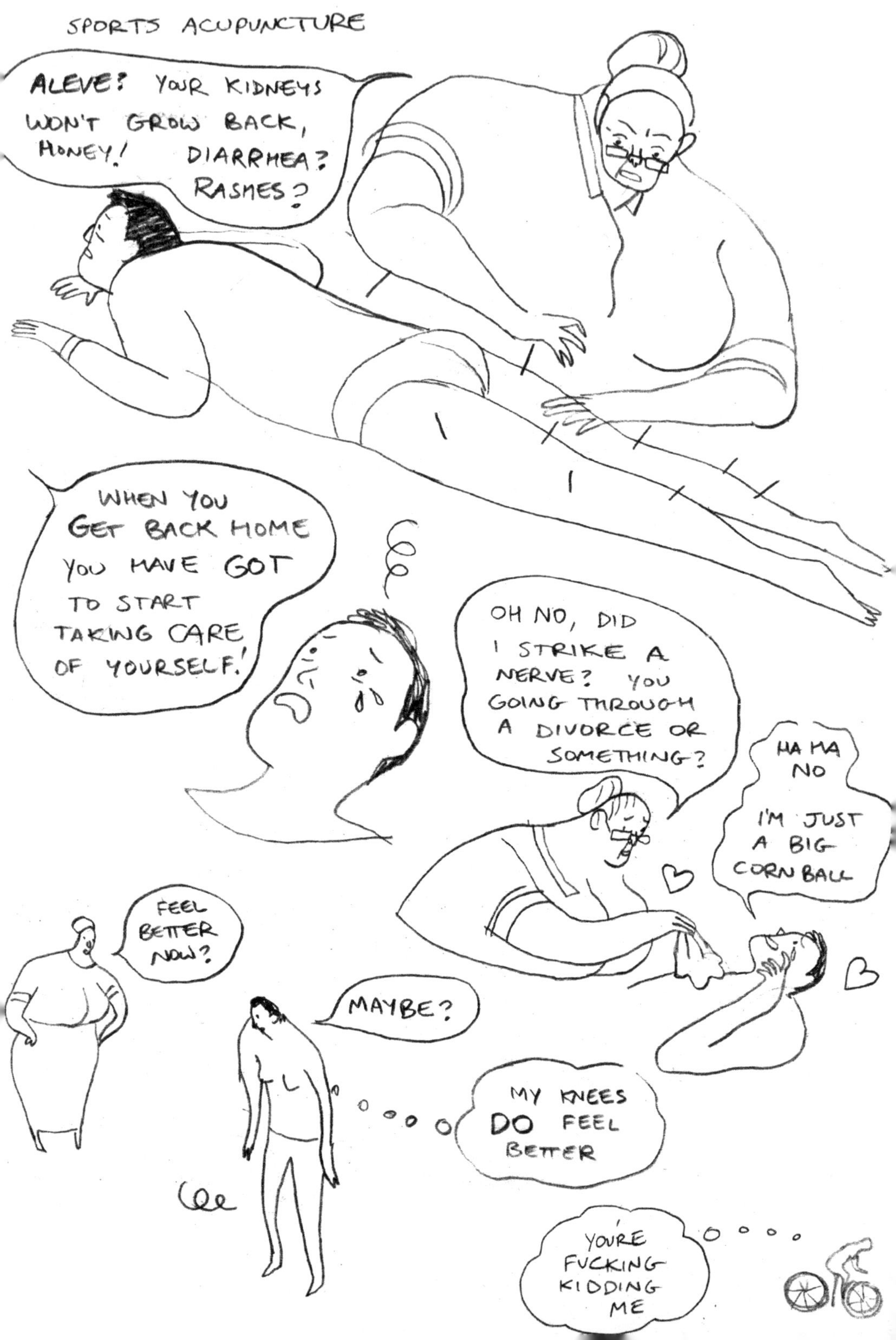
SPORTS ACUPUNCTURE
ALEVE? YOUR KIDNEYS WON'T GROW BACK, HONEY! DIARRHEA? RASHES?
WHEN YOU GET BACK HOME YOU HAVE GOT TO START TAKING CARE OF YOURSELF!
OH NO, DID I STRIKE A NERVE? YOU GOING THROUGH A DIVORCE OR SOMETHING?
HA HA NO
I'M JUST A BIG CORNBALL
FEEL BETTER NOW?
MAYBE?
MY KNEES DO FEEL BETTER
YOU'RE FUCKING KIDDING ME

DAY 27 — APRIL 11TH

ALPINE TO MARATHON, 33.5 MILES

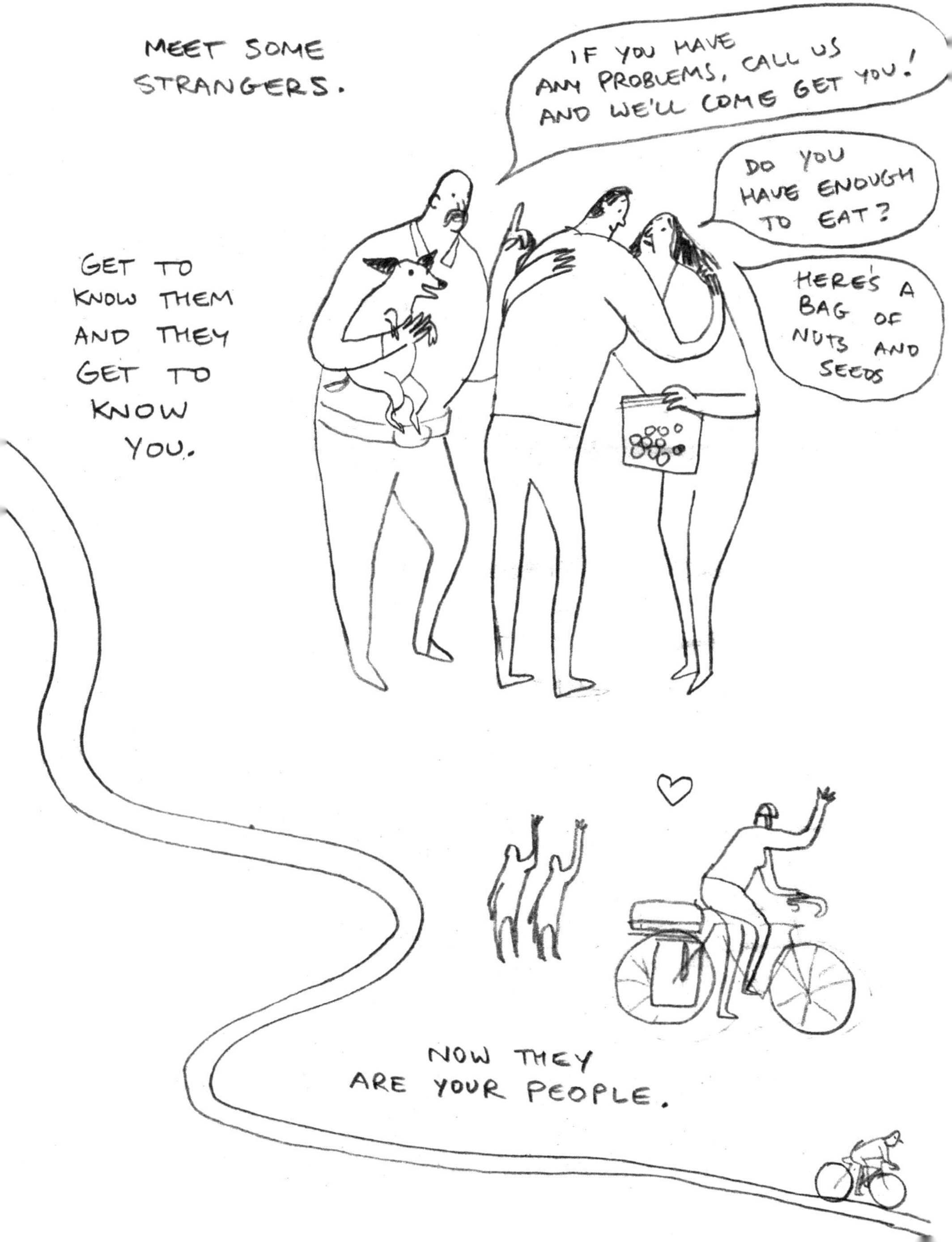
MEET SOME STRANGERS.
IF YOU HAVE ANY PROBLEMS, CALL US AND WE'LL COME GET YOU!
DO YOU HAVE ENOUGH TO EAT?
HERE'S A BAG OF NUTS AND SEEDS
GET TO KNOW THEM AND THEY GET TO KNOW YOU.
NOW THEY ARE YOUR PEOPLE.

DAY 29 — APRIL 13TH

MARATHON TO SANDERSON - 52 MILES

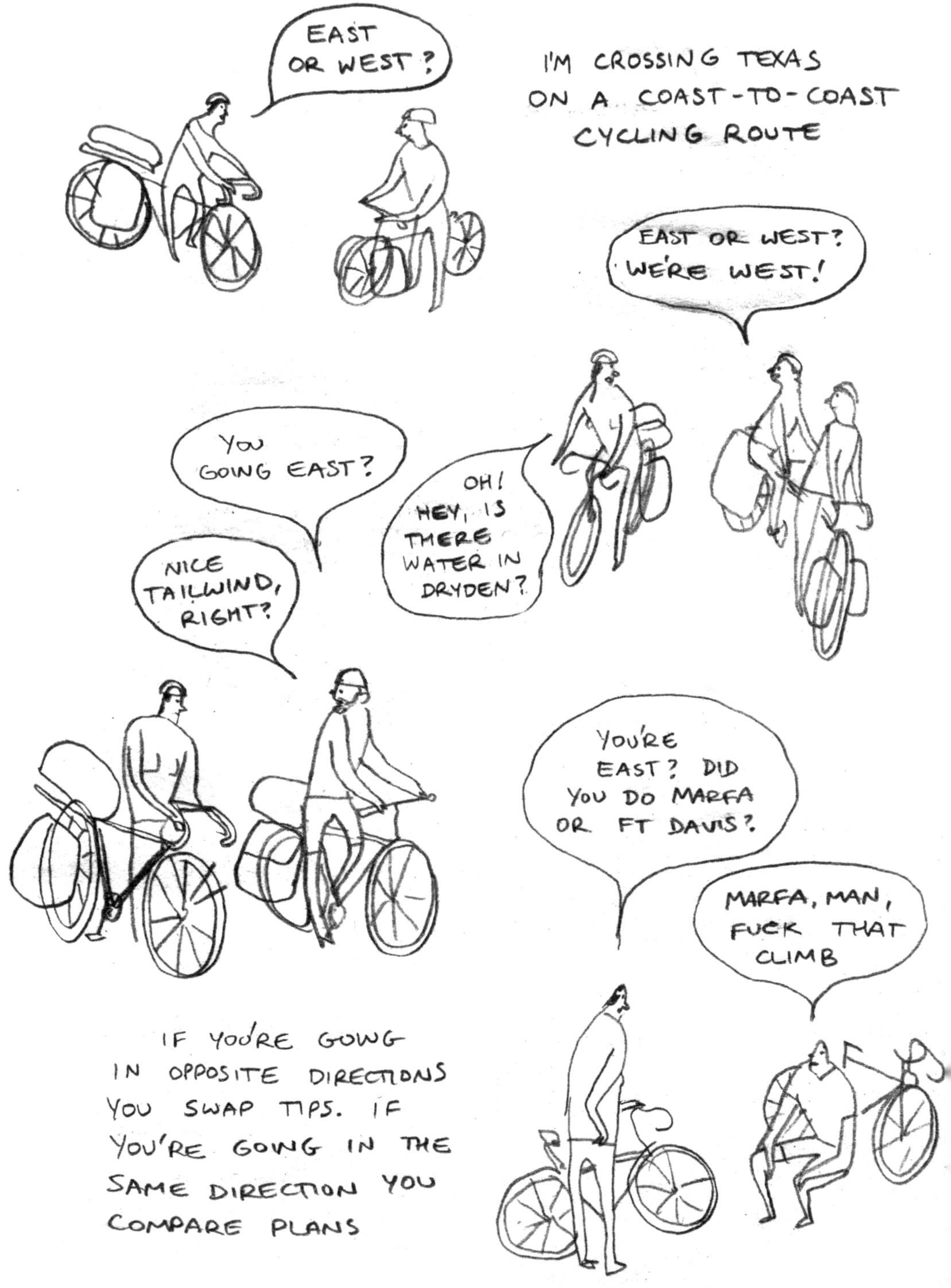
EAST OR WEST?
I'M CROSSING TEXAS ON A COAST-TO-COAST CYCLING ROUTE
EAST OR WEST? WE'RE WEST!
OH! HEY, IS THERE WATER IN DRYDEN?
YOU GOING EAST?
NICE TAILWIND, RIGHT?
YOU'RE EAST? DID YOU DO MARFA OR FT DAVIS?
MARFA, MAN, FUCK THAT CLIMB
IF YOU'RE GOING IN OPPOSITE DIRECTIONS YOU SWAP TIPS. IF YOU'RE GOING IN THE SAME DIRECTION YOU COMPARE PLANS

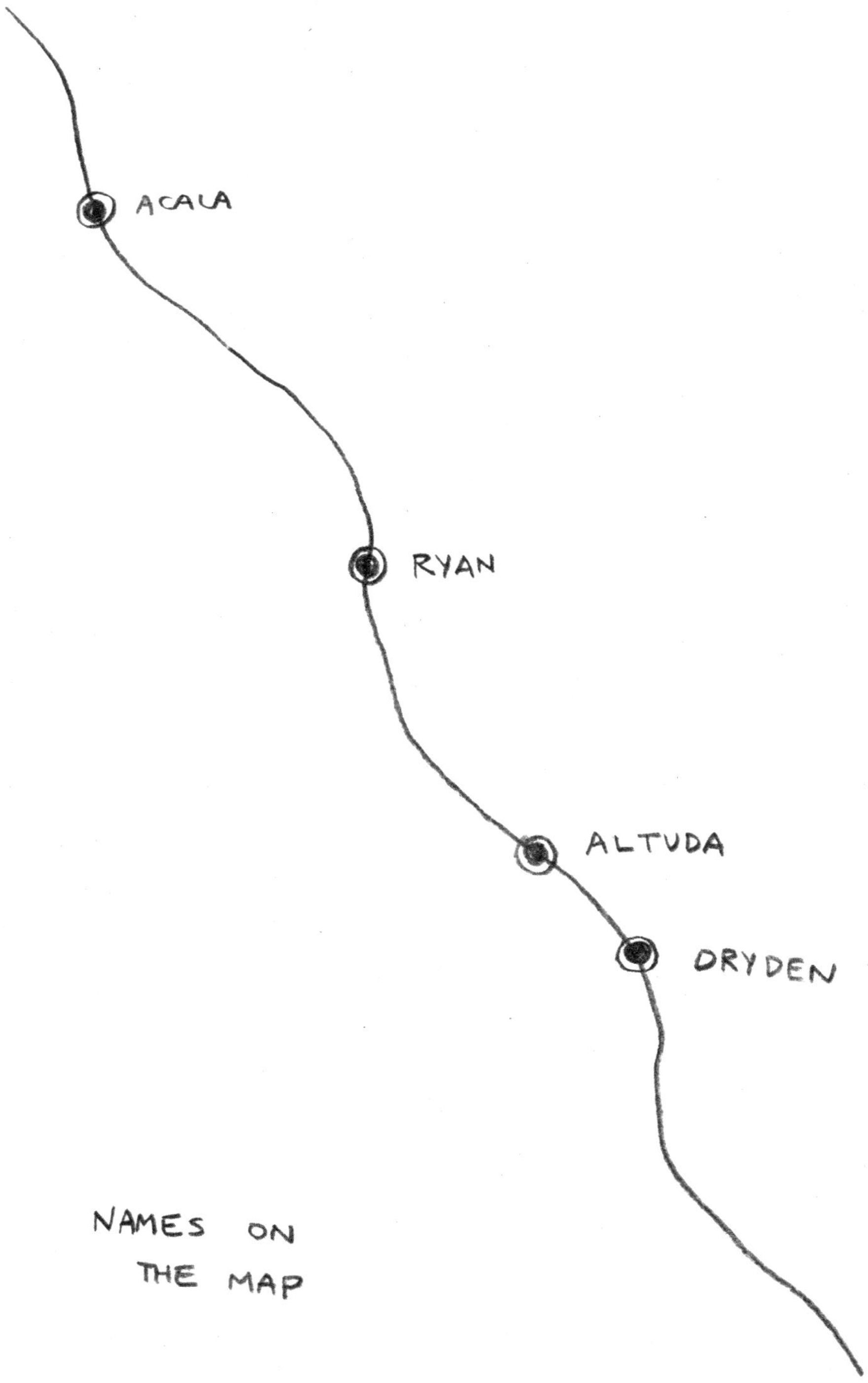
ACALA
RYAN
ALTUDA
DRYDEN
NAMES ON
THE MAP

BARK BARK

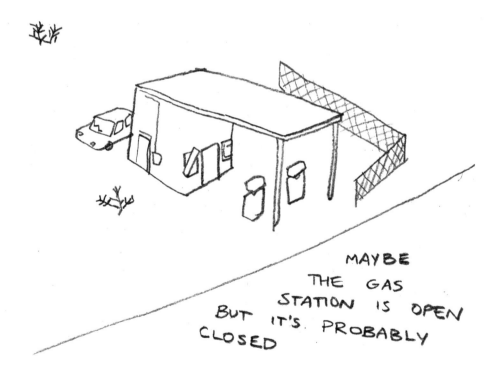

WHEN YOU GET
TO THEM THERE
ARE A FEW HOUSES.

MAYBE
THE GAS
STATION IS OPEN
BUT IT'S PROBABLY
CLOSED

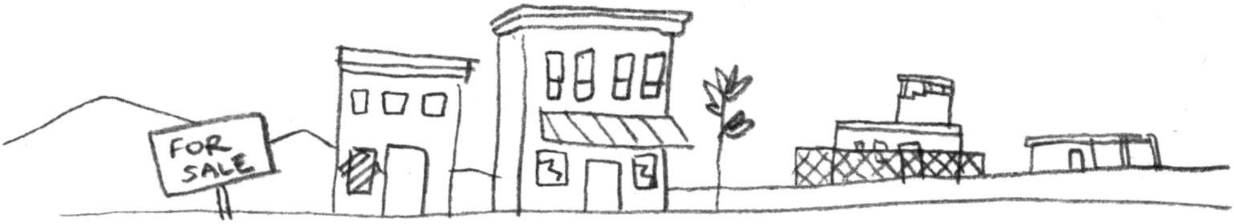
FOR SALE

AMTRAC
USED TO HAVE
A SHIFT CHANGE
HERE BUT NOW
IT DOESN'T

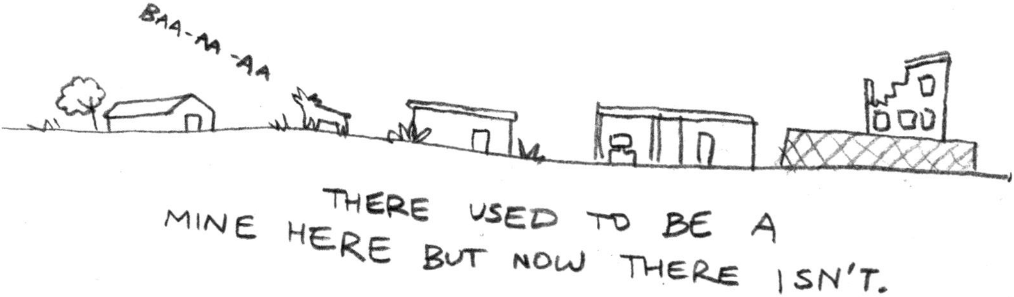
BAA-AA-AA

THERE USED TO BE A
MINE HERE BUT NOW THERE ISN'T.

DAY 30 – APRIL 14TH

SANDERSON TO CAMP OUTSIDE OF LANGTRY – 50 MILES

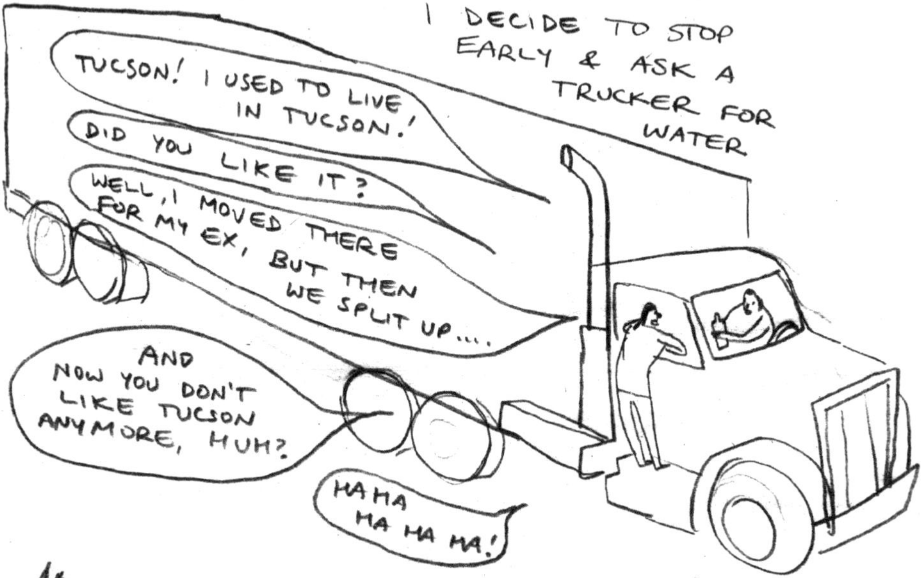
I DECIDE TO STOP EARLY & ASK A TRUCKER FOR WATER
TUCSON! I USED TO LIVE IN TUCSON!
DID YOU LIKE IT?
WELL, I MOVED THERE FOR MY EX, BUT THEN WE SPLIT UP....
AND NOW YOU DON'T LIKE TUCSON ANYMORE, HUH?
HA HA HA HA HA!

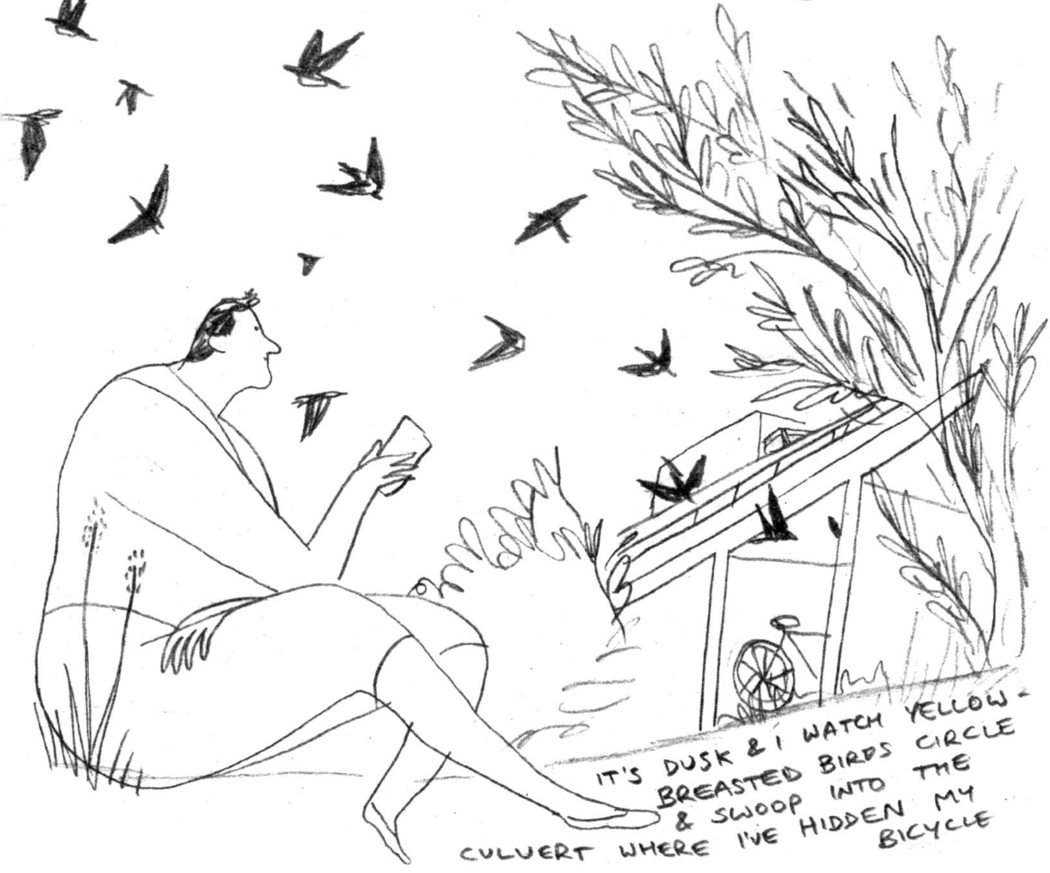
IT'S DUSK & I WATCH YELLOW-BREASTED BIRDS CIRCLE & SWOOP INTO THE CULVERT WHERE I'VE HIDDEN MY BICYCLE

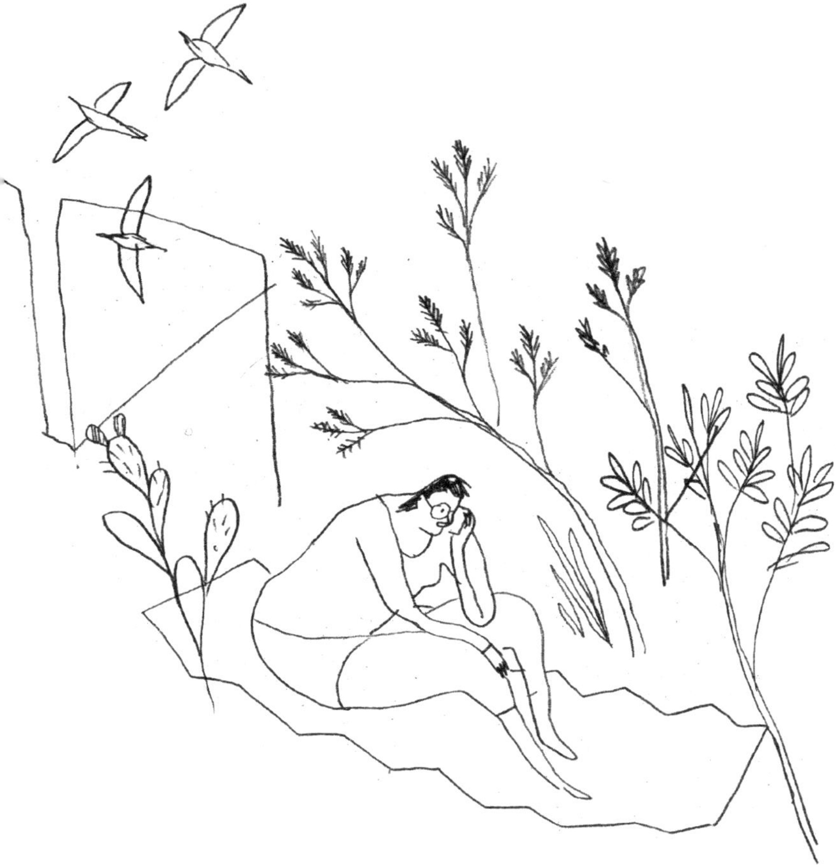

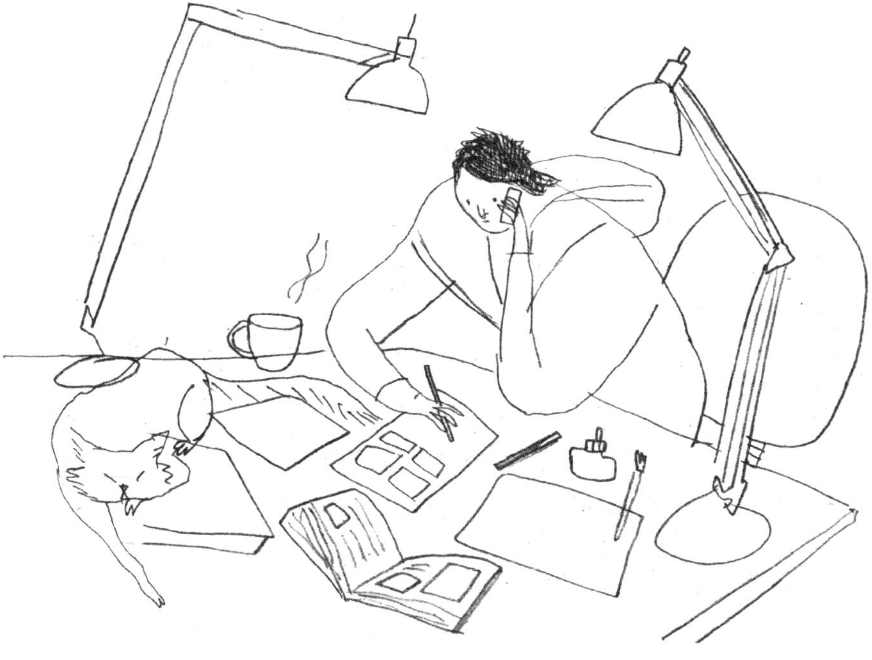

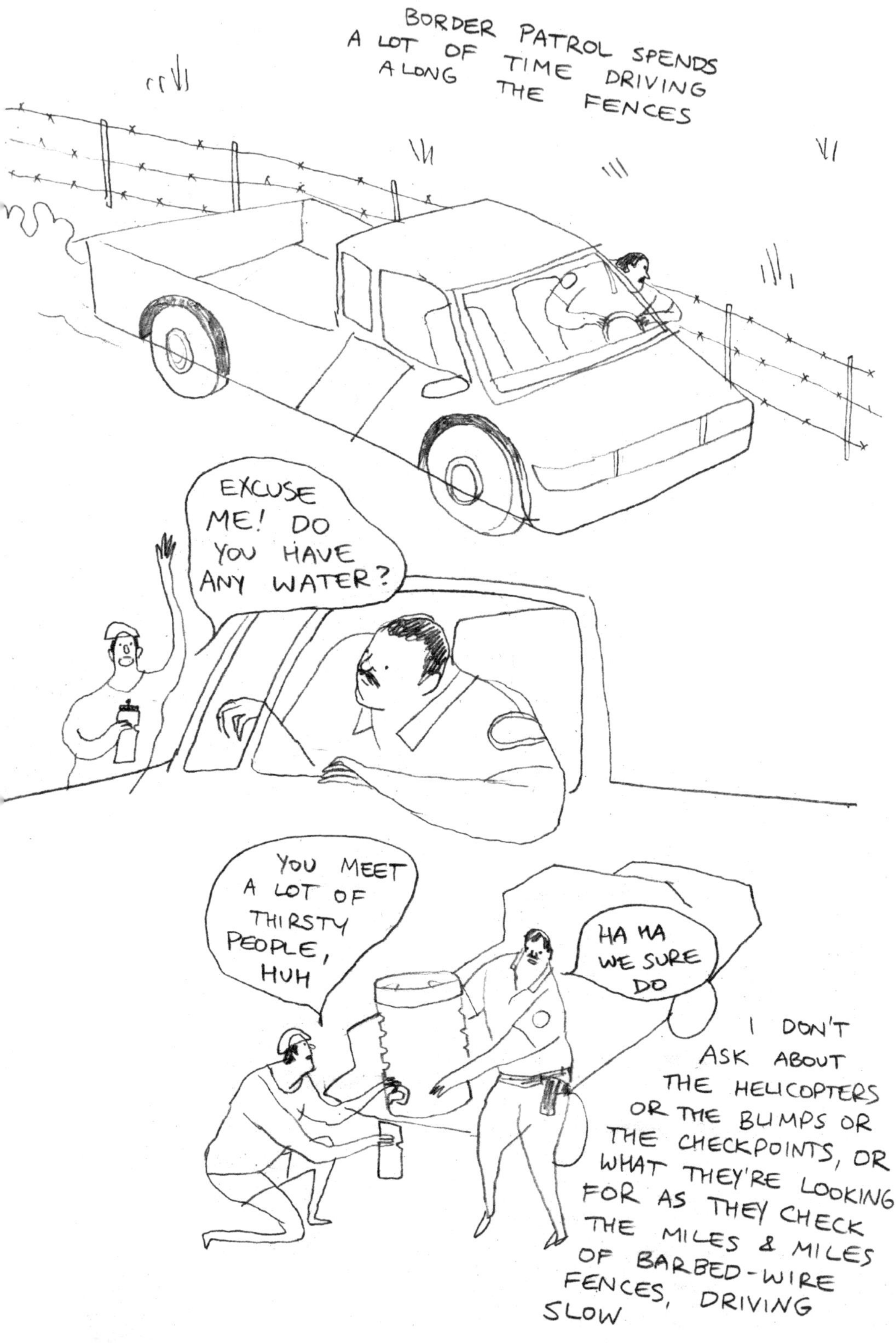
BORDER PATROL SPENDS A LOT OF TIME DRIVING ALONG THE FENCES
EXCUSE ME! DO YOU HAVE ANY WATER?
YOU MEET A LOT OF THIRSTY PEOPLE, HUH
HA HA WE SURE DO
I DON'T ASK ABOUT THE HELICOPTERS OR THE BLIMPS OR THE CHECKPOINTS, OR WHAT THEY'RE LOOKING FOR AS THEY CHECK THE MILES & MILES OF BARBED-WIRE FENCES, DRIVING SLOW

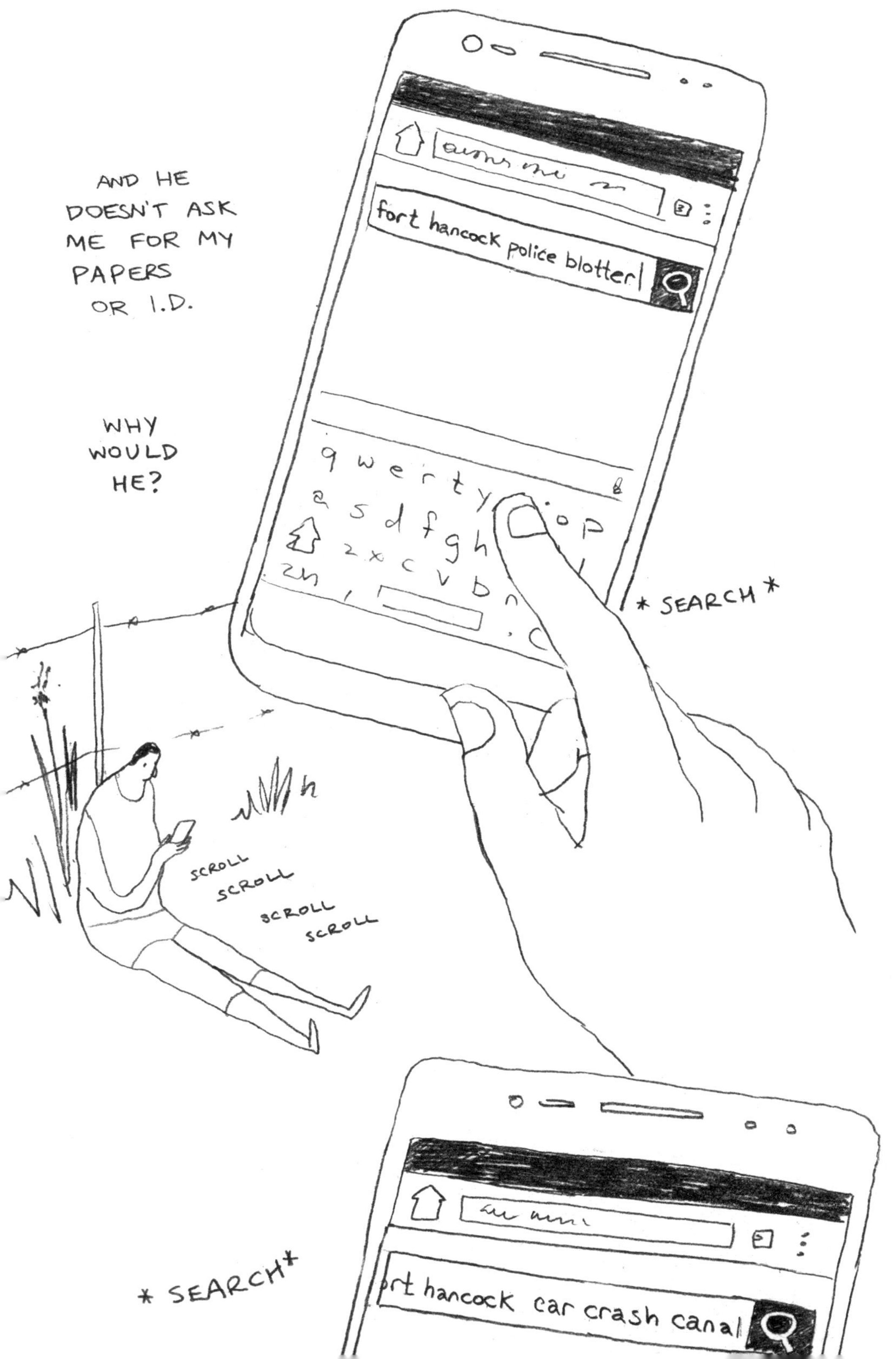
AND HE DOESN'T ASK ME FOR MY PAPERS OR I.D.
WHY WOULD HE?
fort hancock police blotter
* SEARCH *
SCROLL
SCROLL
SCROLL
SCROLL
* SEARCH*
rt hancock car crash canal

DAY 31 - APRIL 15TH

DESERT CAMP TO LANGTRY - 11 MILES

25 MPH HEADWIND

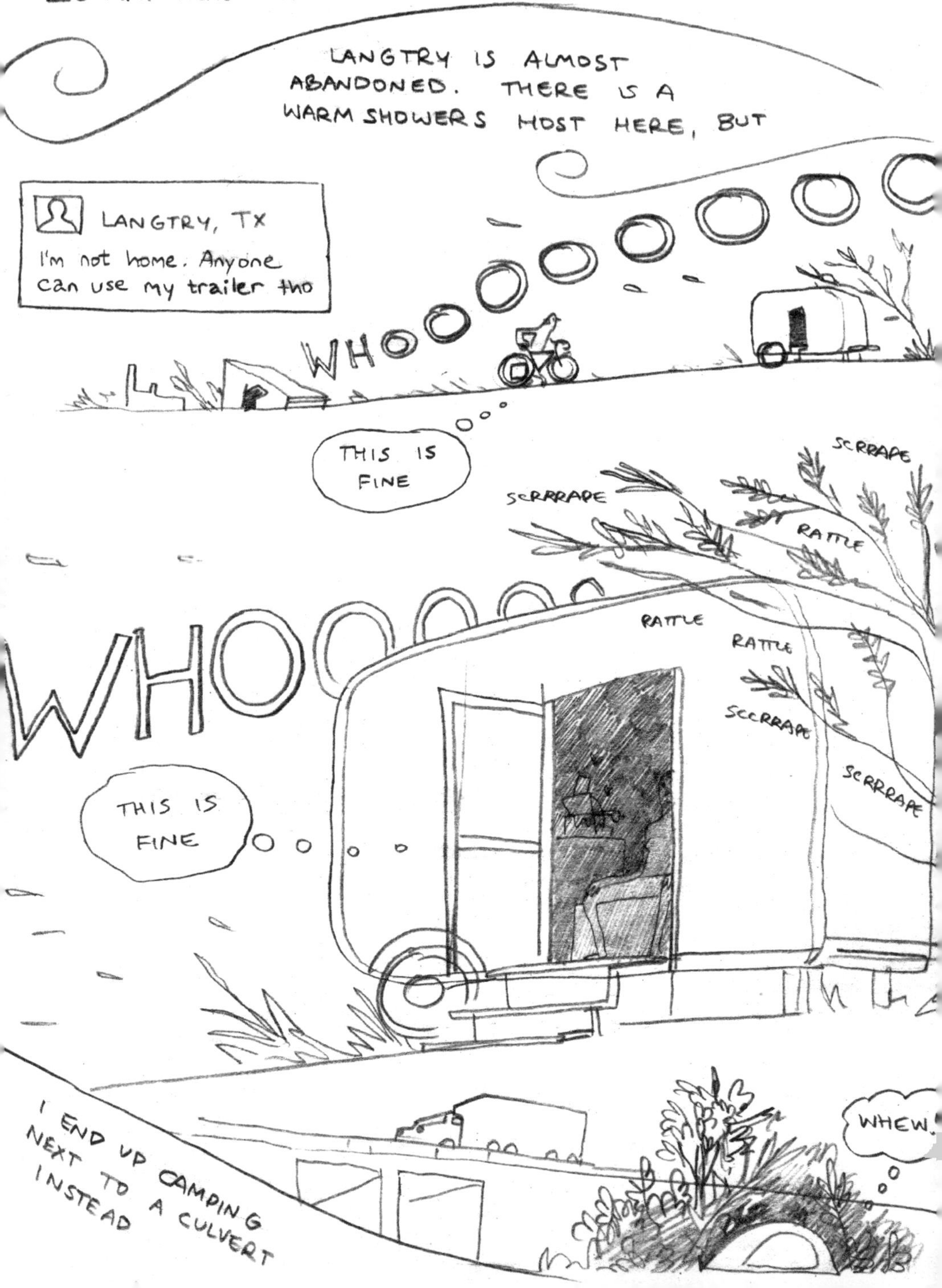

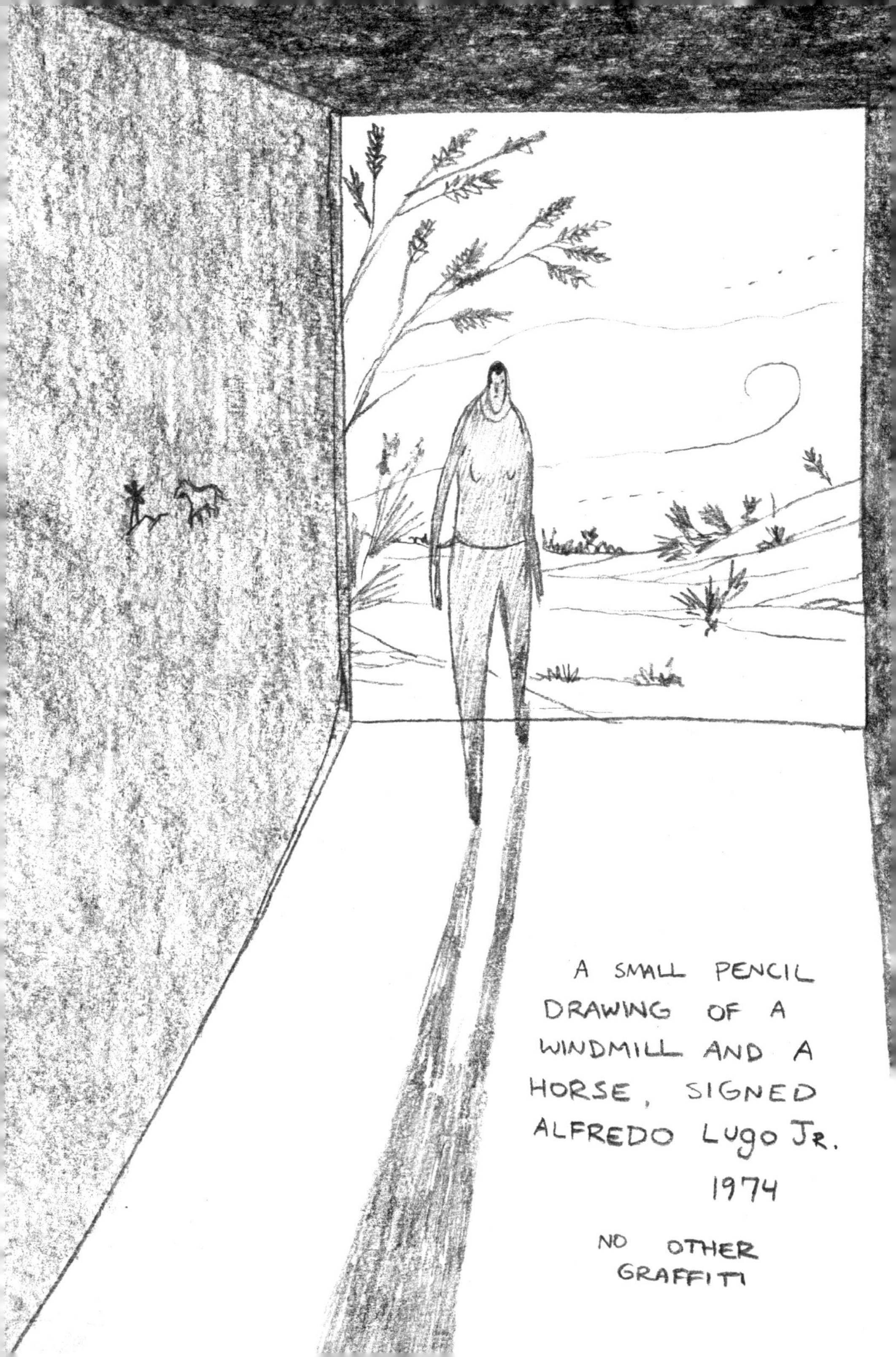
A SMALL PENCIL DRAWING OF A WINDMILL AND A HORSE, SIGNED ALFREDO Lugo Jr. 1974
NO OTHER GRAFFITI

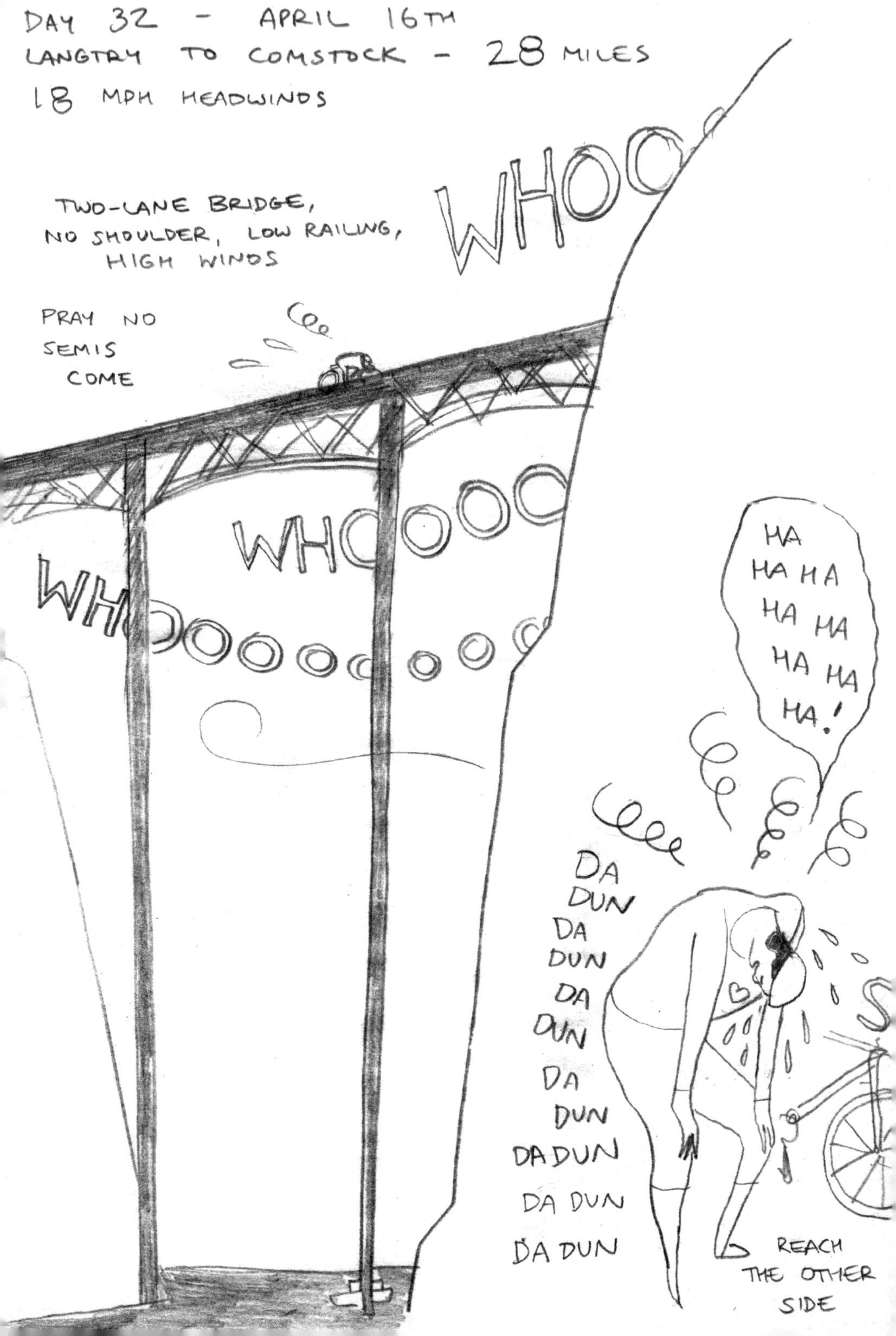
DAY 32 - APRIL 16TH
LANGTRY TO COMSTOCK - 28 MILES
18 MPH HEADWINDS
TWO-LANE BRIDGE, NO SHOULDER, LOW RAILING, HIGH WINDS
PRAY NO SEMIS COME
WHOO
WHOOOOO
WHOOOOOOOOOOO
HA HA HA HA HA HA HA HA!
DA DUN DA DUN DA DUN DA DUN DADUN DA DUN DA DUN
REACH THE OTHER SIDE

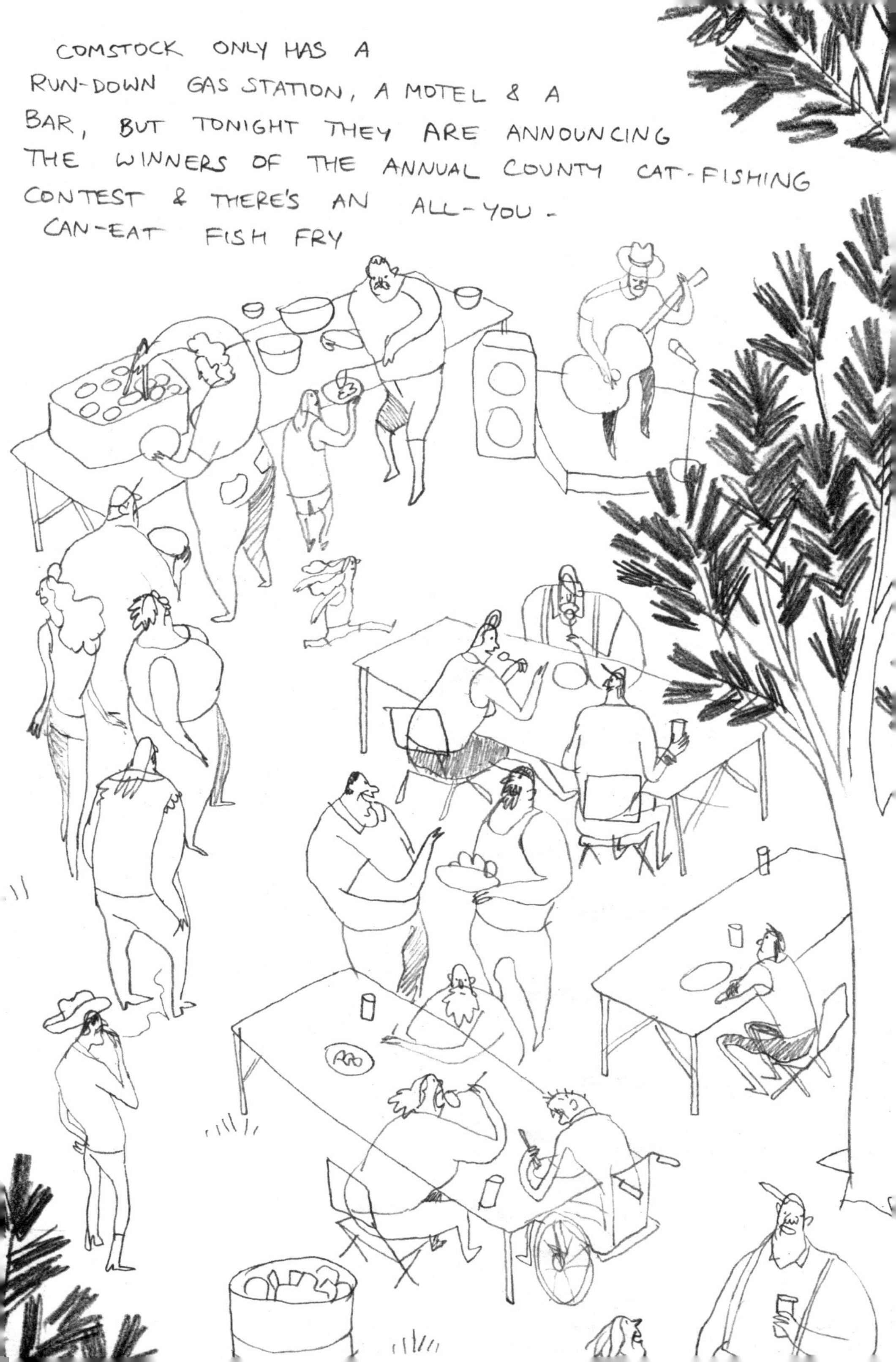
COMSTOCK ONLY HAS A RUN-DOWN GAS STATION, A MOTEL & A BAR, BUT TONIGHT THEY ARE ANNOUNCING THE WINNERS OF THE ANNUAL COUNTY CAT-FISHING CONTEST & THERE'S AN ALL-YOU-CAN-EAT FISH FRY

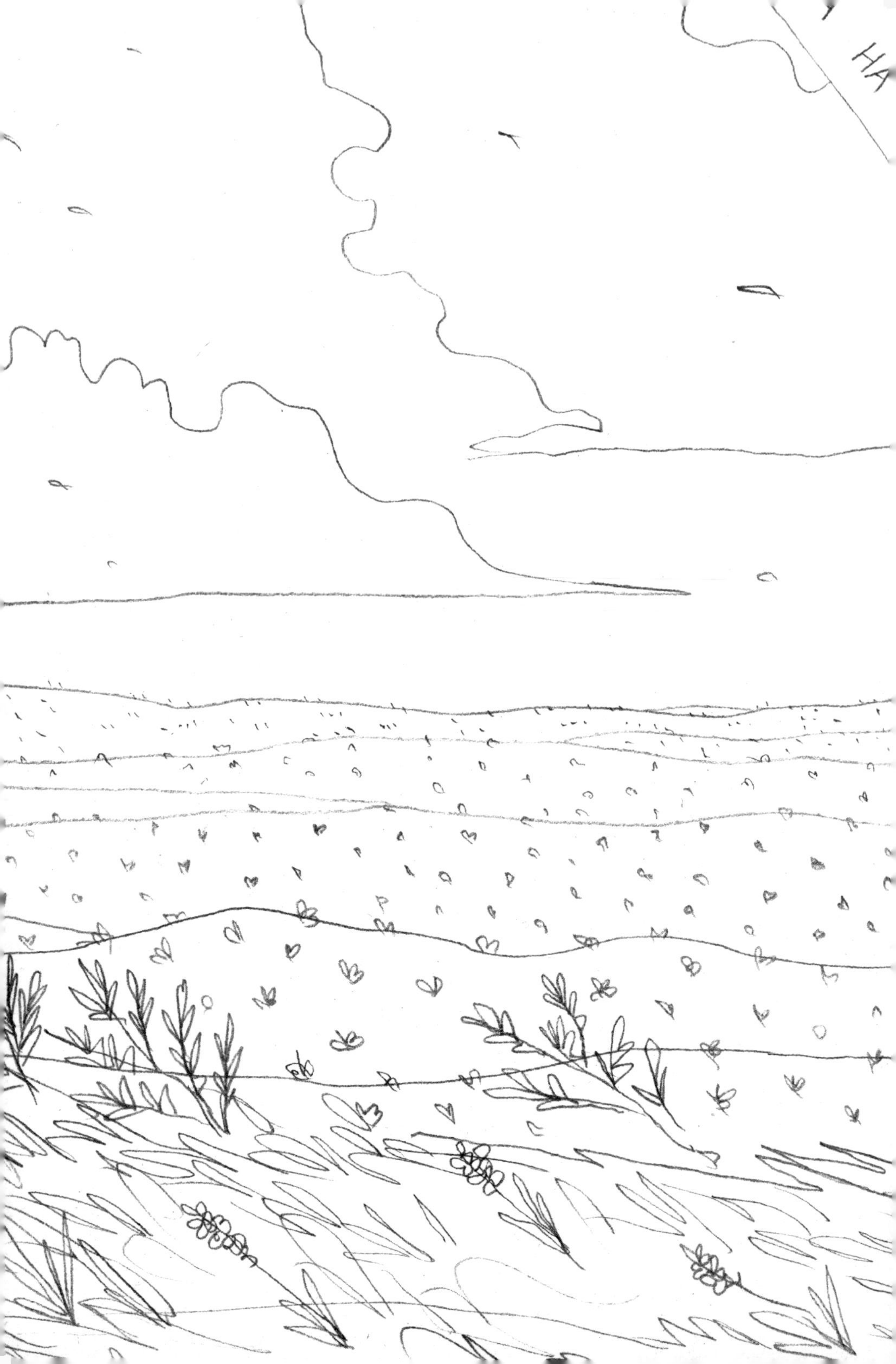
HA

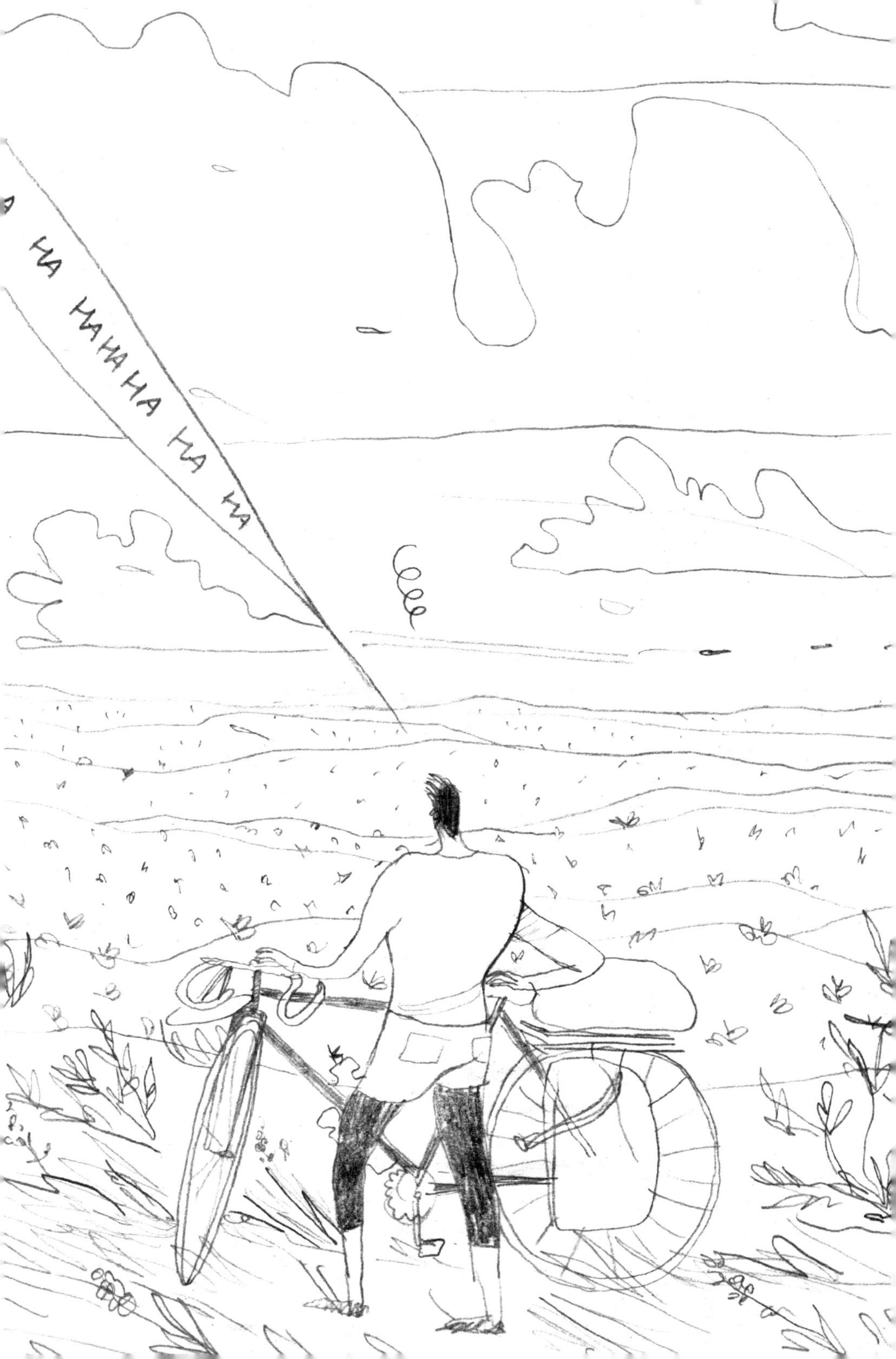
HA HA HAHAHAHA HA HA HA

TURN YOUR
HEAD

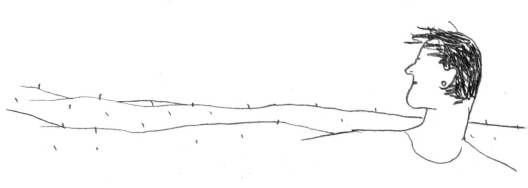

HORIZON

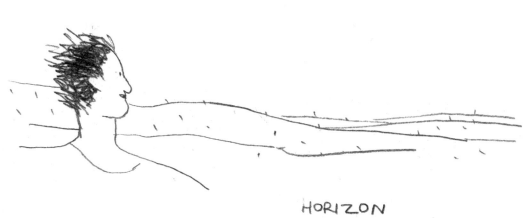

HORIZON

YOUR
SOVEREIGN
BODY

GOD'S
THRILLING
INDIFFERENCE.

DAY 33 — APRIL 17TH
COMSTOCK TO BRACKETTVILLE — 60 MILES

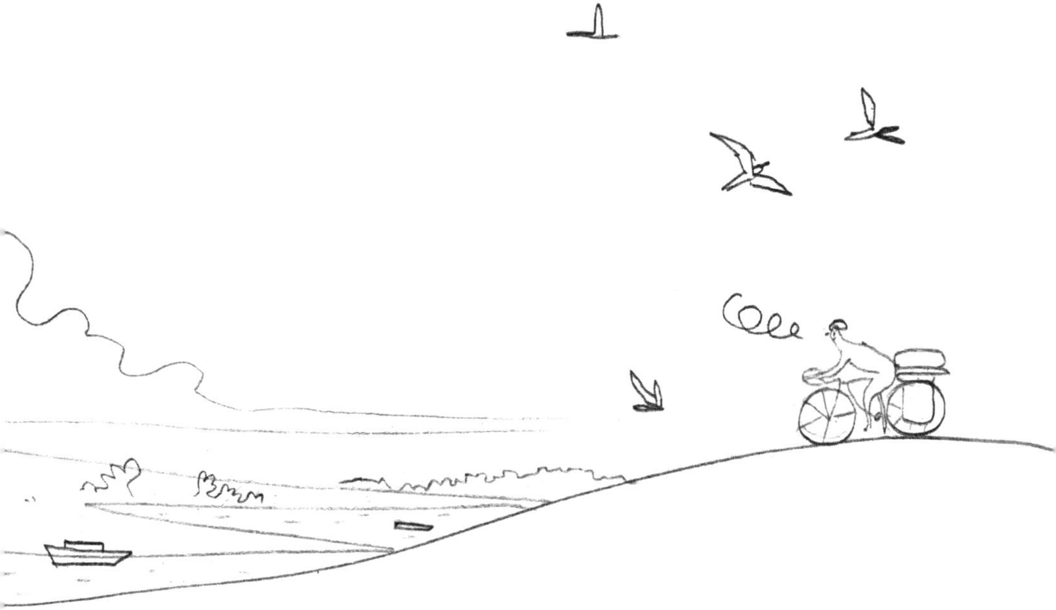

AFTER 30 DAYS OF DESERT
I REACH WETLANDS, BOATS,
PALMTREES, SEABIRDS.

AT AN EMPTY BAR IN BRACKETTVILLE
WELL MY WIFE HAD DIED OF CANCER - 25 YEARS MARRIED - AND I COME TO BRACKETTVILLE AND MEET THIS LOVELY LADY HERE
PICKLES
MY HUSBAND HAD DIED IN A HEAD-ON TRAIN COLLISION
PCCHTS!
40 YEARS MARRIED
AND I THOUGHT... SHE LIKES BARS, MAYBE IF I OWN A BAR, SHE'LL LIKE ME!

DAY 34 - APRIL 18TH

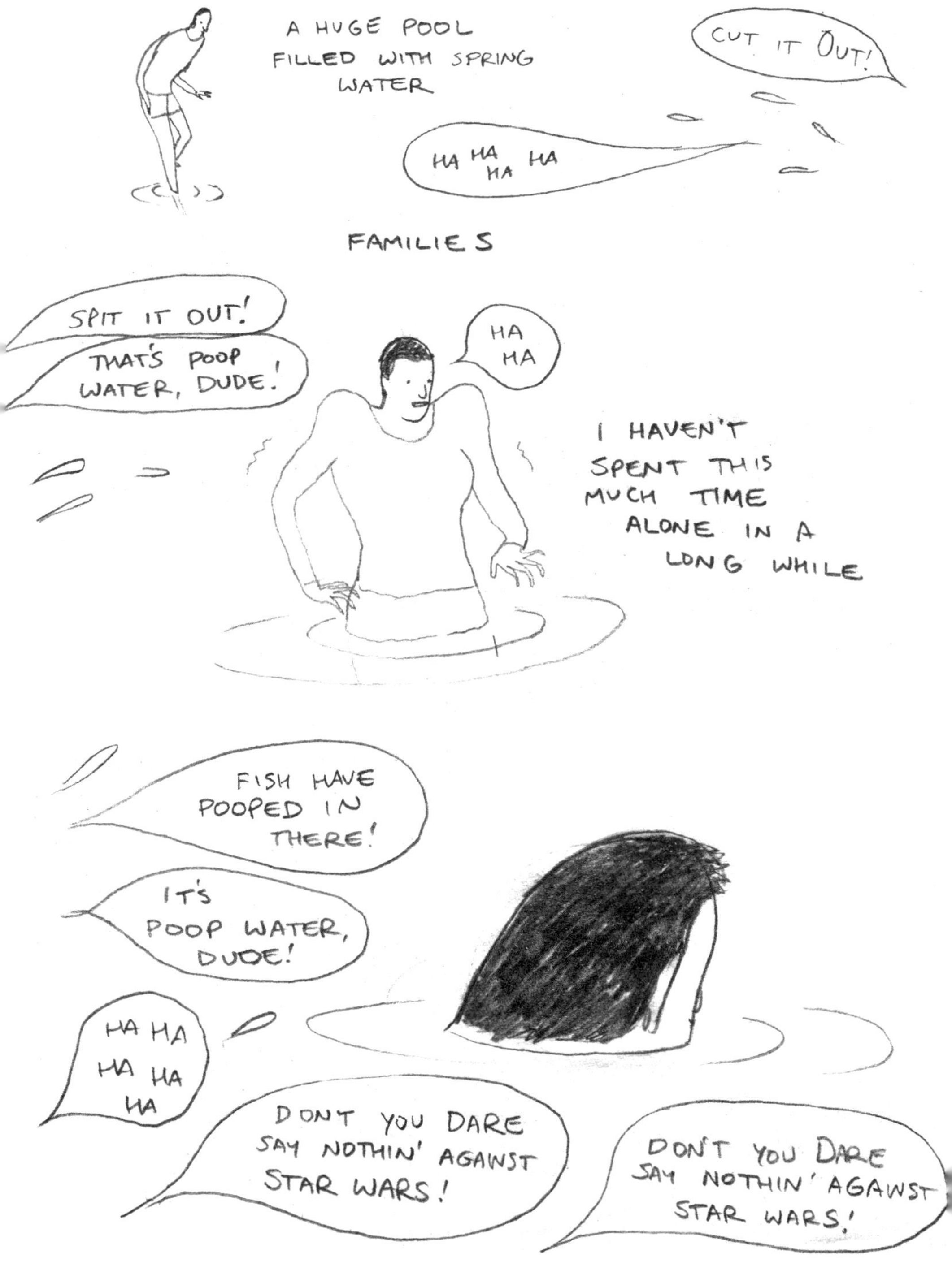
A HUGE POOL FILLED WITH SPRING WATER
CUT IT OUT!
HA HA HA HA
FAMILIES
SPIT IT OUT!
THAT'S POOP WATER, DUDE!
HA HA
I HAVEN'T SPENT THIS MUCH TIME ALONE IN A LONG WHILE
FISH HAVE POOPED IN THERE!
IT'S POOP WATER, DUDE!
HA HA HA HA HA
DON'T YOU DARE SAY NOTHIN' AGAINST STAR WARS!
DON'T YOU DARE SAY NOTHIN' AGAINST STAR WARS!

DAY 35 - APRIL 19TH

BRACKETTVILLE TO UVALDE - 48 MILES

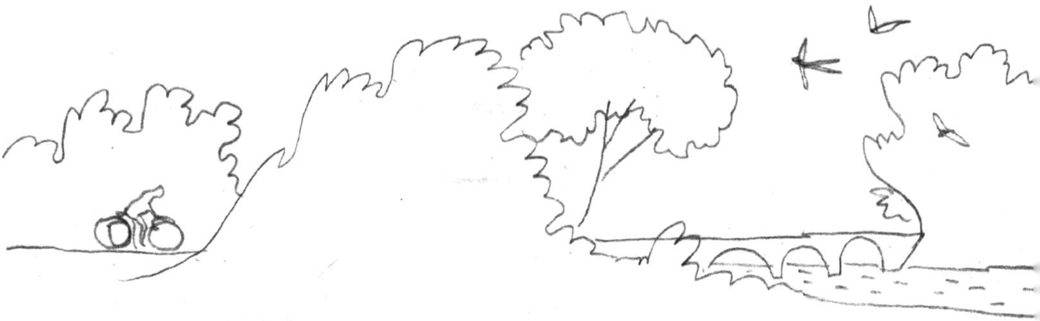

THE AIR IS THICK & MOIST, NOW

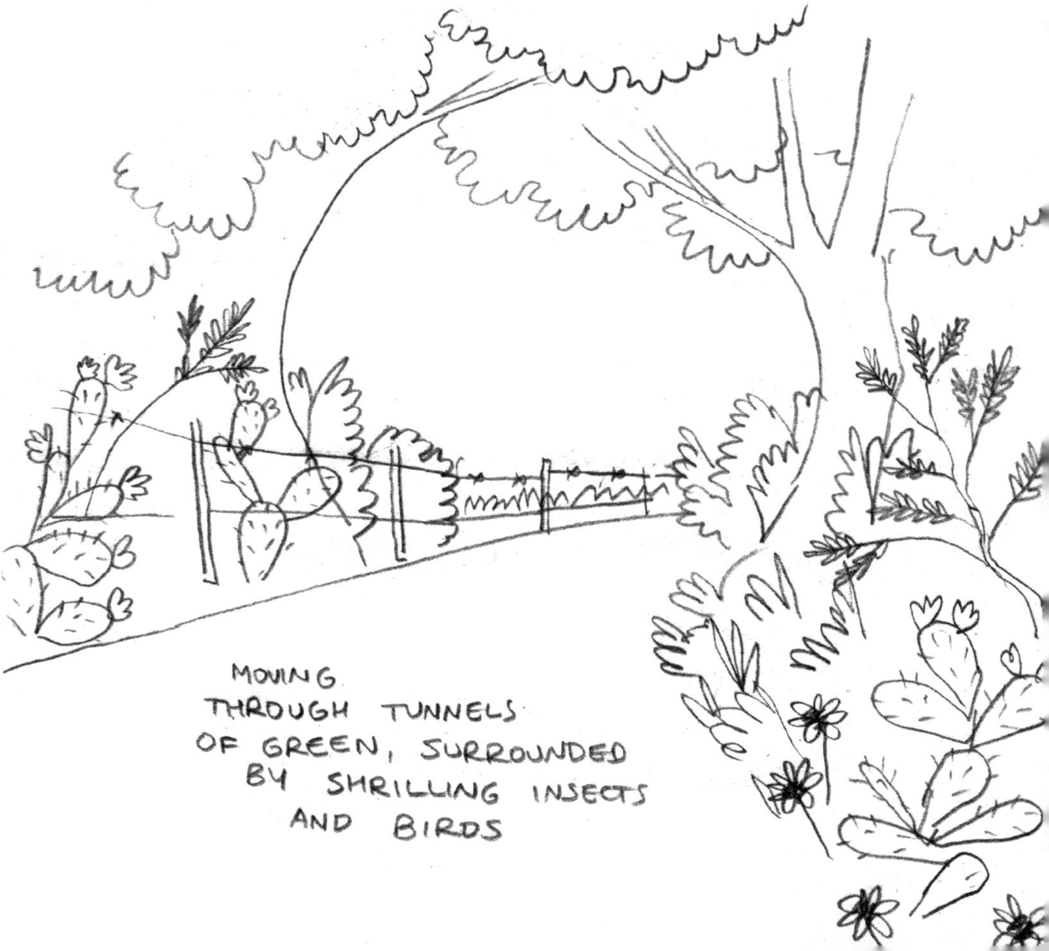

MOVING THROUGH TUNNELS OF GREEN, SURROUNDED BY SHRILLING INSECTS AND BIRDS

WHEAT FIELDS,
    CLEAR CREEKS,
      EVERYTHING
        BLOOMING

                    BIG OAK TREES
                  GROWING NEXT TO
                      MESQUITE

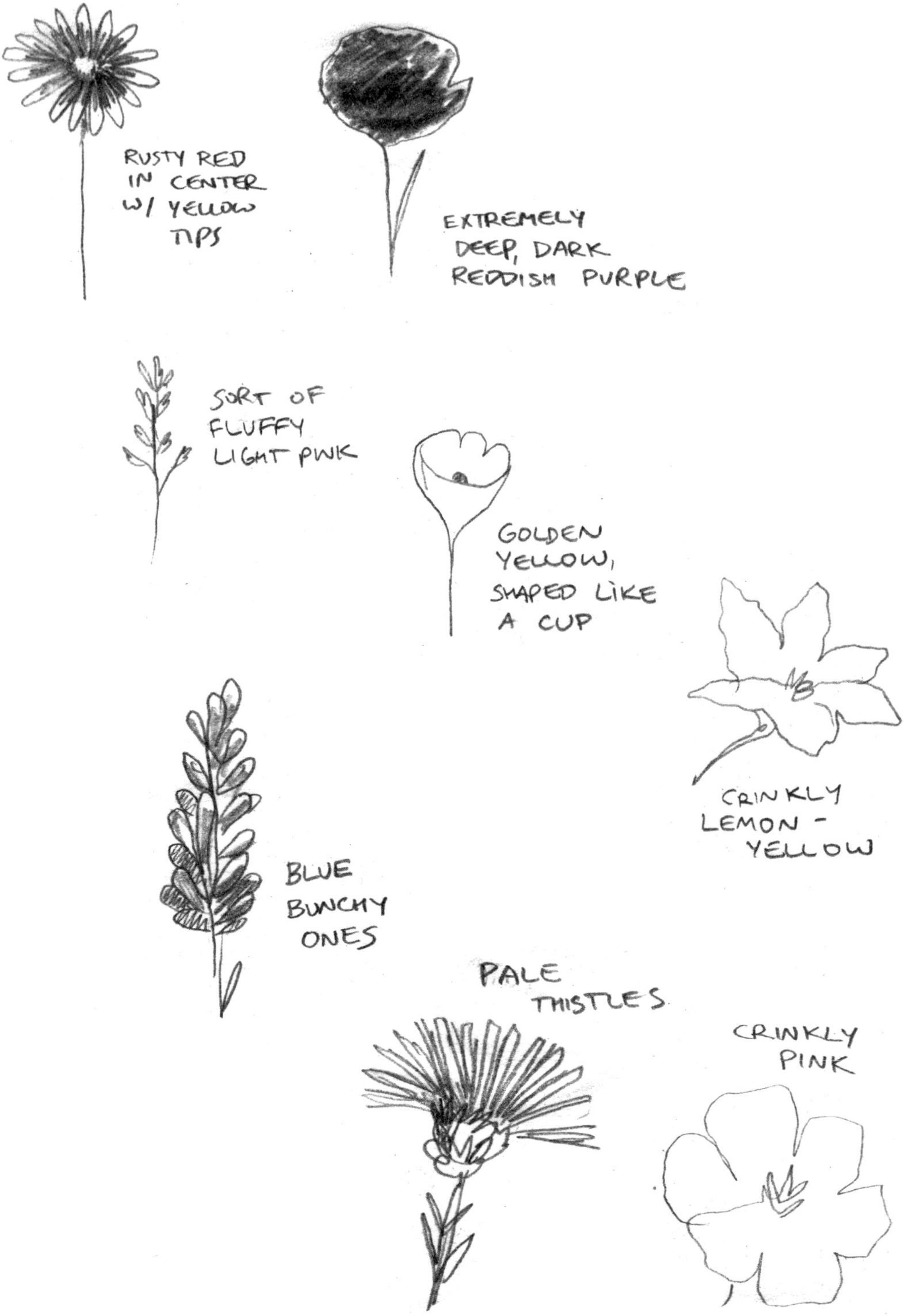
RUSTY RED IN CENTER W/ YELLOW TIPS
EXTREMELY DEEP, DARK REDDISH PURPLE
SORT OF FLUFFY LIGHT PINK
GOLDEN YELLOW, SHAPED LIKE A CUP
CRINKLY LEMON-YELLOW
BLUE BUNCHY ONES
PALE THISTLES
CRINKLY PINK

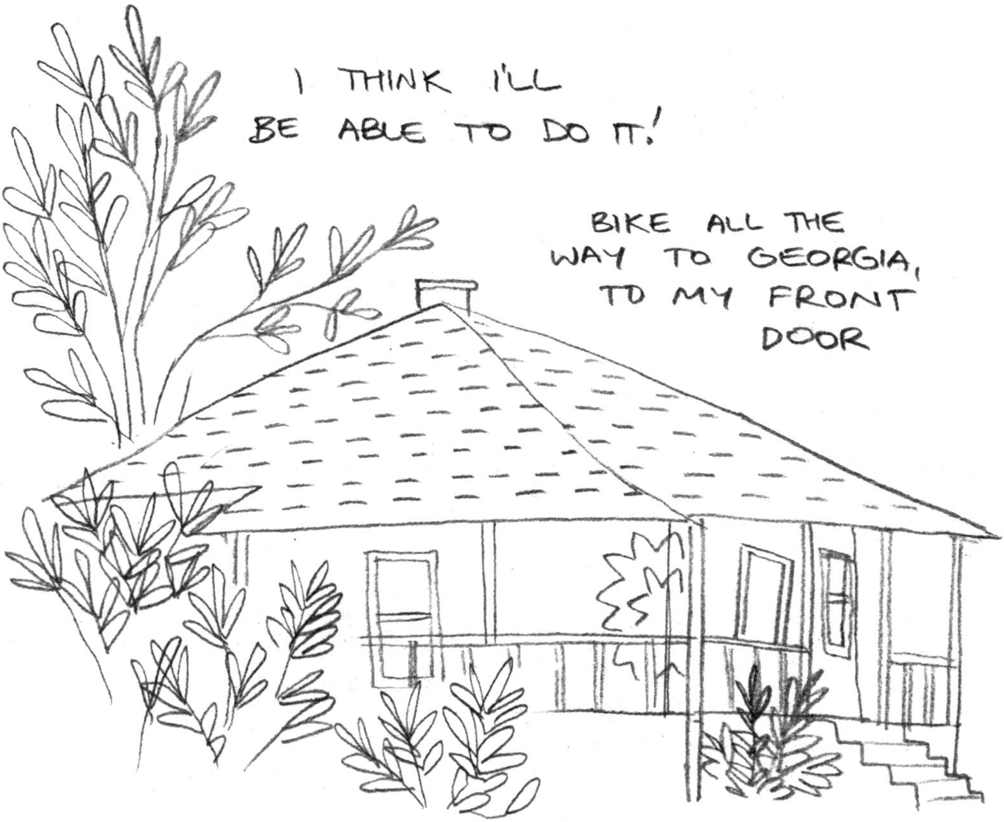
I THINK I'LL
BE ABLE TO DO IT!
BIKE ALL THE
WAY TO GEORGIA,
TO MY FRONT
DOOR

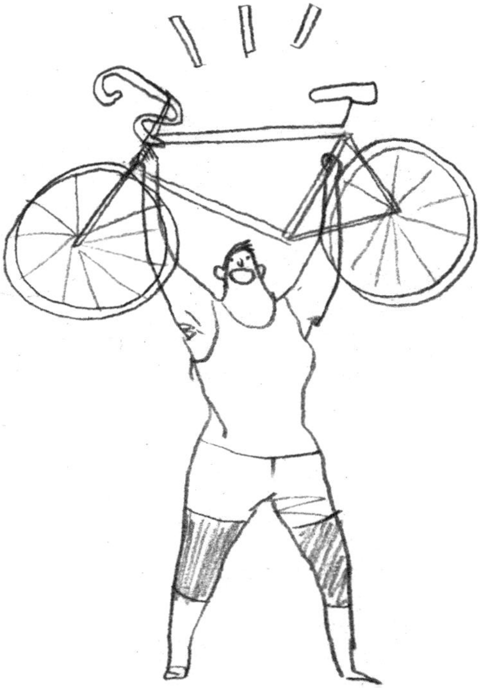

DAY 36 – APRIL 20TH

UVALDE TO HONDO, 45 MILES

OUTSIDE D'HANIS IS A BRICK FACTORY, CAKED IN BRICK DUST

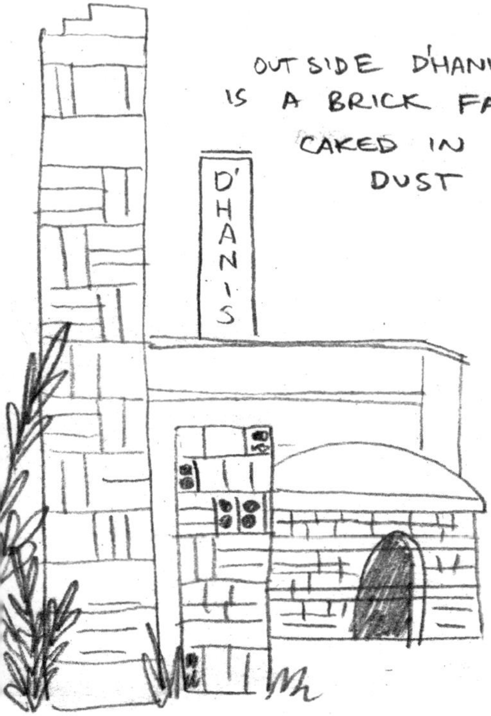
D'HANIS

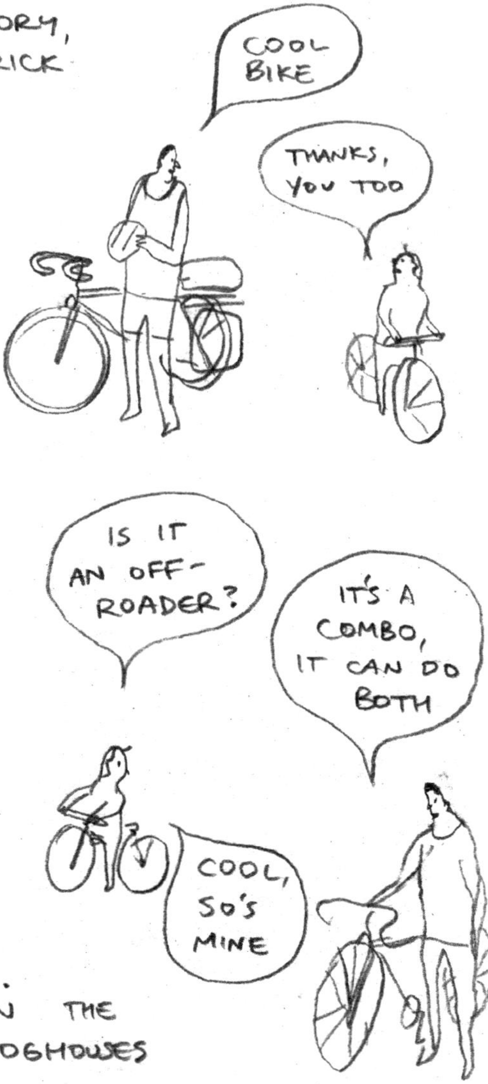
COOL BIKE
THANKS, YOU TOO
IS IT AN OFF-ROADER?
IT'S A COMBO, IT CAN DO BOTH
COOL, SO'S MINE

IN D'HANIS EVERYTHING IS MADE OUT OF BRICK. EVEN THE SHEDS, EVEN THE DOGHOUSES

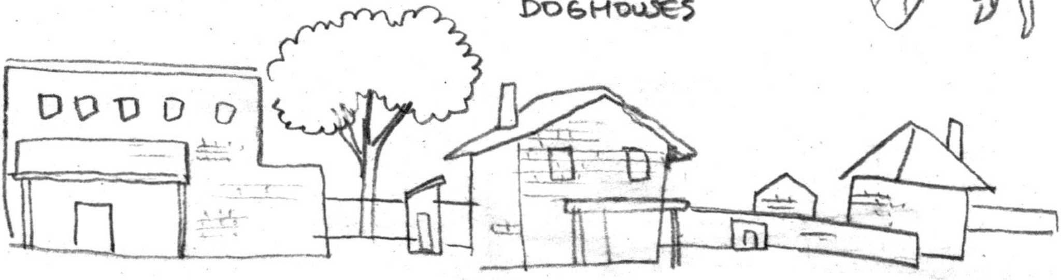

I AM MOSTLY STAYING AT RV PARKS OR CAMPGROUNDS, BUT
MAKE YOURSELF AT HOME!
NO OTHER PEOPLE FOR MILES
RV
$60 FOR A MOTEL

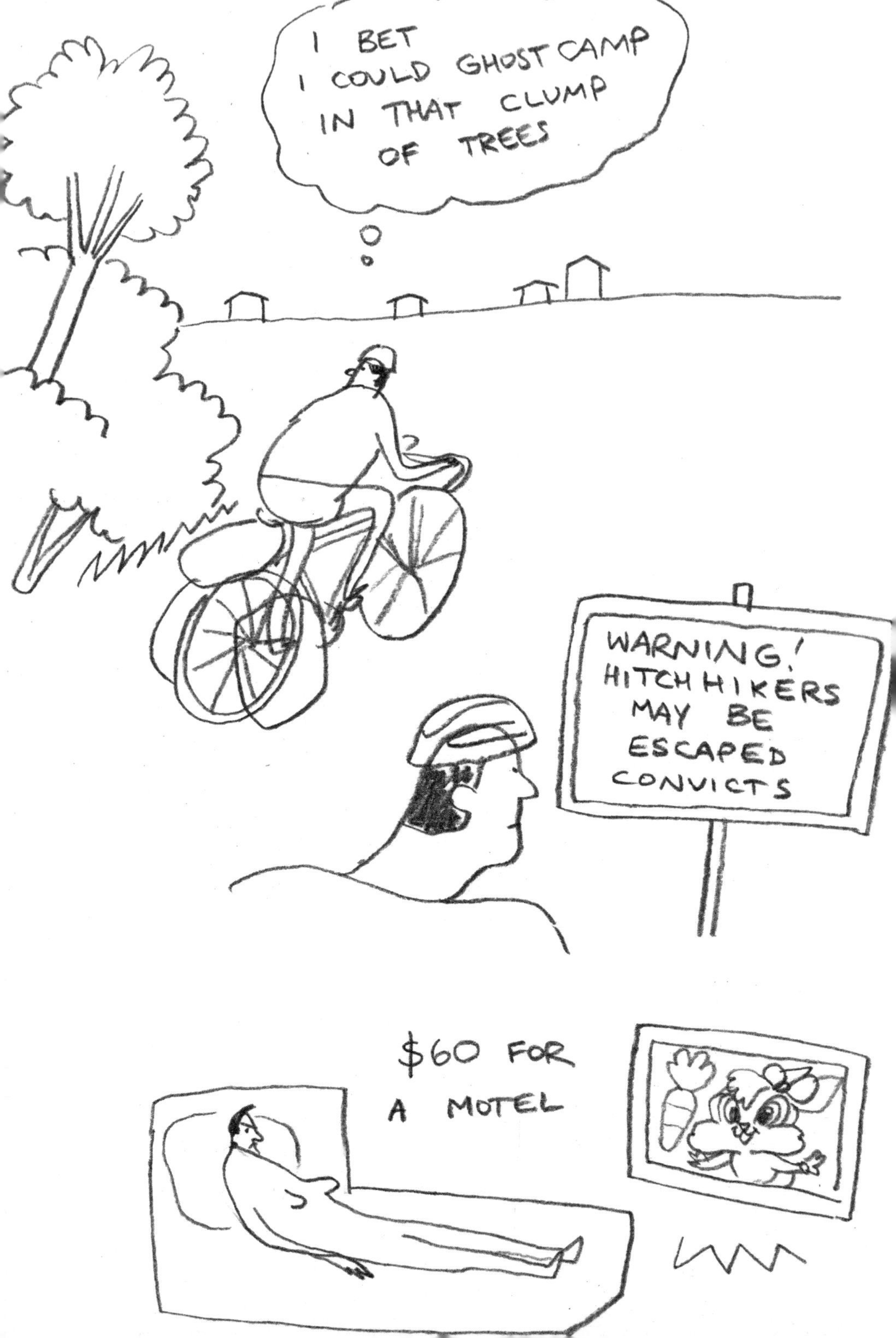
I BET I COULD GHOST CAMP IN THAT CLUMP OF TREES
WARNING! HITCHHIKERS MAY BE ESCAPED CONVICTS
$60 FOR A MOTEL

DAY 37 - APRIL 21ST

HONDO TO SAN ANTONIO, 46 MILES

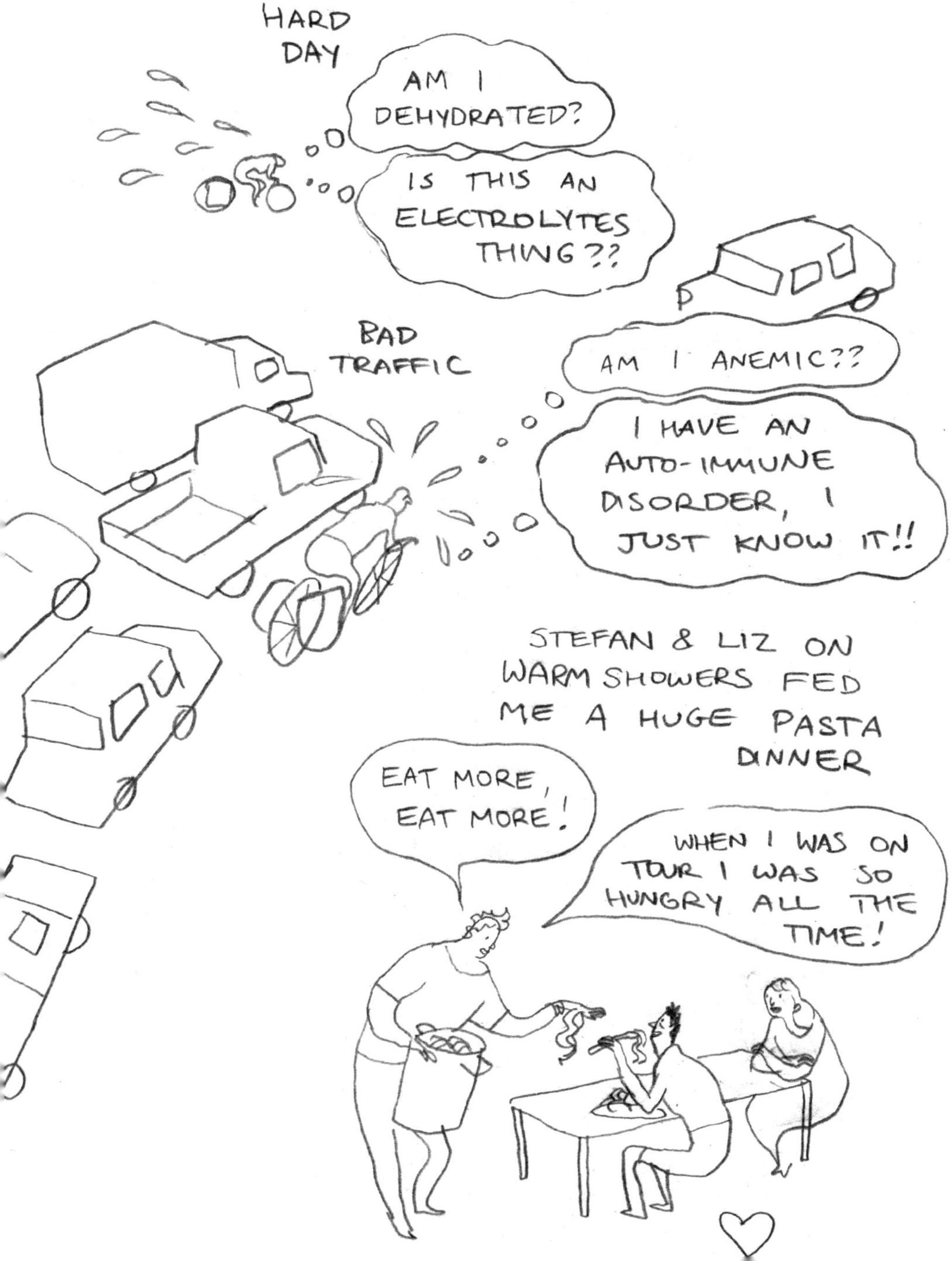

DAY 38 - APRIL 22ND
SAN AN. TO NEW BRAUNFELS
55.5 MILES
SATURDAY NIGHT
HONK!
OH NO- THIS IS A PARTY AREA!
SWERVE!
WALKING MY BIKE THROUGH THE DITCH BY THE ROAD A WOMAN PULLS OFF IN FRONT OF ME
WHAT ARE YOU DOING?? PUT YOUR BIKE IN MY CAR!
HER NAME WAS SUKIE
!
THERE ARE DRUNK DRIVERS! AND SNAKES!
I GET IT THO- YOU'RE ON AN ADVENTURE!

DAY 39 – APRIL 23RD
NEW BRAUNFELS TO AUSTIN – 45 MILES

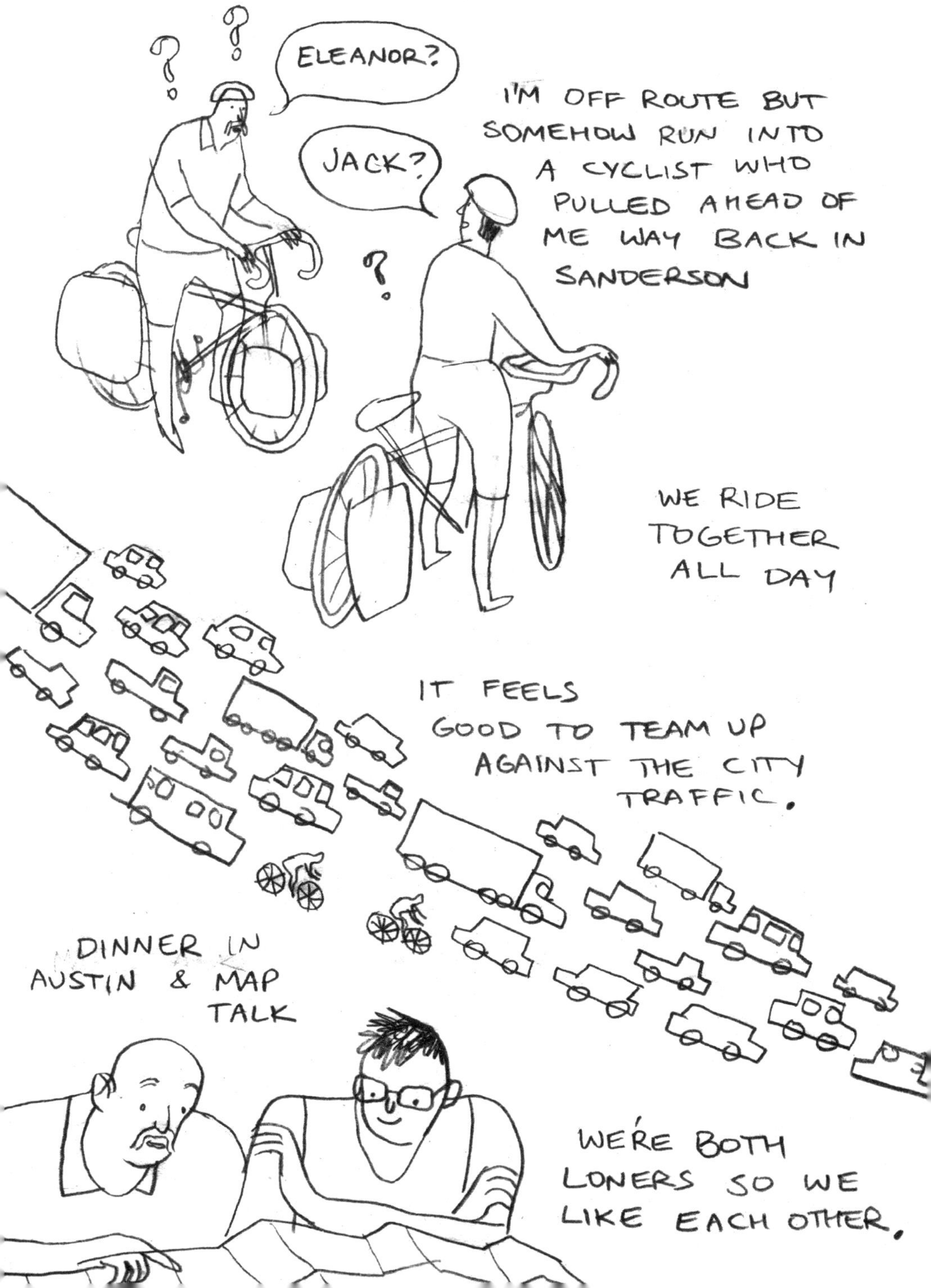
ELEANOR?
JACK?
I'M OFF ROUTE BUT SOMEHOW RUN INTO A CYCLIST WHO PULLED AHEAD OF ME WAY BACK IN SANDERSON
WE RIDE TOGETHER ALL DAY
IT FEELS GOOD TO TEAM UP AGAINST THE CITY TRAFFIC.
DINNER IN AUSTIN & MAP TALK
WE'RE BOTH LONERS SO WE LIKE EACH OTHER.

DAY 39 4/24
BREAK DAY IN AUSTIN
I'M DESTROYING THIS SMALL PLANET & I CAN DESTROY YOUR SMALL BODY ALSO
BUT YOU CAN'T LIVE WITHOUT ME
WITHOUT ME YOU'RE SO WEAK.
THIS IS WHAT CARS TELL US, LIKE SOME DUMB CARTOON VILLAIN.
IT FEELS GOOD TO STAND AGAINST THAT SHITTY TRICK.
IT FEELS GOOD TO MOVE YOUR OWN SMALL BODY THROUGH SPACE
ANOTHER DAY SPENT UNDESTROYED.

DAY 40 4/25

BREAK IN AUSTIN

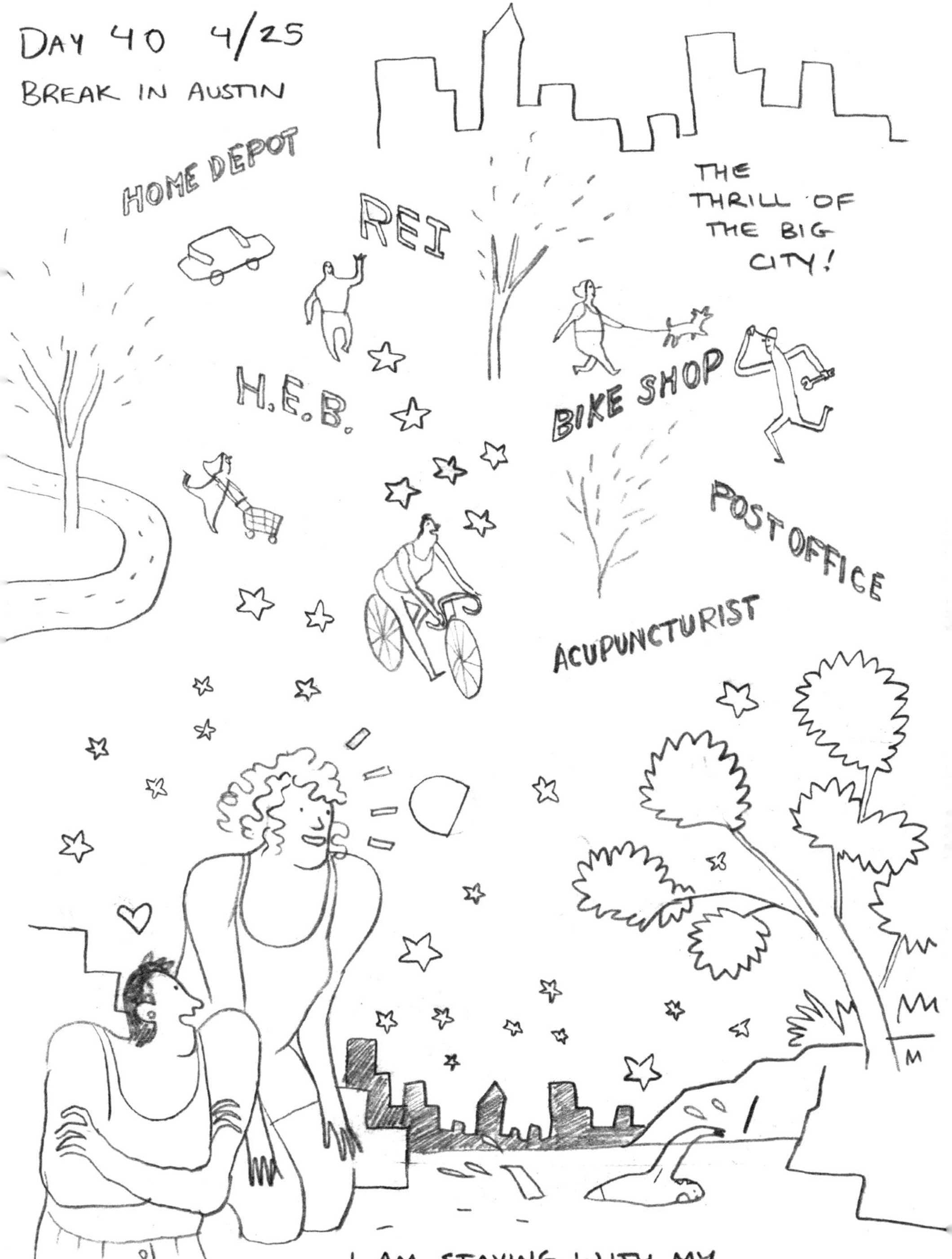
HOME DEPOT
REI
THE THRILL OF THE BIG CITY!
H.E.B.
BIKE SHOP
POST OFFICE
ACUPUNCTURIST
M

I AM STAYING WITH MY FRIEND AMANDA. SHE TAKES ME TO BARTON SPRINGS AT NIGHT. THE TREES ARE LIT UP FROM BELOW & THE SKY IS DEEP PURPLE-RED.

DAY 41 4/26 55.5 MILES

AUSTIN TO BUESCHER STATE PARK

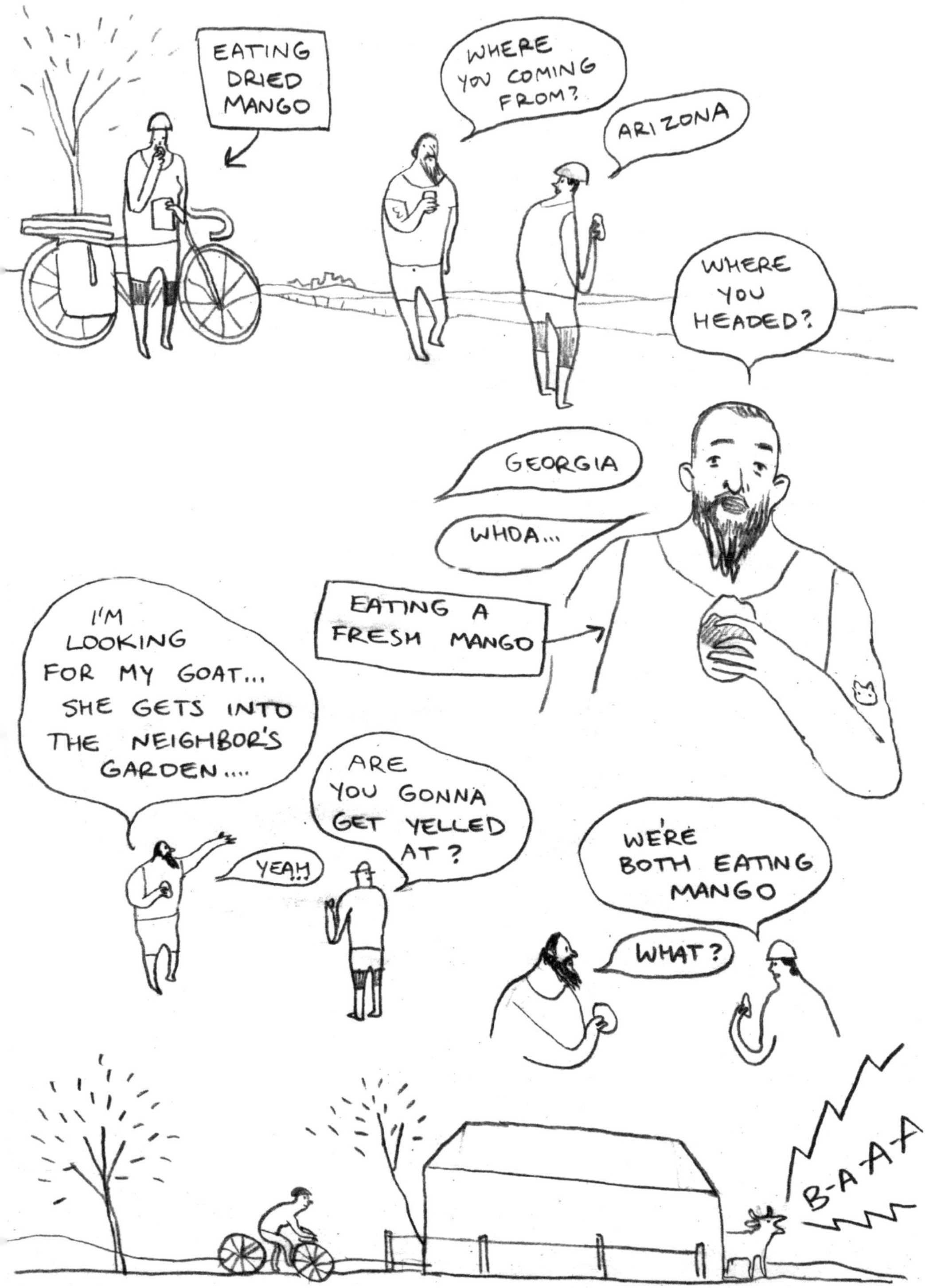

DAY 42 - 4/27
BUESCHER TO YEGUA S.P.
55 MILES
IT RAINS IN THE NIGHT & I WAKE UP IN A PUDDLE
WHY DO YOU SPEND MONEY ON THIS SHIT, YOU DUMB BITCH
SPORTS GOOP
ENERGY POWDER
YOU STUPID CUNT
TIME FOR A LITTLE SOLO THERAPY SESH
ELEANOR YOU WOULD NEVER USE THAT LANGUAGE WITH ANYONE ELSE SO PLEASE DONT USE IT ON YOURSELF!
ETC
ETC
HA HA HA HA HA HA HA HA!
BUT BY THE AFTERNOON I'M SKIMMING THROUGH STREAMS IN HYSTERICS

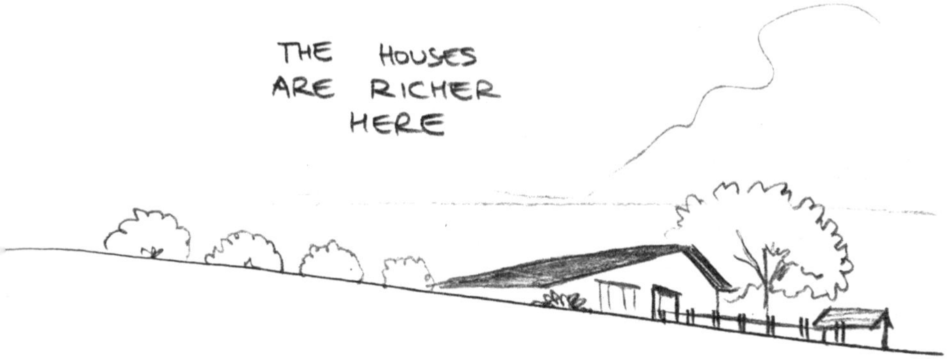
THE HOUSES
ARE RICHER
HERE

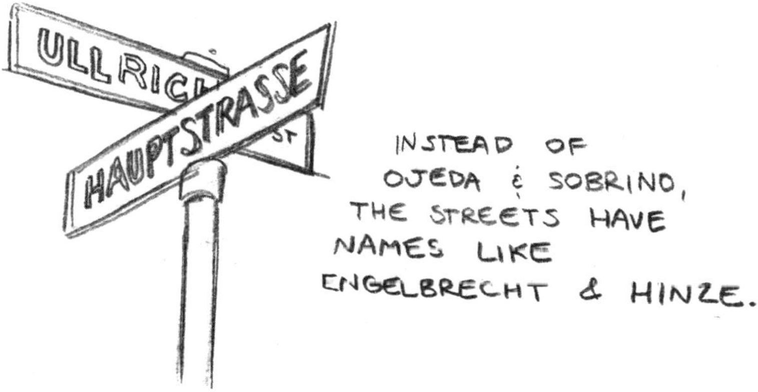
HAUPTSTRASSE
ST
INSTEAD OF
OJEDA & SOBRINO,
THE STREETS HAVE
NAMES LIKE
ENGELBRECHT & HINZE.

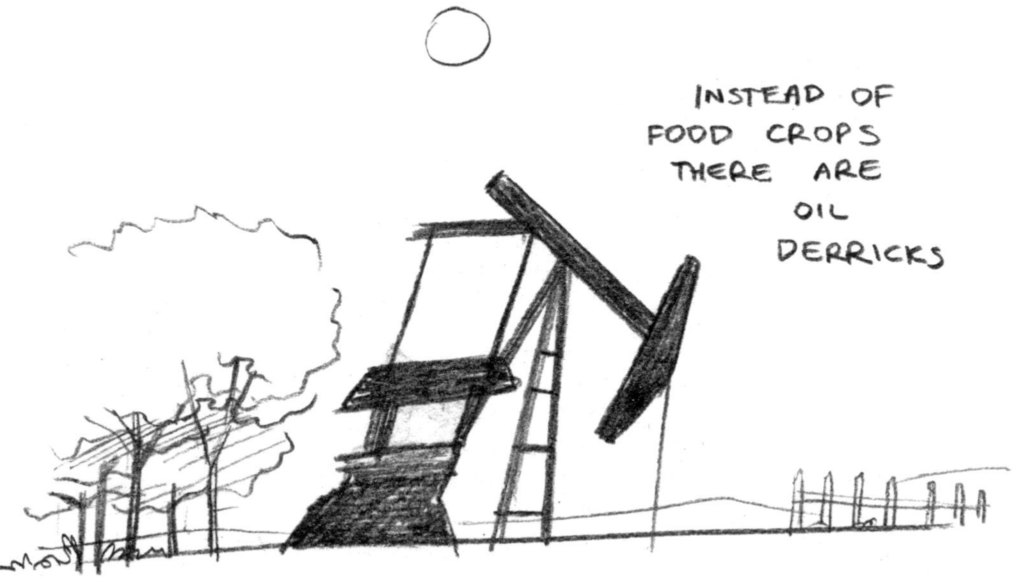
INSTEAD OF
FOOD CROPS
THERE ARE
OIL
DERRICKS

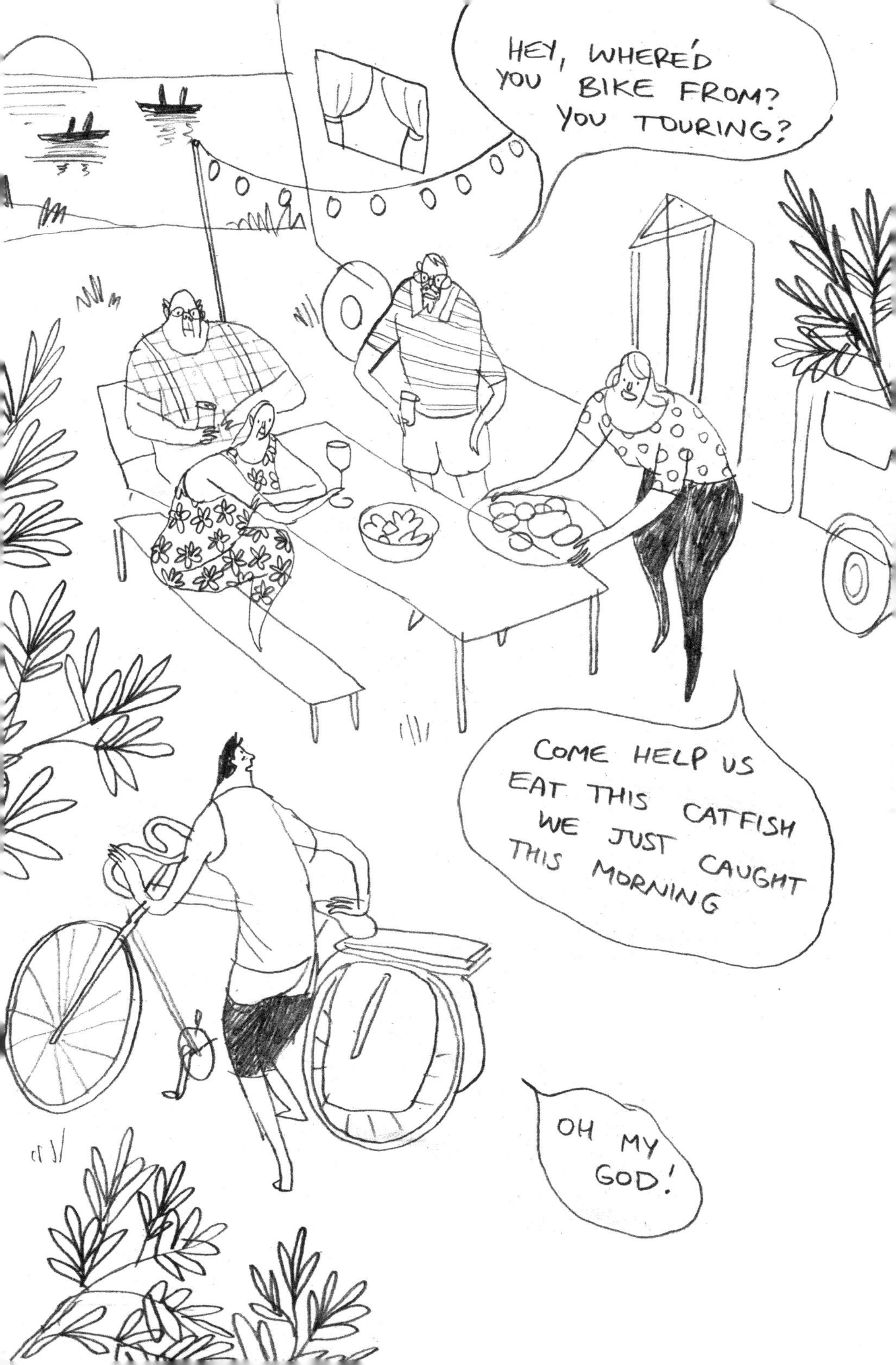
HEY, WHERE'D YOU BIKE FROM? YOU TOURING?
COME HELP US EAT THIS CATFISH WE JUST CAUGHT THIS MORNING
OH MY GOD!

DAY 43 - 4/28
YEGUA TO RICHARDS 55.5 MILES
IN THE BACK OF MY MIND:
I'LL BE HOME IN ABOUT A MONTH!
BUT WHEN I TRIED TO SIT DOWN & PLAN IT ALL OUT
IT'S GONNA TAKE ME A MONTH TO GET HOME!
JUST, WAKE UP IN THE MORNING
GONNA GO FIFTY MILES TODAY
BIKE
SLEEP
DO IT AGAIN
GONNA GO FIFTY MILES TODAY

DAY 44 4/29

RICHARDS TO OUTSIDE OF COLDSPRING

43 MILES

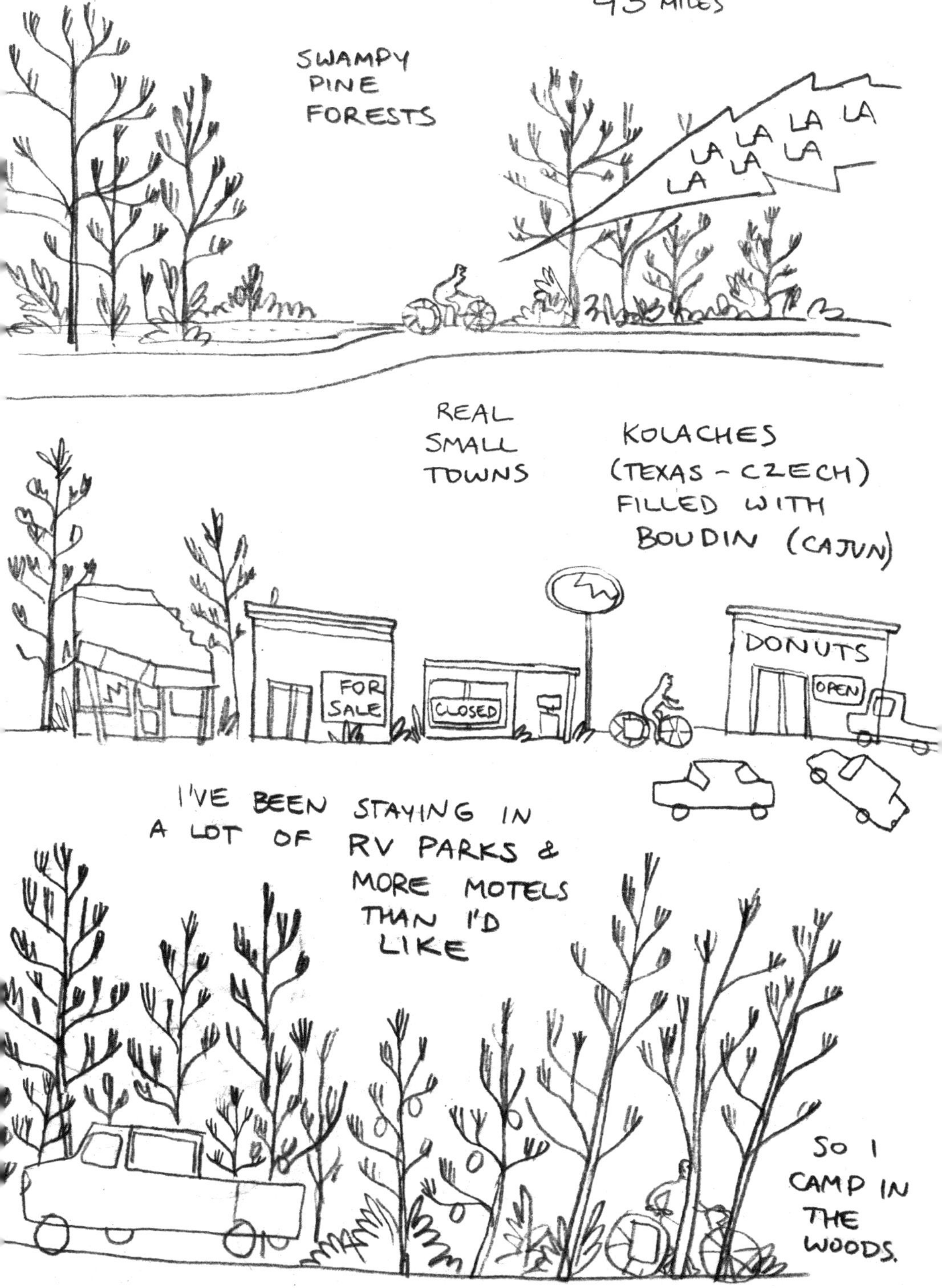
SWAMPY PINE FORESTS
LA LA LA LA LA LA LA
REAL SMALL TOWNS
KOLACHES (TEXAS - CZECH) FILLED WITH BOUDIN (CAJUN)
FOR SALE
CLOSED
DONUTS
OPEN
I'VE BEEN STAYING IN A LOT OF RV PARKS & MORE MOTELS THAN I'D LIKE
SO I CAMP IN THE WOODS.

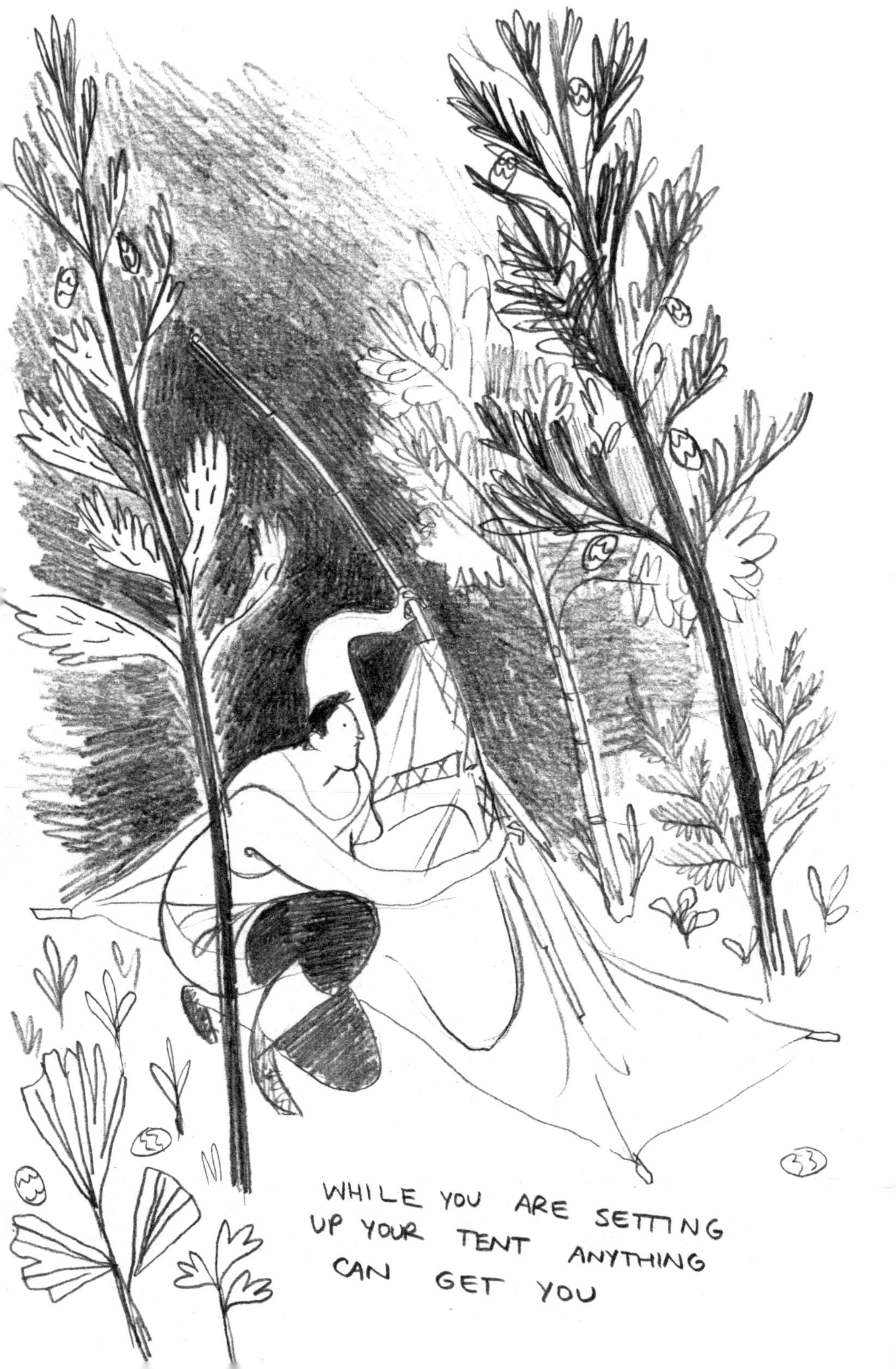

WHILE YOU ARE SETTING UP YOUR TENT ANYTHING CAN GET YOU

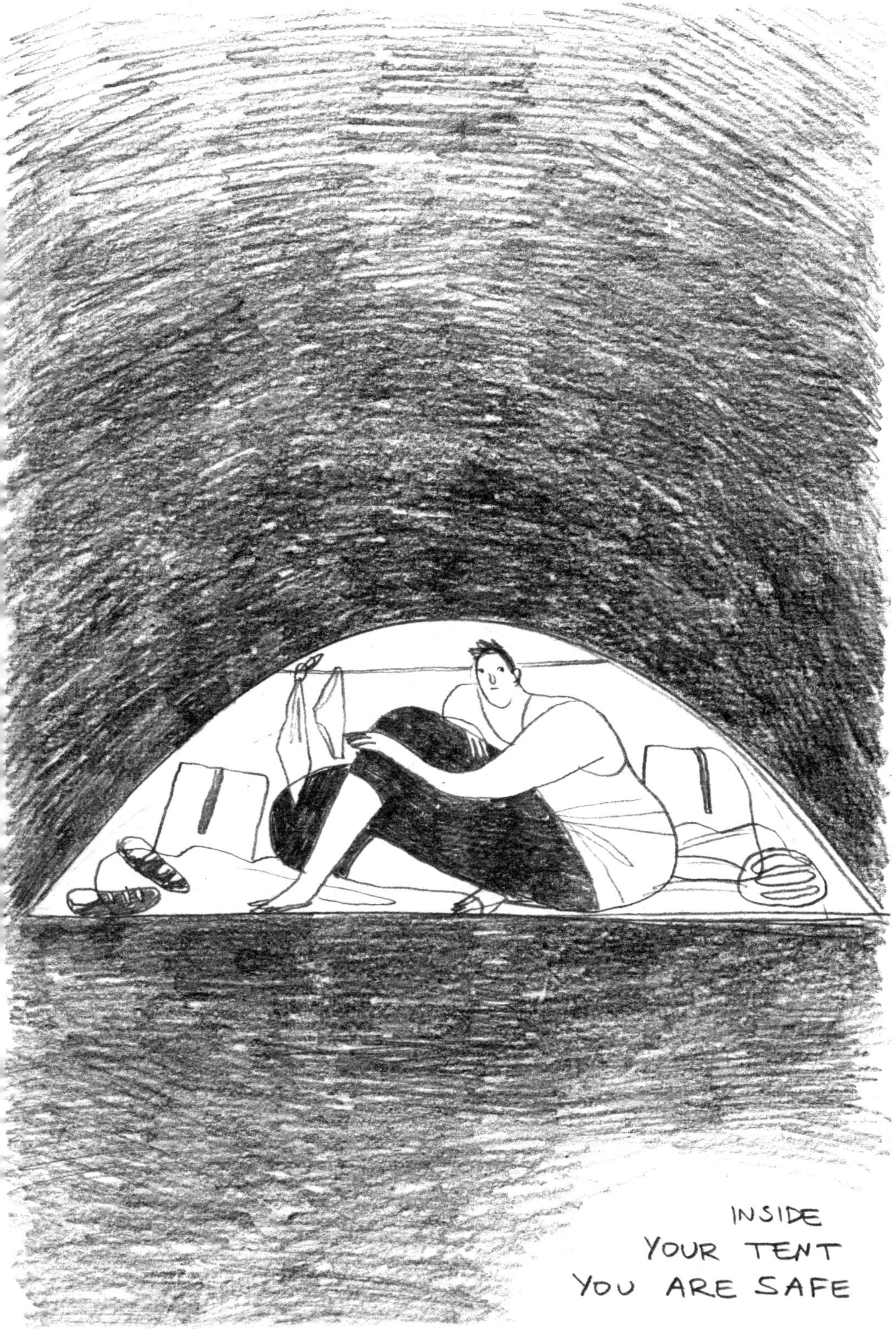
INSIDE
YOUR TENT
YOU ARE SAFE

DAY 45 4/30
OUTSIDE COLDSPRING TO SHEPHERD - 17 MILES

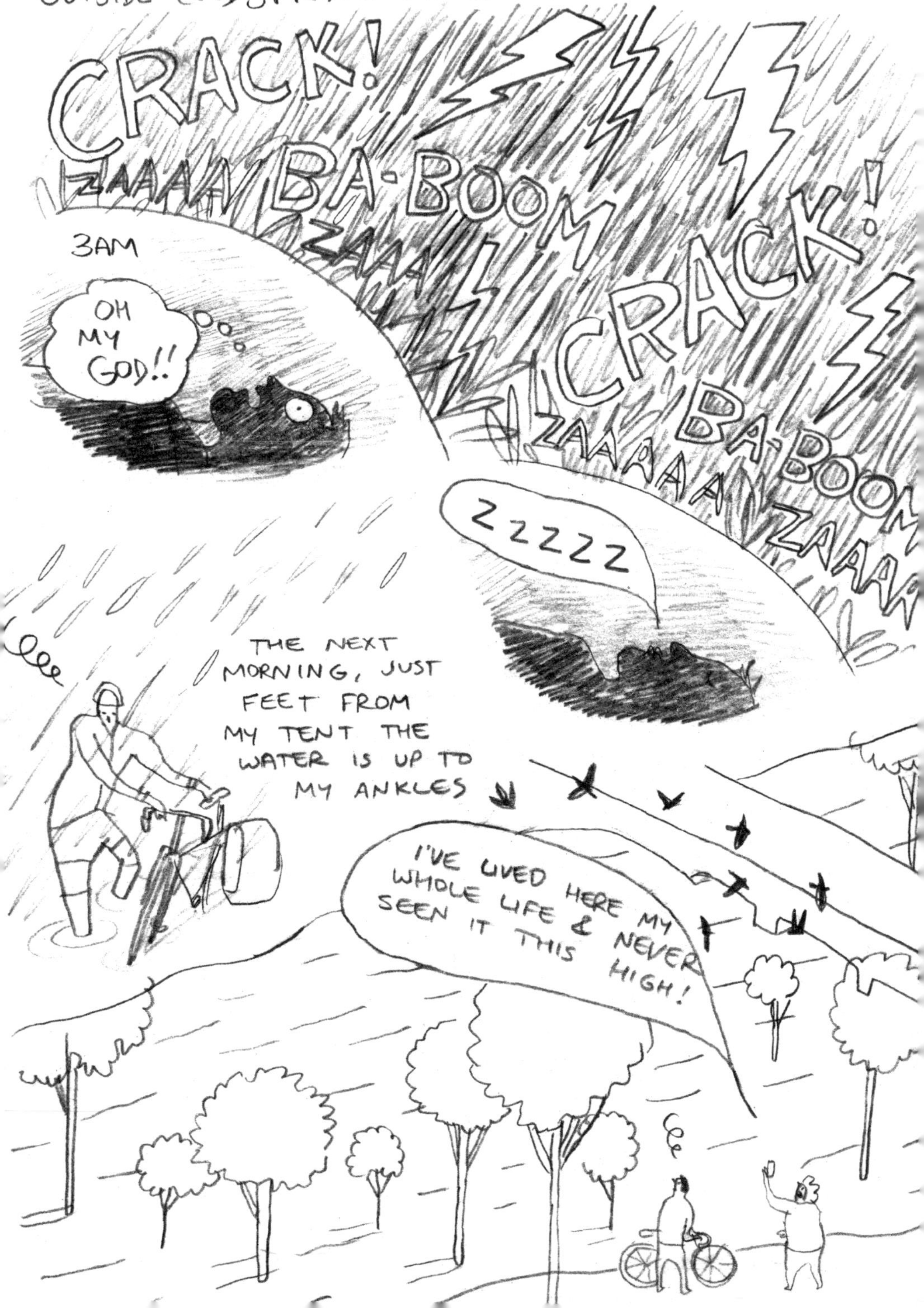

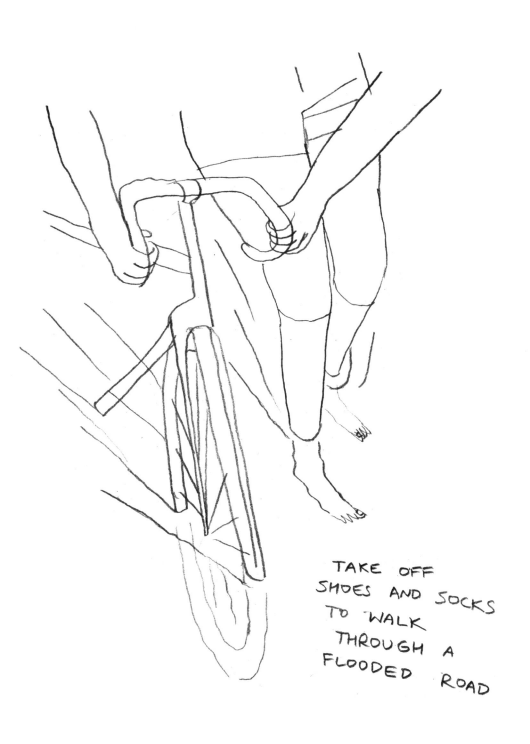

TAKE OFF
SHOES AND SOCKS
TO WALK
THROUGH A
FLOODED ROAD

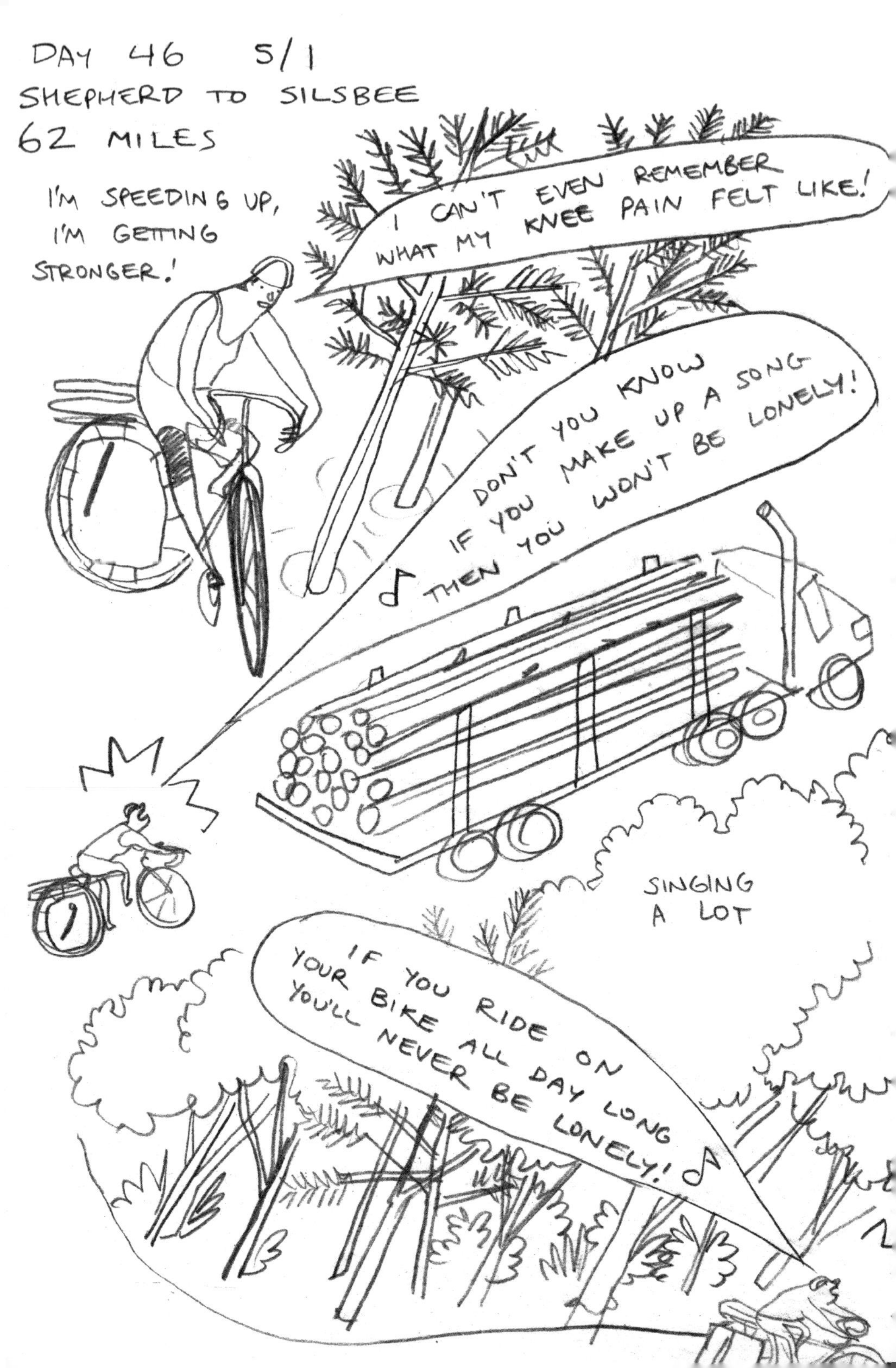
DAY 46 5/1
SHEPHERD TO SILSBEE
62 MILES
I'M SPEEDING UP, I'M GETTING STRONGER!
I CAN'T EVEN REMEMBER WHAT MY KNEE PAIN FELT LIKE!
DON'T YOU KNOW IF YOU MAKE UP A SONG THEN YOU WON'T BE LONELY!
SINGING A LOT
IF YOU RIDE ON YOUR BIKE ALL DAY LONG YOU'LL NEVER BE LONELY!

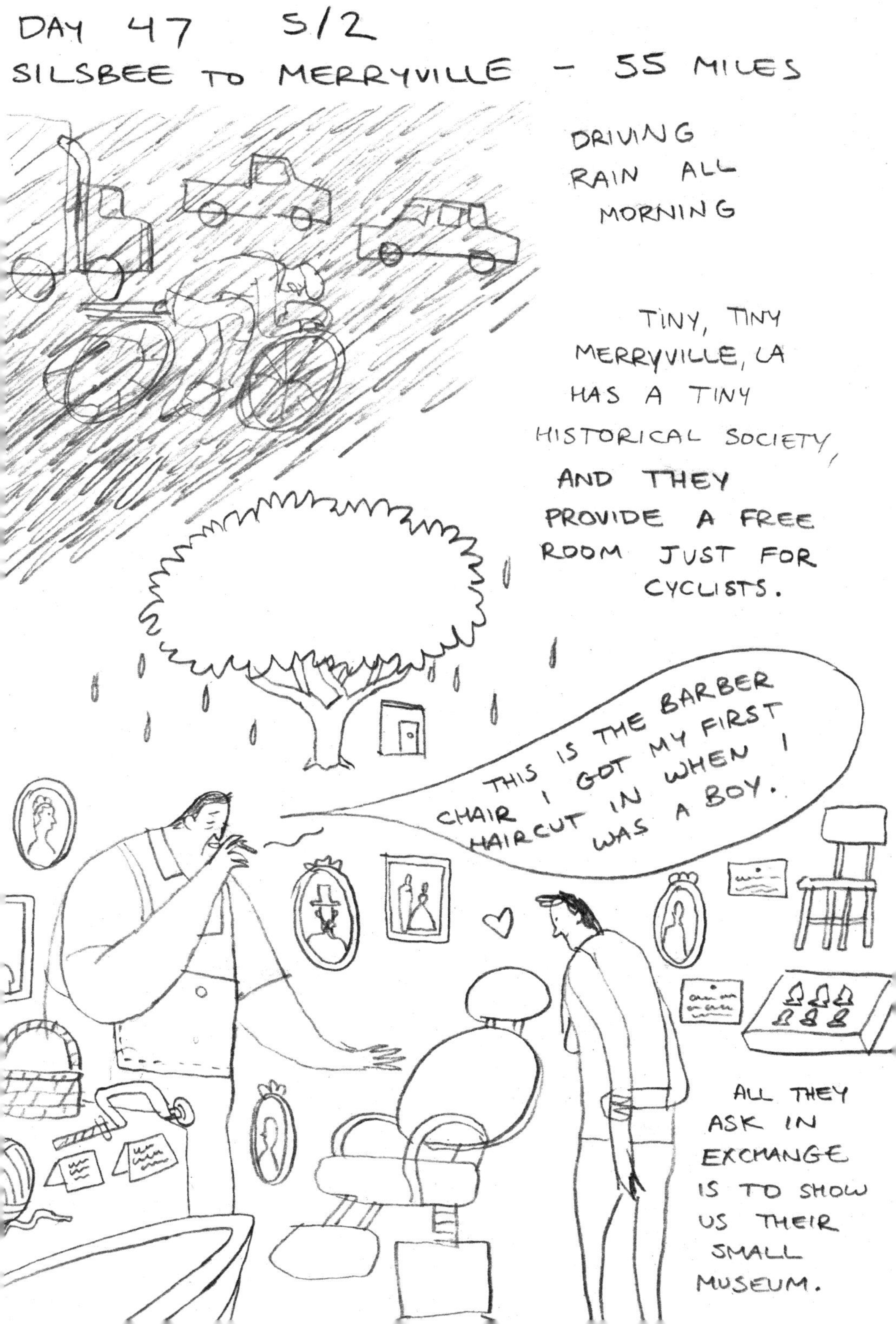
DAY 47 5/2
SILSBEE TO MERRYVILLE - 55 MILES
DRIVING RAIN ALL MORNING
TINY, TINY MERRYVILLE, LA HAS A TINY HISTORICAL SOCIETY, AND THEY PROVIDE A FREE ROOM JUST FOR CYCLISTS.
THIS IS THE BARBER CHAIR I GOT MY FIRST HAIRCUT IN WHEN I WAS A BOY.
ALL THEY ASK IN EXCHANGE IS TO SHOW US THEIR SMALL MUSEUM.

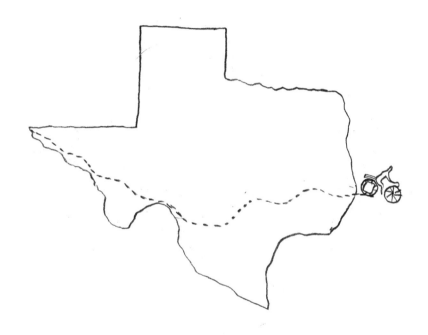

CROSS THE
SABINE RIVER &
GOODBYE, BEAUTIFUL
TEXAS

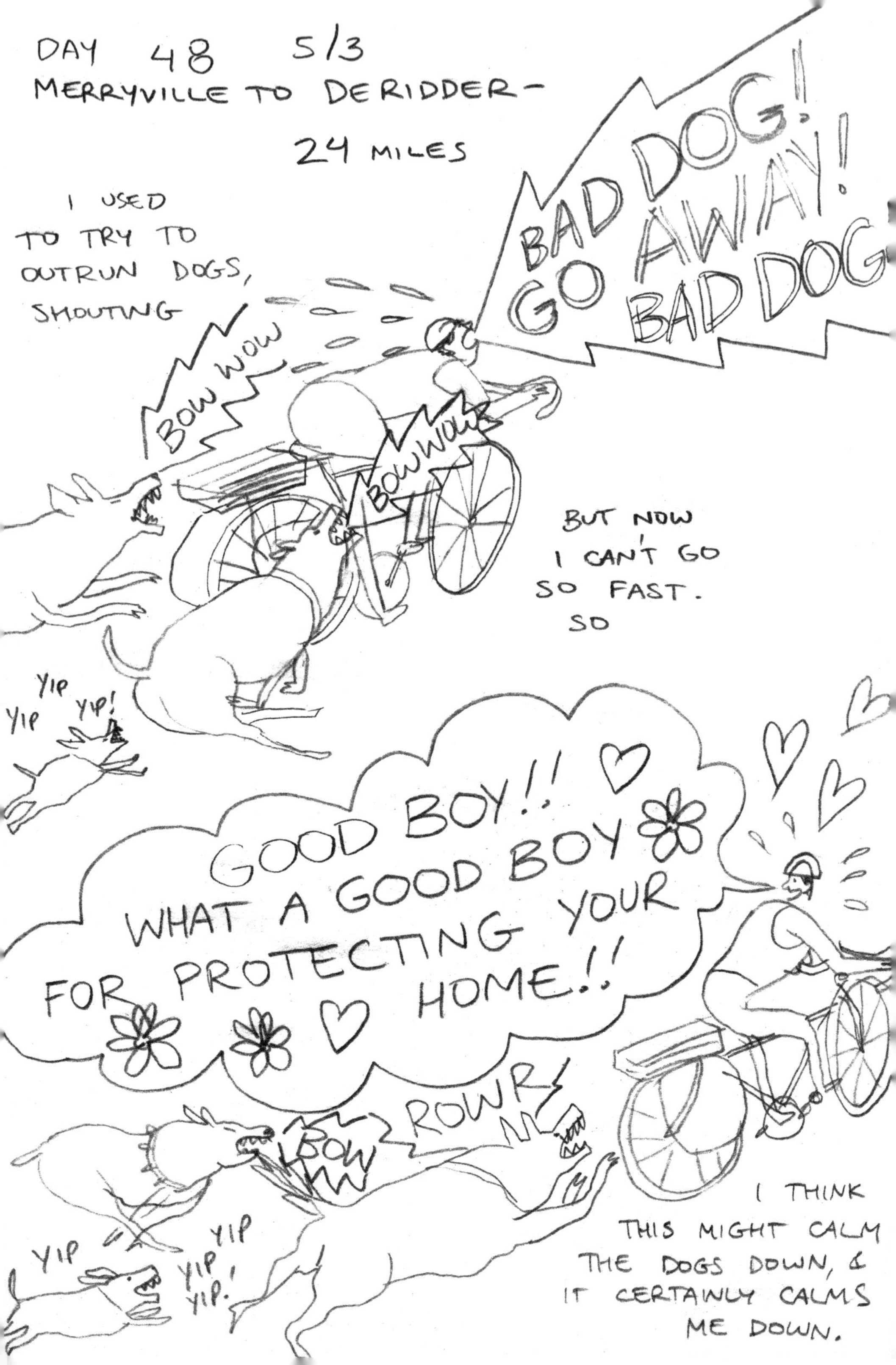

DAY 48 5/3
MERRYVILLE TO DERIDDER -
24 MILES
I USED TO TRY TO OUTRUN DOGS, SHOUTING
BAD DOG! GO AWAY! BAD DOG
BOW WOW
BOW WOW
BOW WOW
BUT NOW I CAN'T GO SO FAST. SO
YIP YIP YIP!
GOOD BOY!! WHAT A GOOD BOY FOR PROTECTING YOUR HOME!!
ROWR
BOW WOW
YIP YIP YIP! YIP.
I THINK THIS MIGHT CALM THE DOGS DOWN, & IT CERTAINLY CALMS ME DOWN.

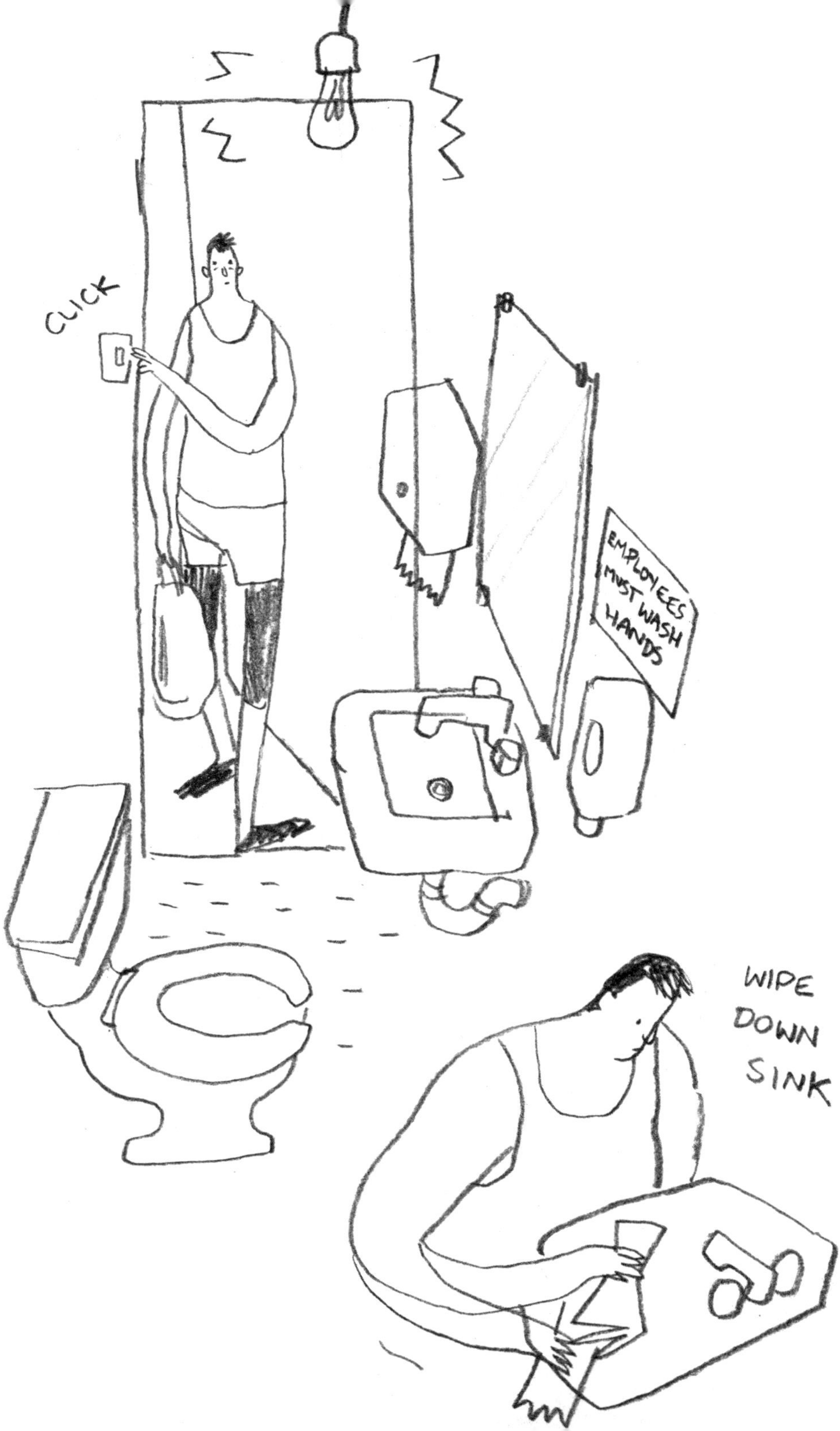
CLICK
EMPLOYEES MUST WASH HANDS
WIPE DOWN SINK

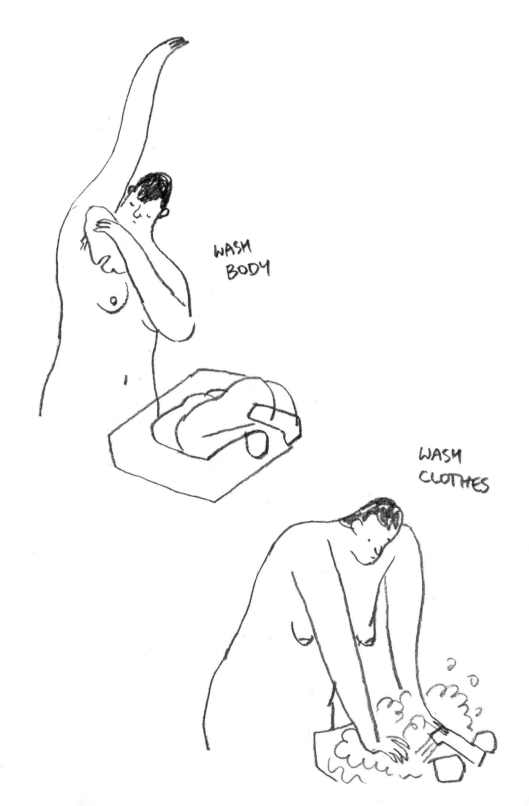

WASH
BODY

WASH
CLOTHES

DAY 49 - 5/4
DE RIDDER TO FULLERTON - 39 MILES
THEY'RE HURTING AGAIN, AND IT'S SO BORING.
WHAT DID I DO WRONG
WHAT DID I DO WRONG
WHAT DID I DO WRONG
I'M TAKING A BIG RISK ON A SHORTCUT THROUGH A MILITARY RESERVE TOMORROW MORNING
121
FORT POLK
NAT'L FOREST
FULLERTON RD
IF IT'S IMPASSABLE I HAVE NO BACK-UP PLAN.
CRYING IN AN UNKIND PINE FOREST.

DAY 50 - 5/5
FULLERTON TO ALEXANDRIA - 35 MILES

THE DIRT ROAD THROUGH THE MILITARY RESERVE IS CLEAR.

دخول ميناء
استقبال نقطة
PORT OF ENTRY AHEAD

PINE FOREST RIDDLED WITH PATHS

اسلام اباد
PAKISTAN

كندهار
KANDAHAR

MAZAR-I-SHARIF
مزار شريف

HERAT
هرات

AND SIGNS IN ARABIC

IN THE
CENTER IS A
RECREATION OF
AN AFGHAN
TOWN

THE BUILDINGS ARE PAINTED BLUE AND PINK
AND PURPLE. IT'S DAWN.

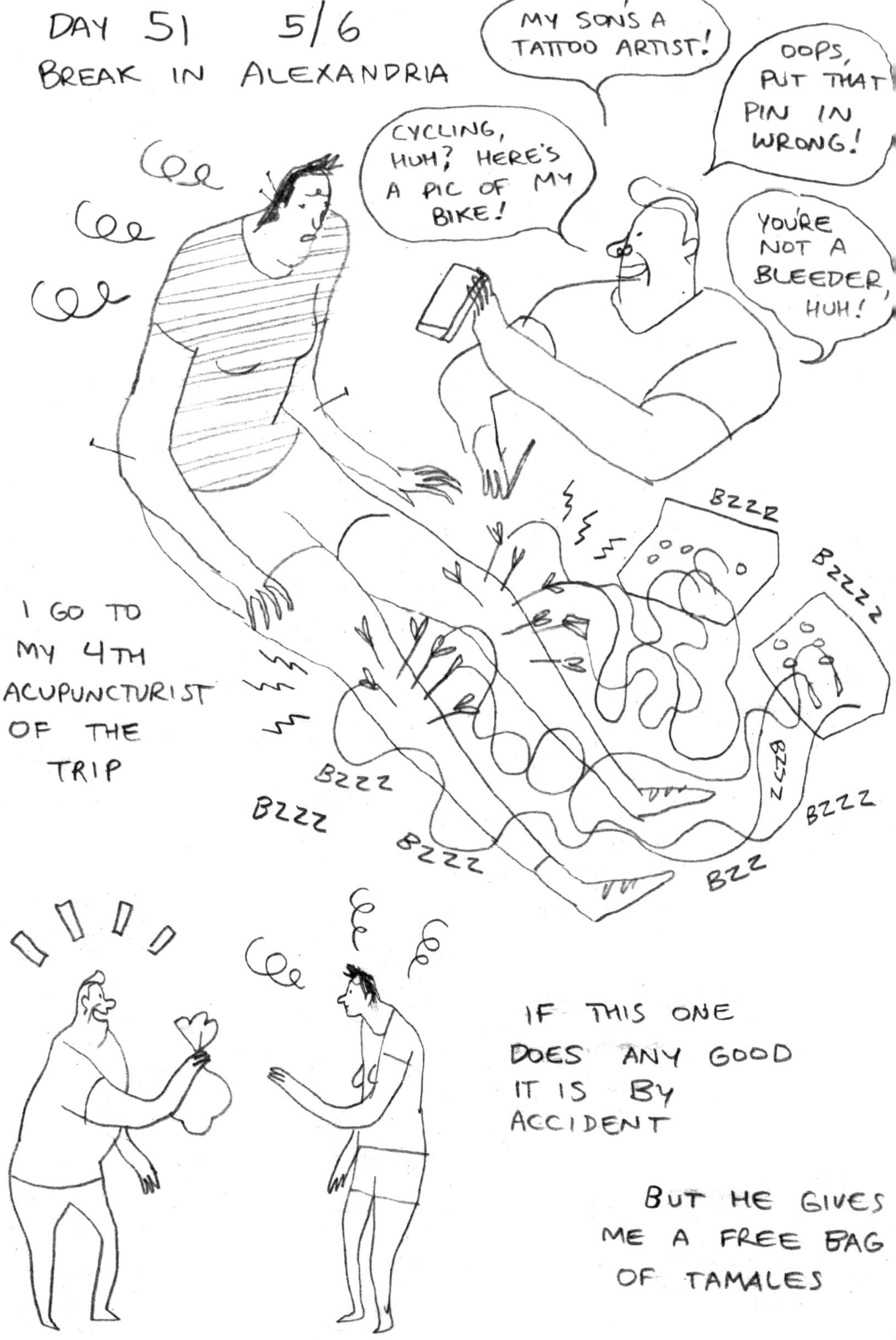
DAY 51 5/6
BREAK IN ALEXANDRIA
MY SON'S A TATTOO ARTIST!
CYCLING, HUH? HERE'S A PIC OF MY BIKE!
OOPS, PUT THAT PIN IN WRONG!
YOU'RE NOT A BLEEDER, HUH!
BZZZ
BZZZZZ
I GO TO MY 4TH ACUPUNCTURIST OF THE TRIP
BZZZ
BZZZ
BZZZ
BZZZ
BZZZ
BZZ
BZZ
IF THIS ONE DOES ANY GOOD IT IS BY ACCIDENT
BUT HE GIVES ME A FREE BAG OF TAMALES

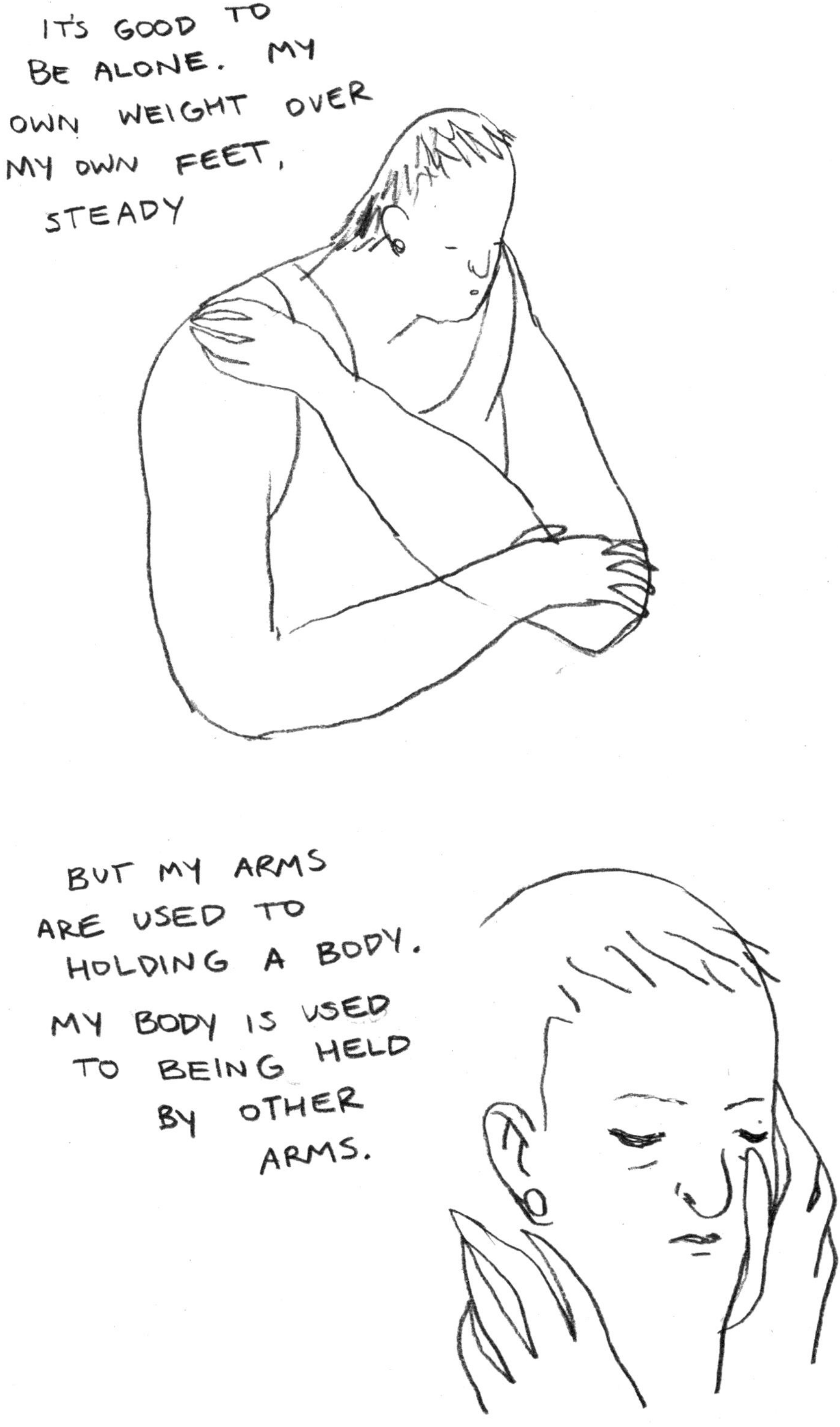
IT'S GOOD TO BE ALONE. MY OWN WEIGHT OVER MY OWN FEET, STEADY
BUT MY ARMS ARE USED TO HOLDING A BODY.
MY BODY IS USED TO BEING HELD BY OTHER ARMS.

DAY 52 5/7 26 MILES
ALEXANDRIA TO POLLACK —
POLLACK, LOUISIANÁ IS SO SMALL, BUT
A TINY GOTH & A TINY PUNK!
HEY, ARE YOU LONELY?
!
I ... I AM!
THEY TEACH ME TEEN TRICKS
IF YOU PROGRAM YOUR iPHONE TO JAN 1ST, 1970, IT'LL BREAK YOUR PHONE!!
IF YOU DRAW A BLACK SQUARE ON YOUR SKIN & PUT YOUR PHONE CAMERA ON IT & TAKE A PHOTO WITH FLASH IT'LL SHOCK YOU!

WE'RE SO CRAZY, RIGHT? YOU PROBABLY THINK WE'RE CRAZY!
UM, SO I WAS WONDERING, HOW FAR HAVE YOU BIKED?
MY WHOLE FAMILY IS CRAZY! MY DAD SHOT OUR NEIGHBOR'S DOG ON CHRISTMAS DAY!
UM, SO I WAS WONDERING, WHAT'S YOUR FAVORITE CITY THAT YOU'VE BEEN TO?
UM, SO
I'M JUST LIKE AMETHYST, I'M SHORT & FAT & LOUD!
I'M SO CRAZY, WE GO TO WALMART & I HIDE BEHIND THE SPONGEBOB PINATAS & YELL "SQUIDWARD!" AT PEOPLE
UM, SO I WAS WONDERING
I RUN AWAY WHEN SHE DOES THAT
MY SISTER IS BIGGER'N ME BUT SHE CAN'T EVEN FIGHT!
I LIKE TO LINE UP THE PLASTIC DINOSAURS IN THE AISLES
MY COUSIN ROBBED A BANK ONCE! AFTERWARDS HE WENT TO APPLEBYS & GOT SOME PIE
I DON'T GET TO GO TO WALMART MUCH, GAS IS TOO EXPENSIVE FOR MY MOM TO DRIVE ME
THAT'S WHERE THE COPS FOUND HIM
HEY, TAKE US WITH YOU!

DAY 53 5/8
POLLACK TO ARCHIE — 43 MILES

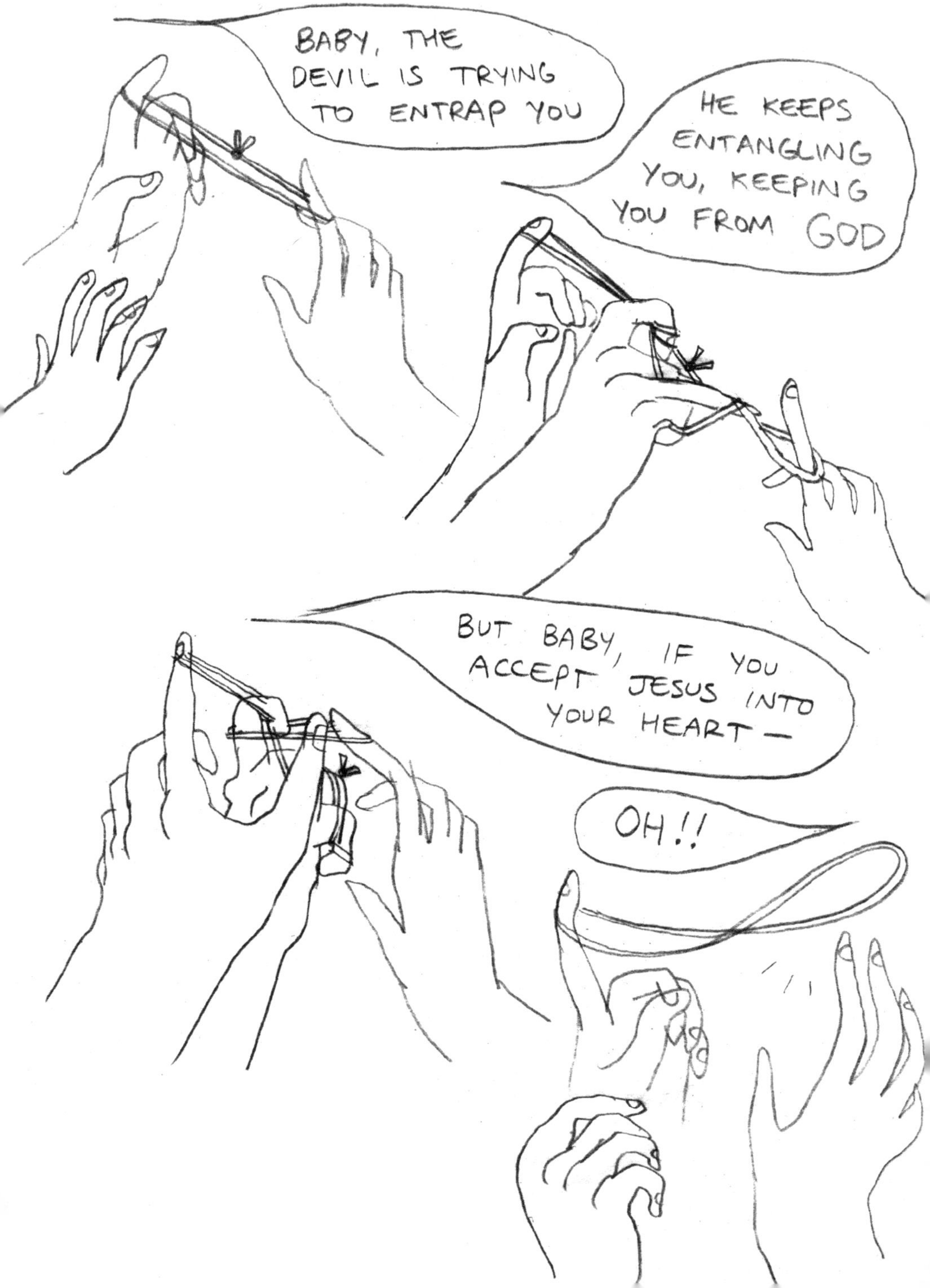

HE IS A PREACHER.
HE & HIS WIFE
GIVE ME A
LIFT PAST 3 MILES
   OF   DANGEROUS ROAD,
AND HE TRIES TO GIVE
   ME HIS   SUNGLASSES
        & SOME MONEY.

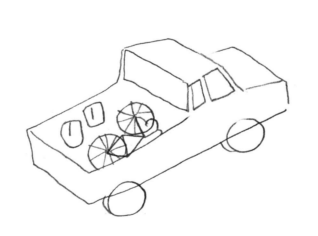

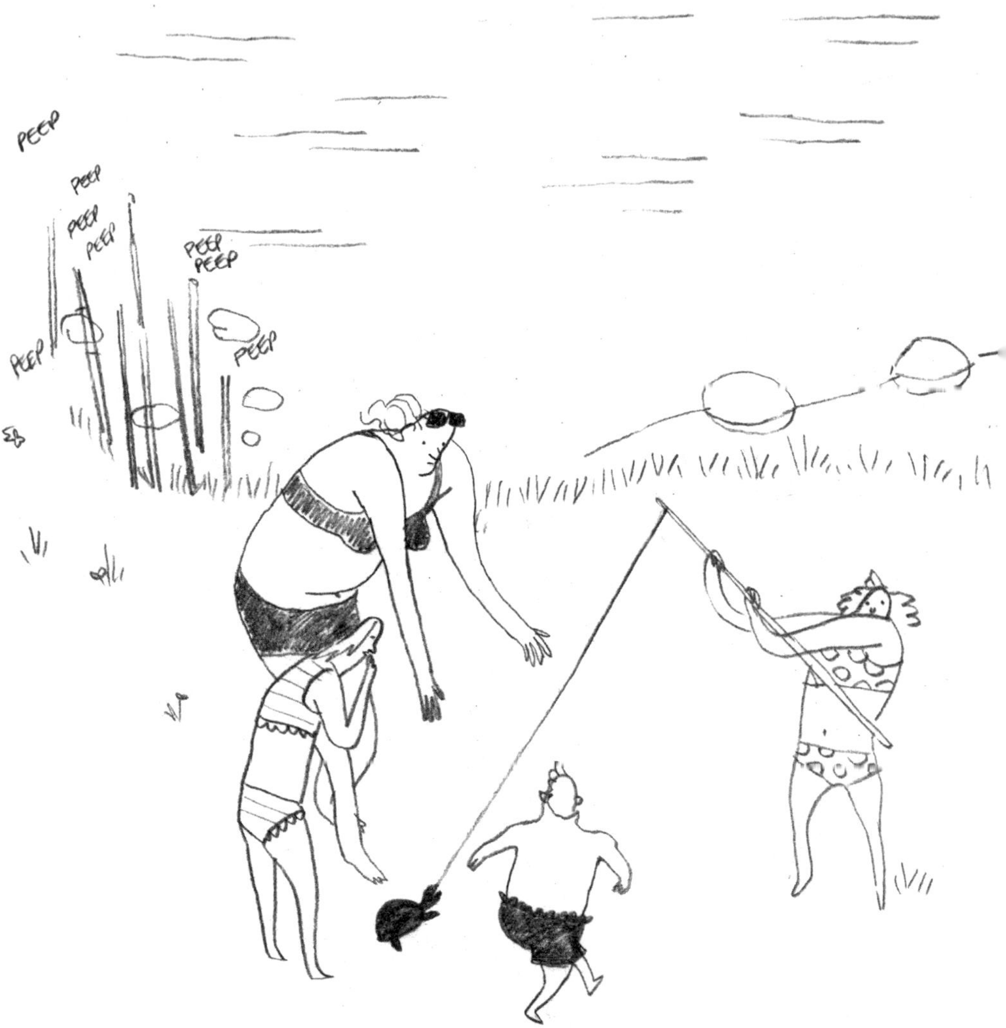
PEEP
PEEP
PEEP
PEEP
PEEP
PEEP
PEEP
PEEP

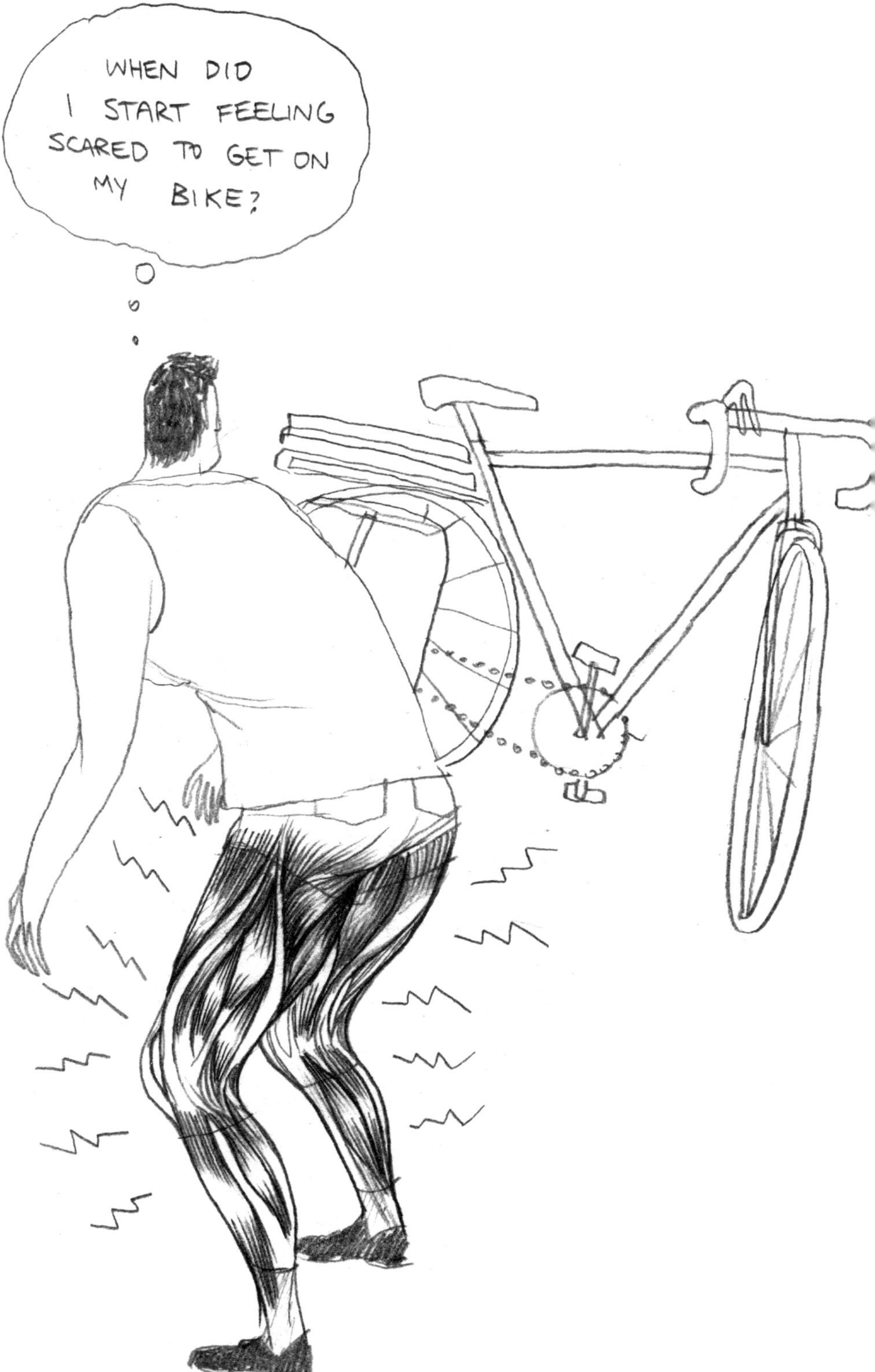
WHEN DID I START FEELING SCARED TO GET ON MY BIKE?

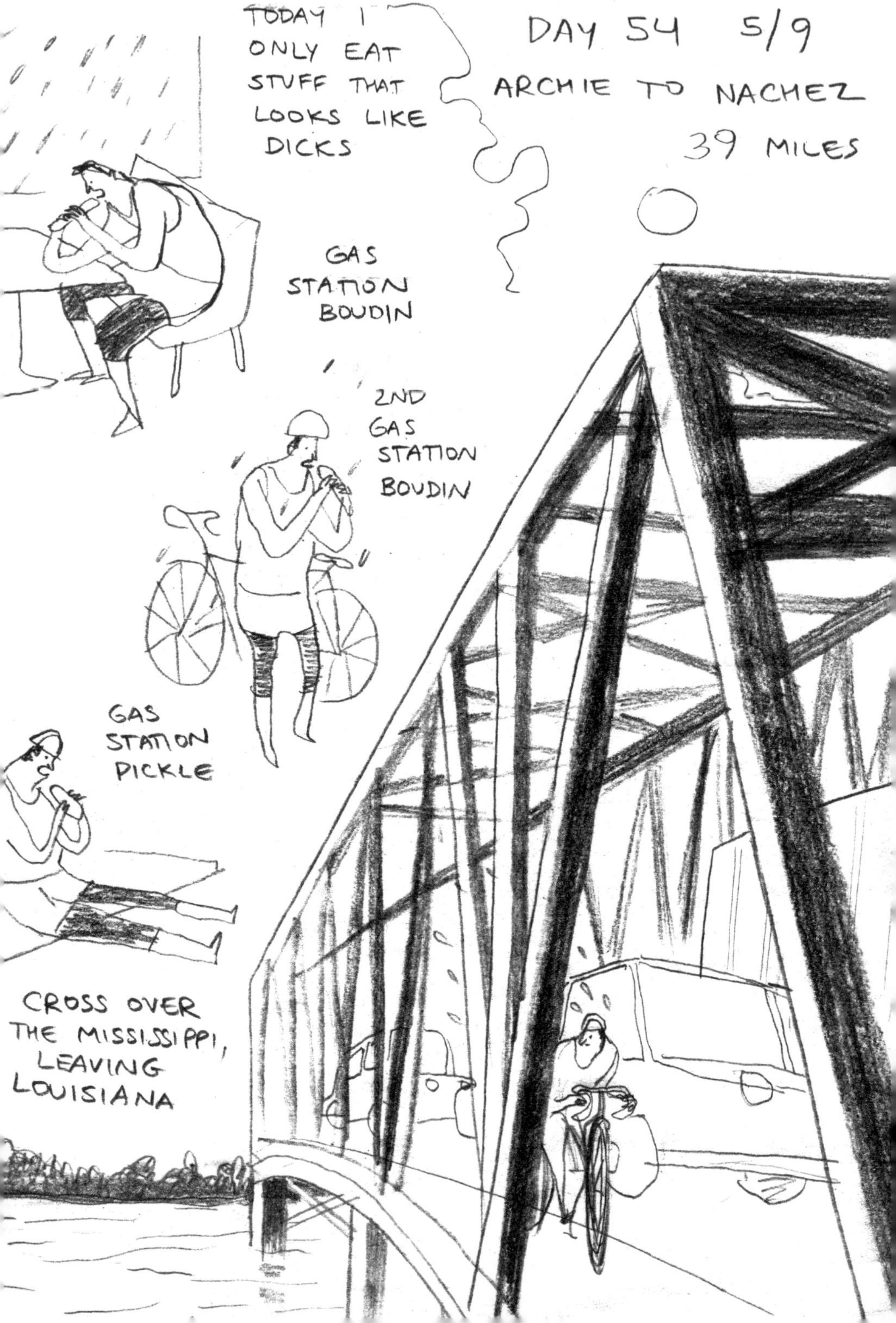

DAY 54 5/9
ARCHIE TO NACHEZ
39 MILES
TODAY I ONLY EAT STUFF THAT LOOKS LIKE DICKS
GAS STATION BOUDIN
2ND GAS STATION BOUDIN
GAS STATION PICKLE
CROSS OVER THE MISSISSIPPI, LEAVING LOUISIANA

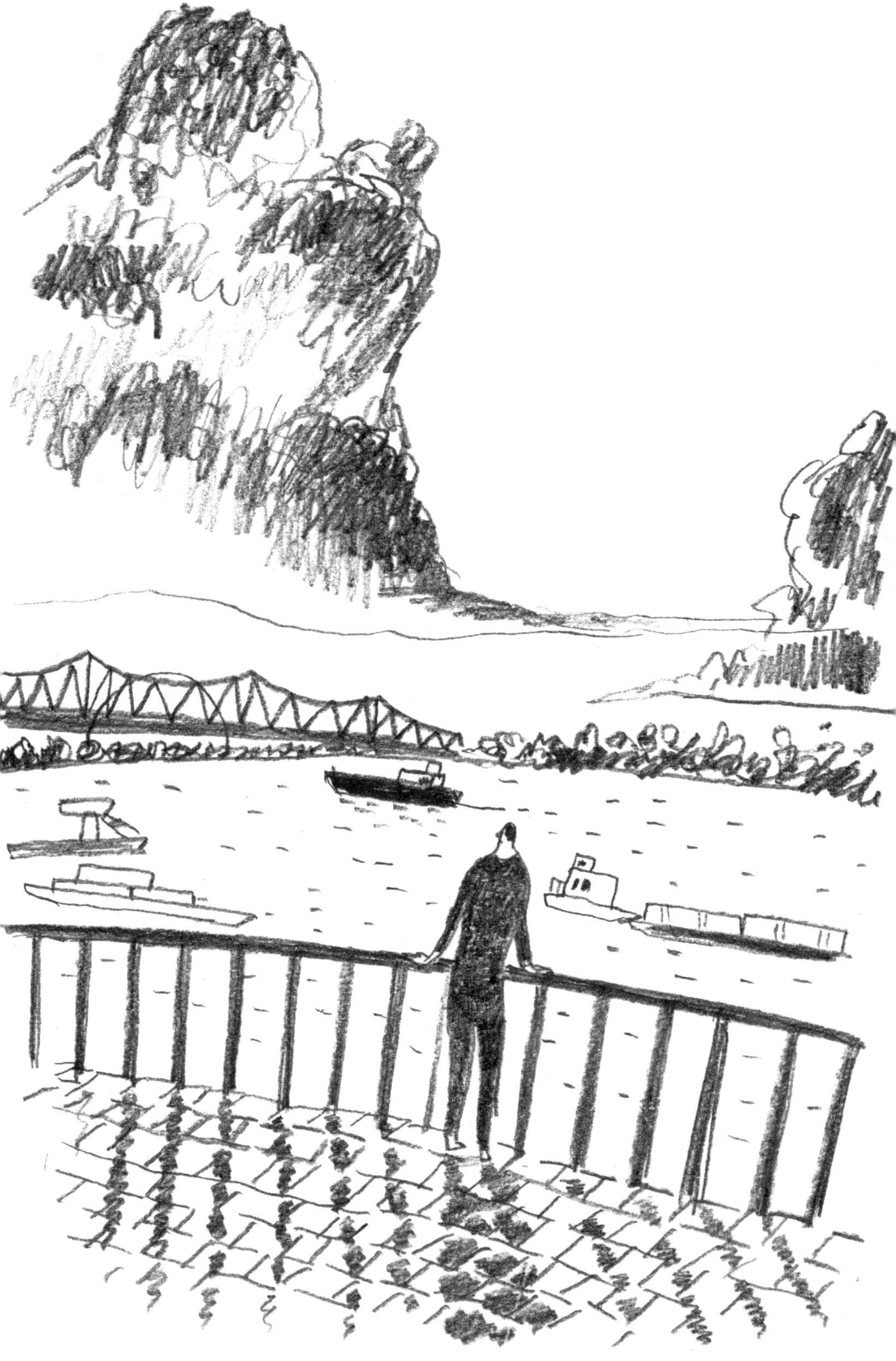

TEXAS MAKES
EVERY OTHER
STATE SEEM
TINY.

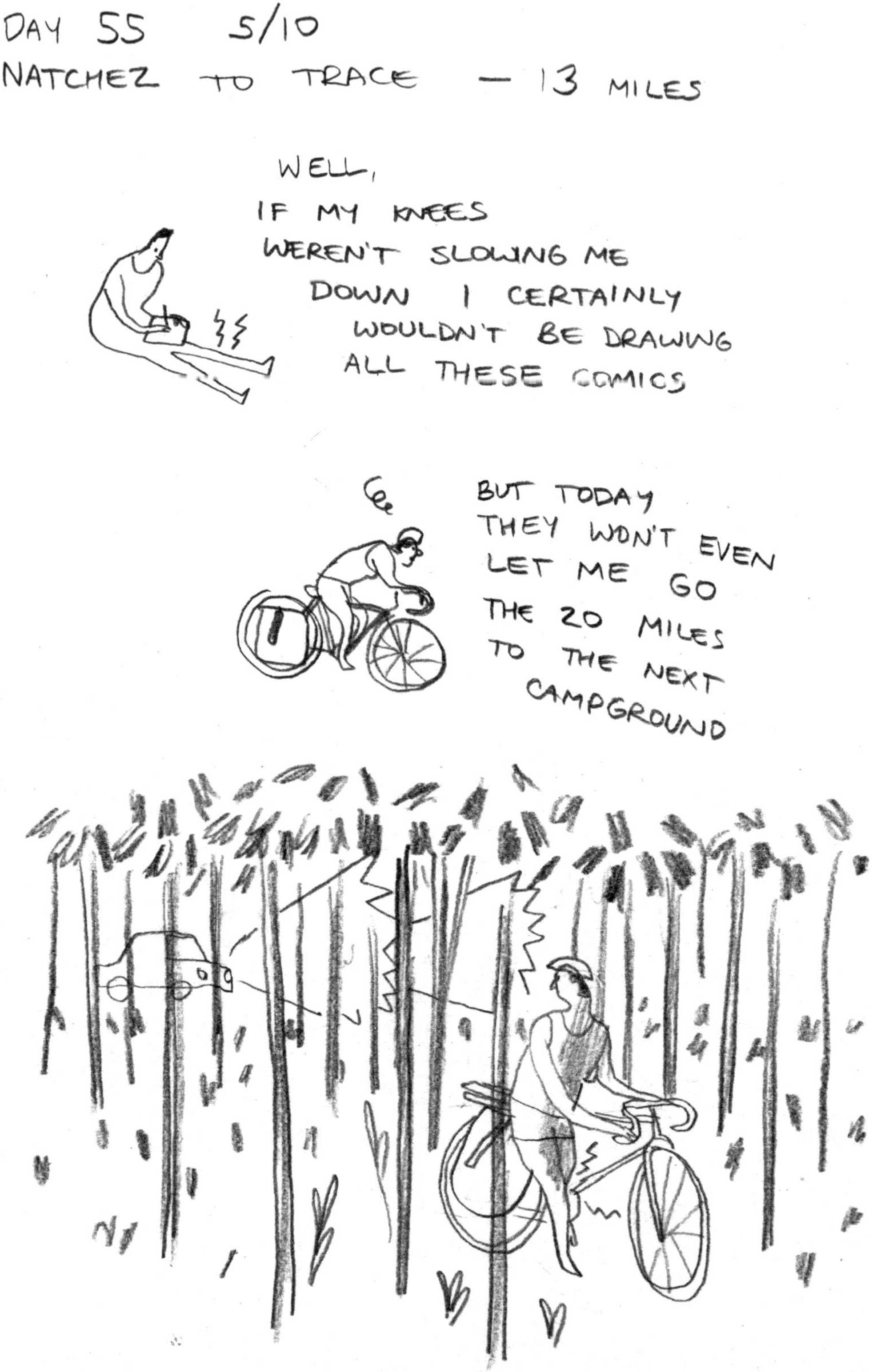
DAY 55 5/10
NATCHEZ TO TRACE — 13 MILES
WELL, IF MY KNEES WEREN'T SLOWING ME DOWN I CERTAINLY WOULDN'T BE DRAWING ALL THESE COMICS
BUT TODAY THEY WON'T EVEN LET ME GO THE 20 MILES TO THE NEXT CAMPGROUND

DAY 56 5/11
TRACE TO ROSSWOOD — 33 MILES

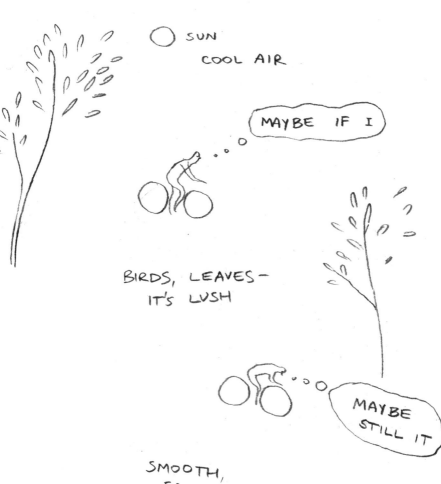

SUN
COOL AIR

MAYBE IF I

BIRDS, LEAVES—
IT'S LUSH

MAYBE
STILL IT

SMOOTH,
SAFE ROAD,
1,700 MILES
BEHIND ME

NO
. . .

MY BODY TOOK ME A LONG WAY
BEEP BOOP
(HUSBAND, HOME)
OH! HELLO SWEETIE!
HA HA I JUST CAN'T MAKE THE LAST 600 MILES

OH! IT WOULD
HAVE FELT SO GOOD
TO BIKE ALL
THE WAY THERE!

BUT IT FEELS
GOOD, TOO, TO
LET MYSELF
STOP.

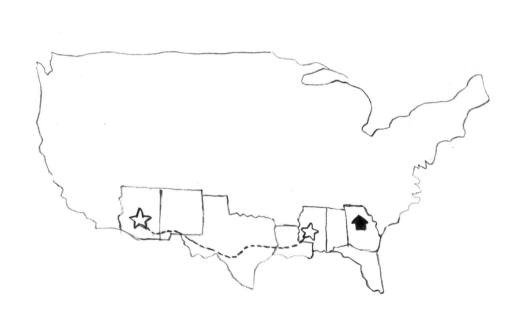

EPILOGUE

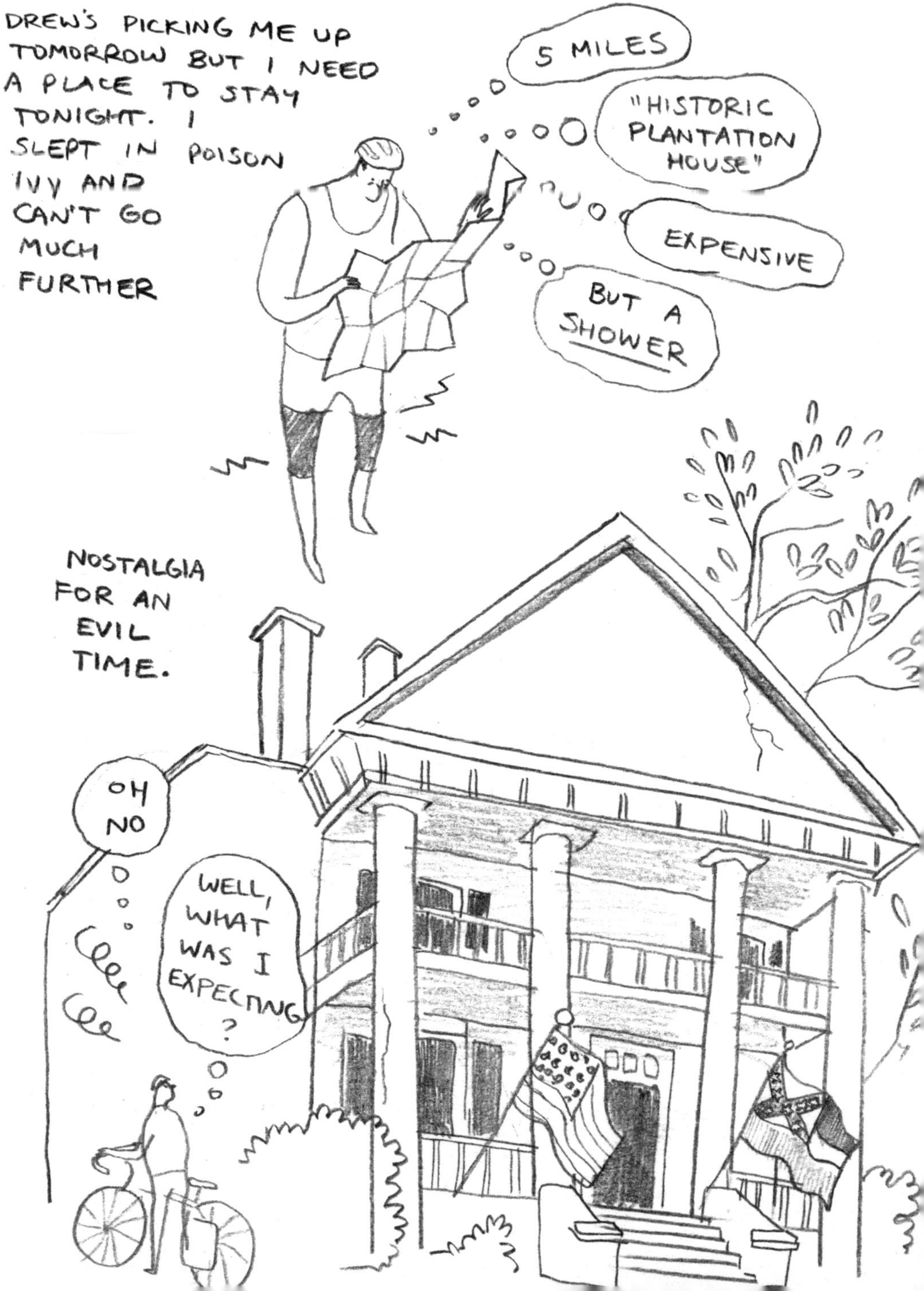
DREW'S PICKING ME UP TOMORROW BUT I NEED A PLACE TO STAY TONIGHT. I SLEPT IN POISON IVY AND CAN'T GO MUCH FURTHER
5 MILES
"HISTORIC PLANTATION HOUSE"
EXPENSIVE
BUT A SHOWER
NOSTALGIA FOR AN EVIL TIME.
OH NO
WELL, WHAT WAS I EXPECTING?

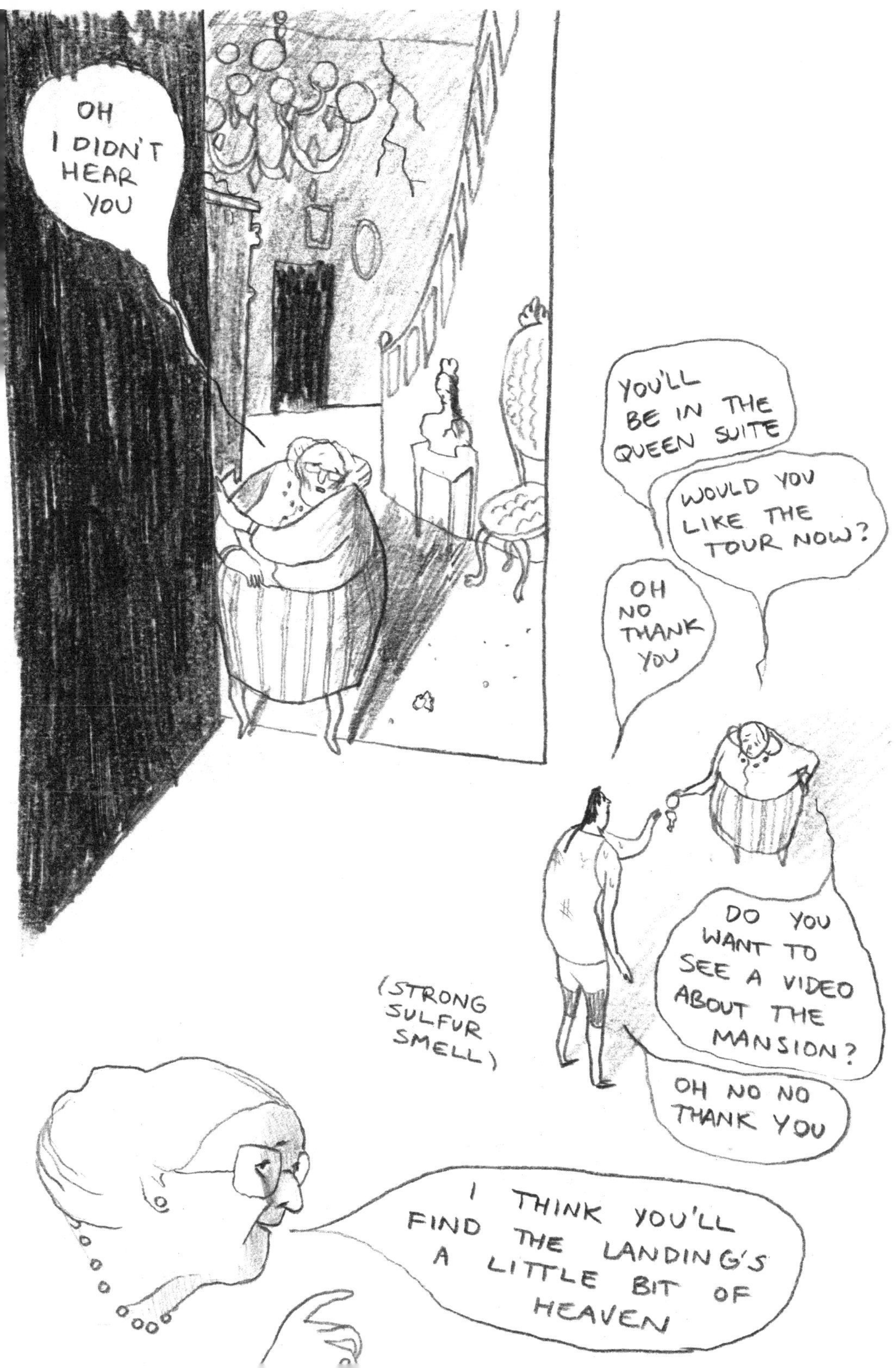
OH I DIDN'T HEAR YOU
YOU'LL BE IN THE QUEEN SUITE
WOULD YOU LIKE THE TOUR NOW?
OH NO THANK YOU
DO YOU WANT TO SEE A VIDEO ABOUT THE MANSION?
OH NO NO THANK YOU
(STRONG SULFUR SMELL)
I THINK YOU'LL FIND THE LANDING'S A LITTLE BIT OF HEAVEN

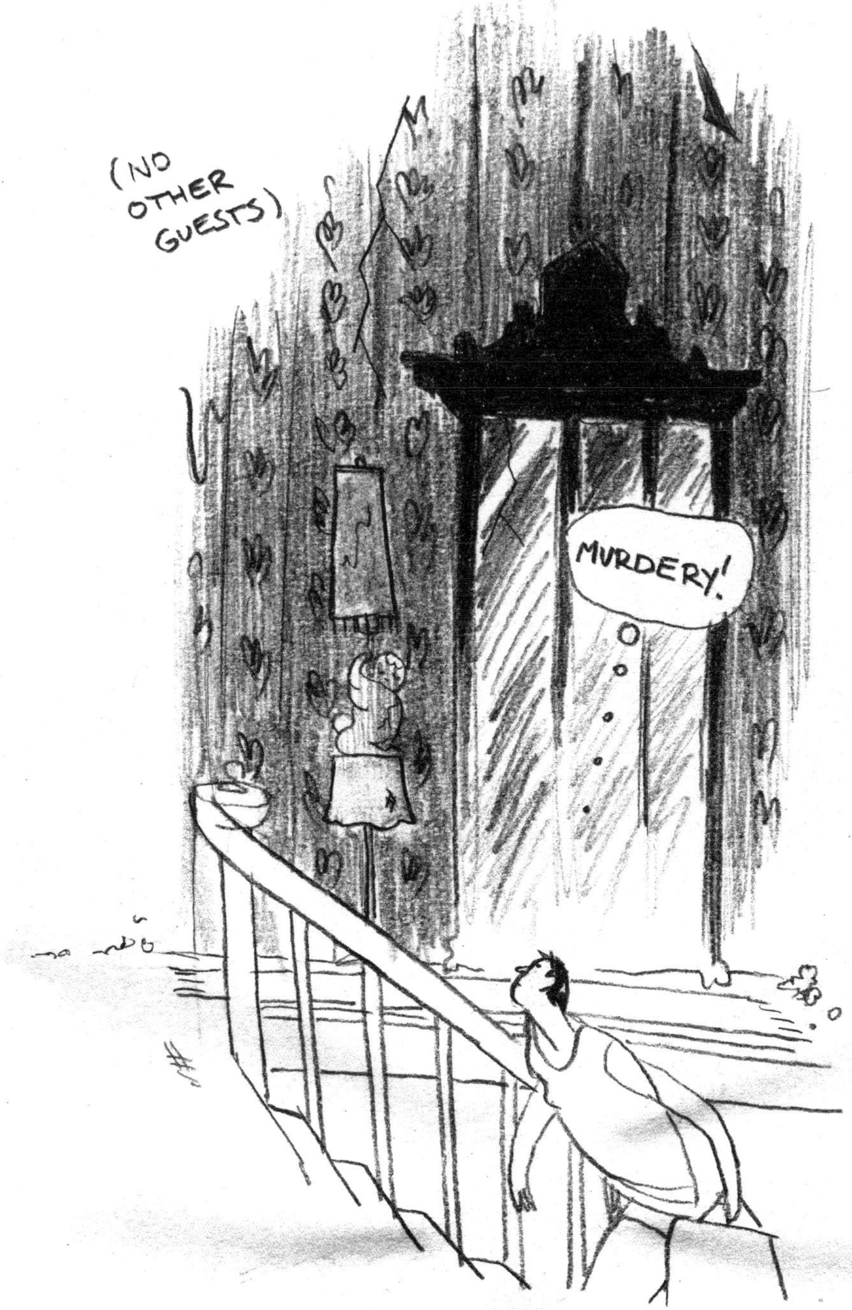
(NO OTHER GUESTS)
MURDERY!

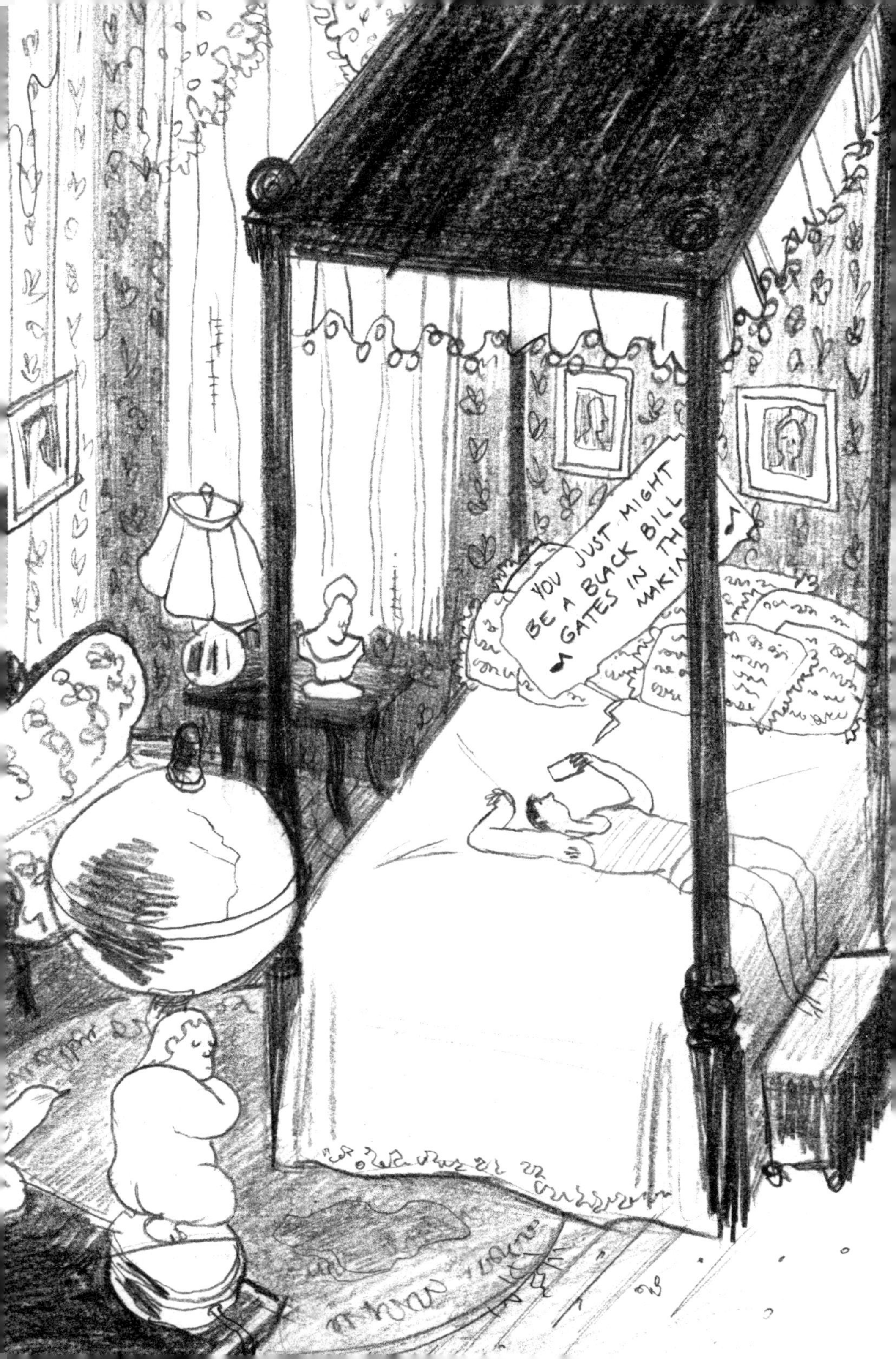
YOU JUST MIGHT BE A BLACK BILL GATES IN THE MAKIN

DAY 57 5/12

ROSSWOOD TO PORT GIBSON - 16 MILES

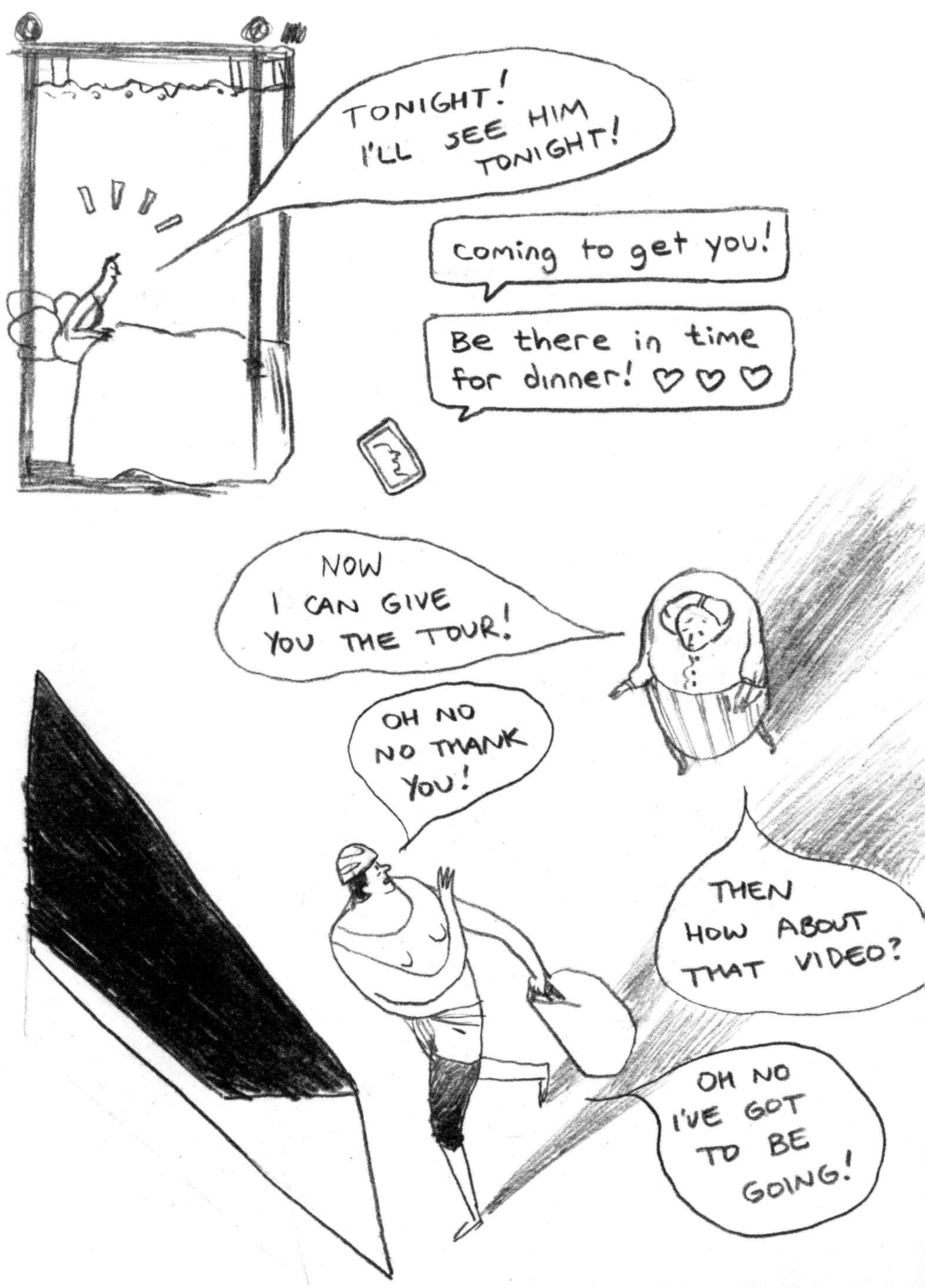
TONIGHT! I'LL SEE HIM TONIGHT!
Coming to get you!
Be there in time for dinner! ♡♡♡
NOW I CAN GIVE YOU THE TOUR!
OH NO NO THANK YOU!
THEN HOW ABOUT THAT VIDEO?
OH NO I'VE GOT TO BE GOING!

SCREEEE!
GIVE THESE TO MISS JEAN.
HOW'S MISS JEAN DOING?
I HAVE TO BE GOING.
IS MISS JEAN OK?
TELL HER I CAME BY.
WHAT ARE YOU TALKING ABOUT?
OBITUARY
PORT GIBSON GAZETTE
YOU DIDN'T HEAR?
COLONEL HIGHLANDER DIED JUST DAY BEFORE YESTERDAY
THEY'D BEEN MARRIED A HUNDRED YEARS.

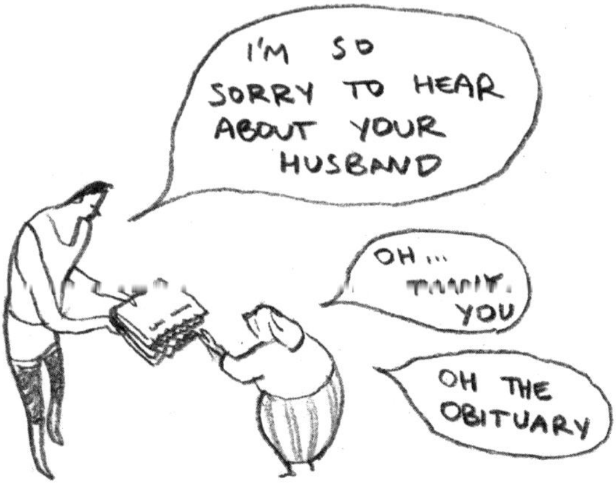
I'M SO SORRY TO HEAR ABOUT YOUR HUSBAND
OH... YOU
OH THE OBITUARY

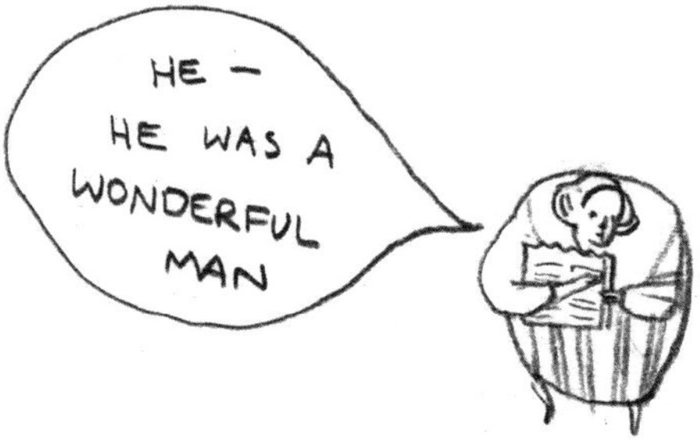
HE – HE WAS A WONDERFUL MAN

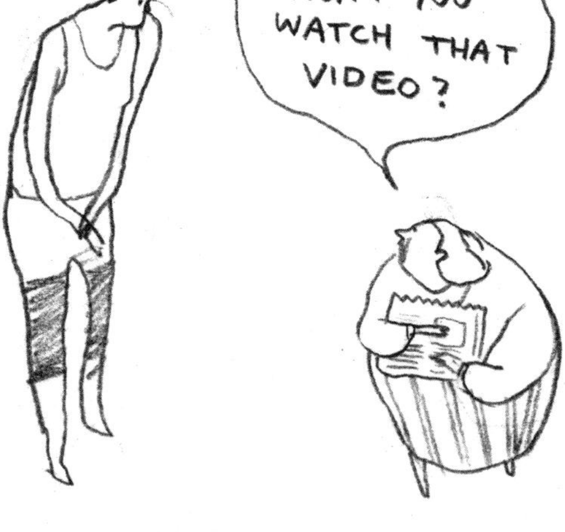
WON'T YOU WATCH THAT VIDEO?

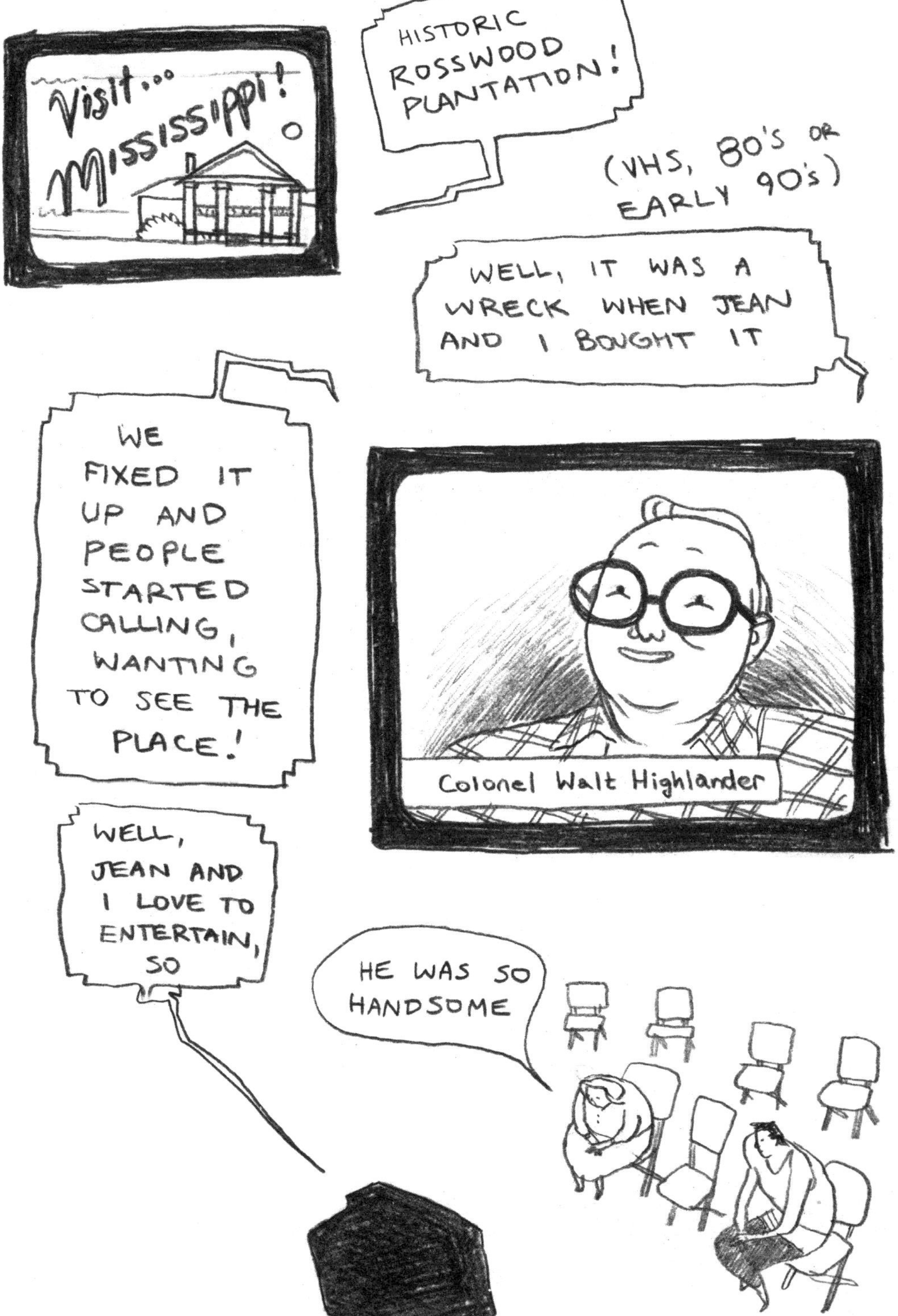
Visit... Mississippi!
HISTORIC ROSSWOOD PLANTATION!
(VHS, 80'S OR EARLY 90'S)
WELL, IT WAS A WRECK WHEN JEAN AND I BOUGHT IT
WE FIXED IT UP AND PEOPLE STARTED CALLING, WANTING TO SEE THE PLACE!
Colonel Walt Highlander
WELL, JEAN AND I LOVE TO ENTERTAIN, SO
HE WAS SO HANDSOME

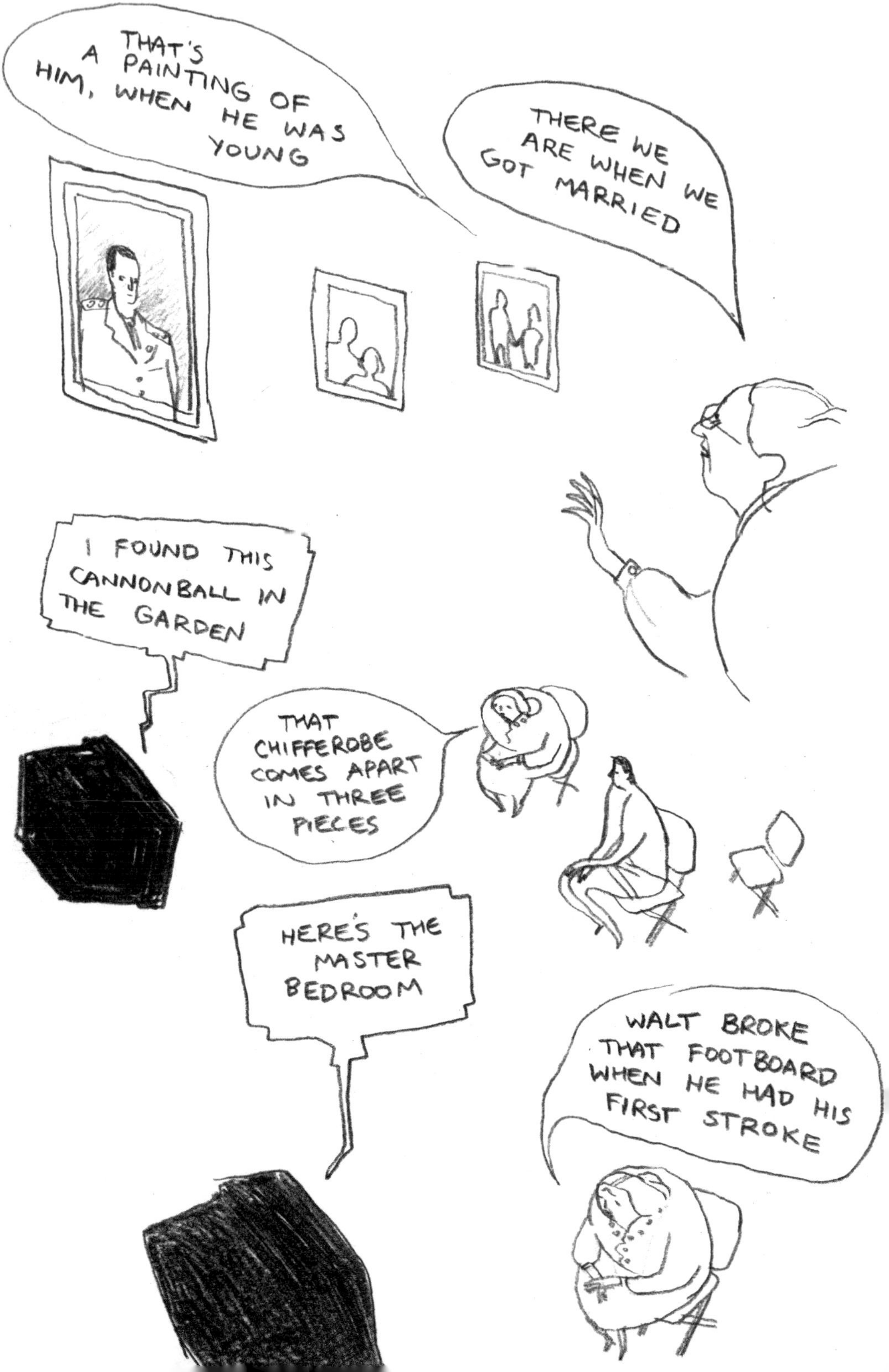
THAT'S A PAINTING OF HIM, WHEN HE WAS YOUNG
THERE WE ARE WHEN WE GOT MARRIED
I FOUND THIS CANNONBALL IN THE GARDEN
THAT CHIFFEROBE COMES APART IN THREE PIECES
HERE'S THE MASTER BEDROOM
WALT BROKE THAT FOOTBOARD WHEN HE HAD HIS FIRST STROKE

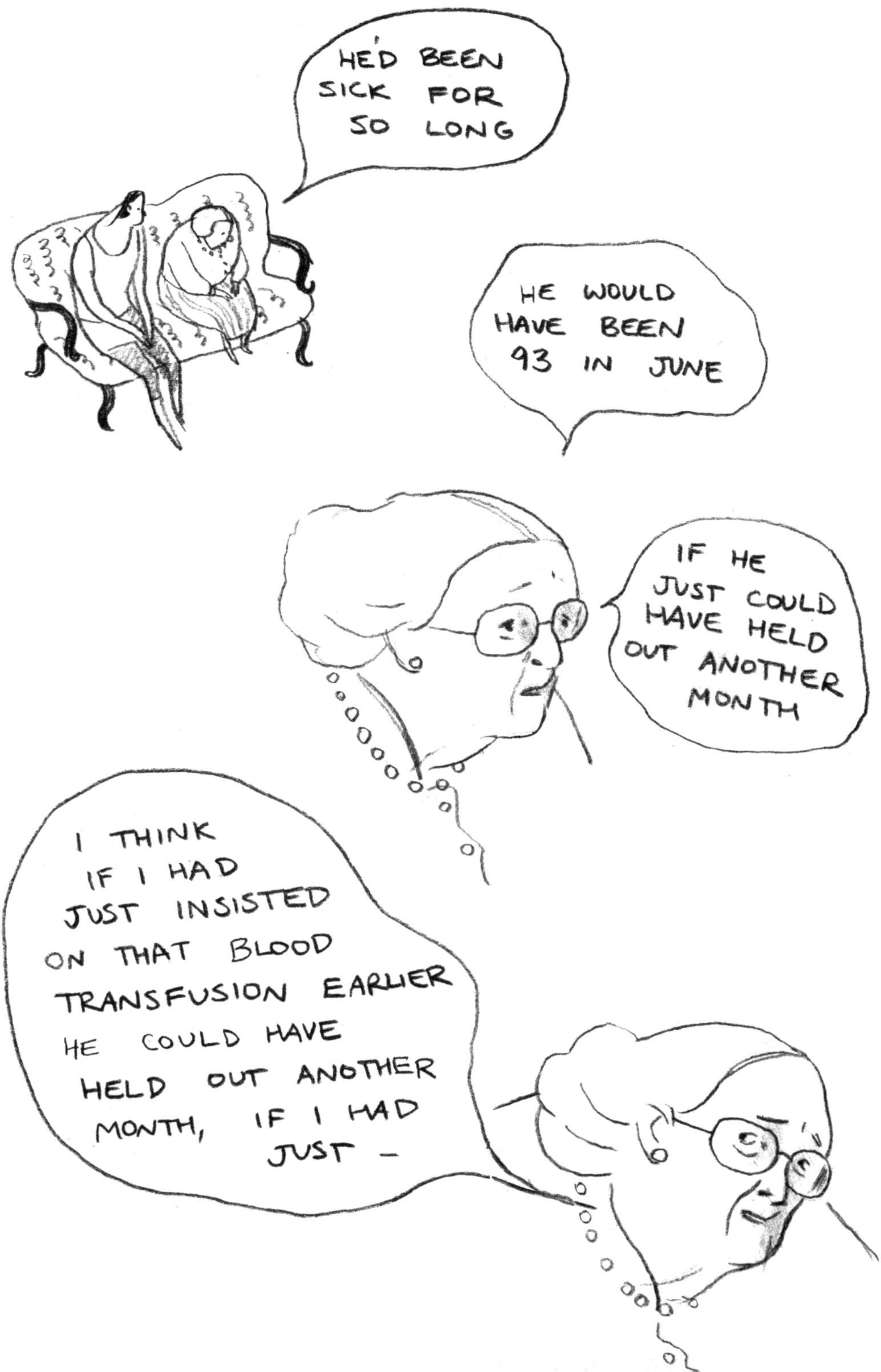
HE'D BEEN SICK FOR SO LONG
HE WOULD HAVE BEEN 93 IN JUNE
IF HE JUST COULD HAVE HELD OUT ANOTHER MONTH
I THINK IF I HAD JUST INSISTED ON THAT BLOOD TRANSFUSION EARLIER HE COULD HAVE HELD OUT ANOTHER MONTH, IF I HAD JUST –

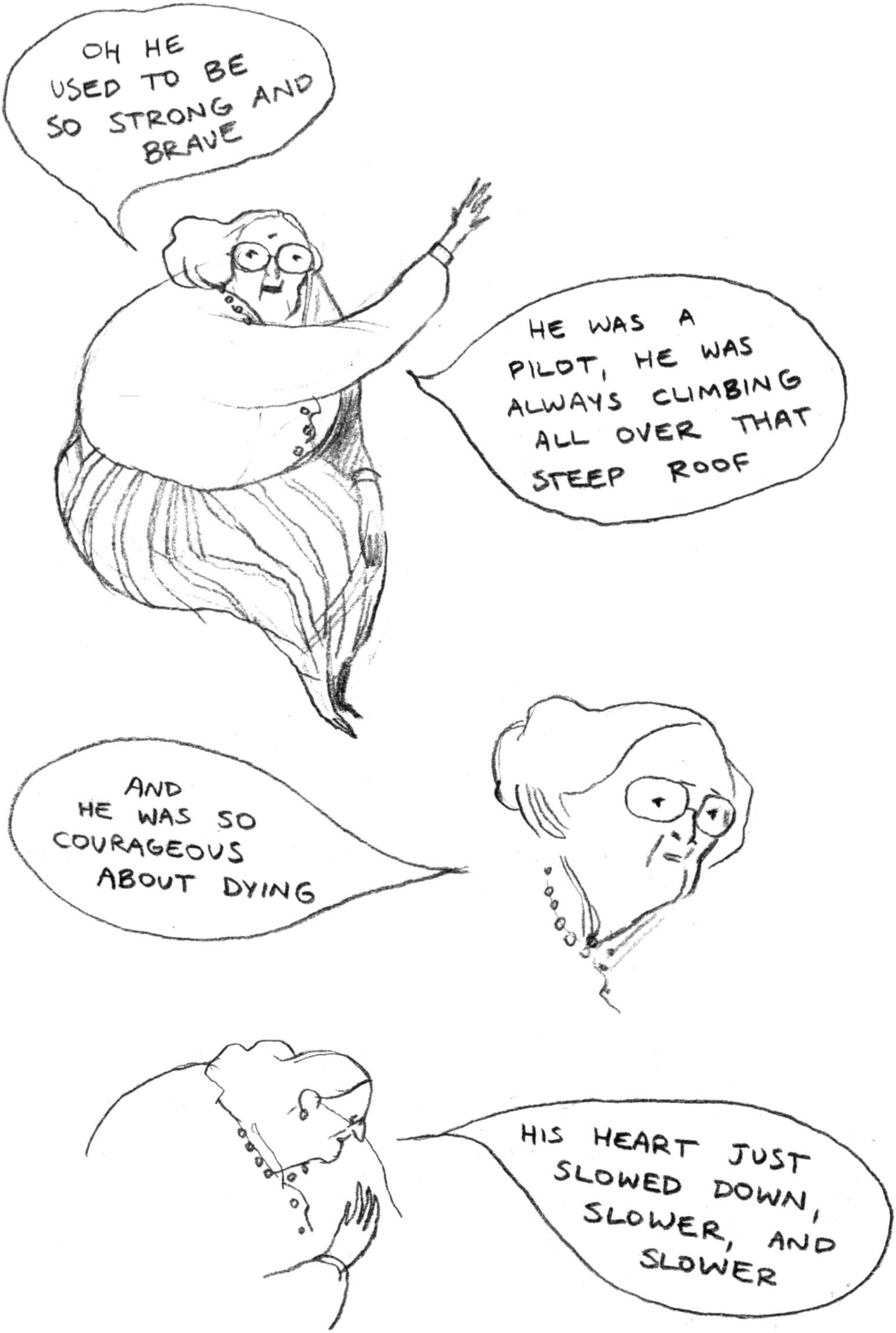
OH HE USED TO BE SO STRONG AND BRAVE
HE WAS A PILOT, HE WAS ALWAYS CLIMBING ALL OVER THAT STEEP ROOF
AND HE WAS SO COURAGEOUS ABOUT DYING
HIS HEART JUST SLOWED DOWN, SLOWER, AND SLOWER

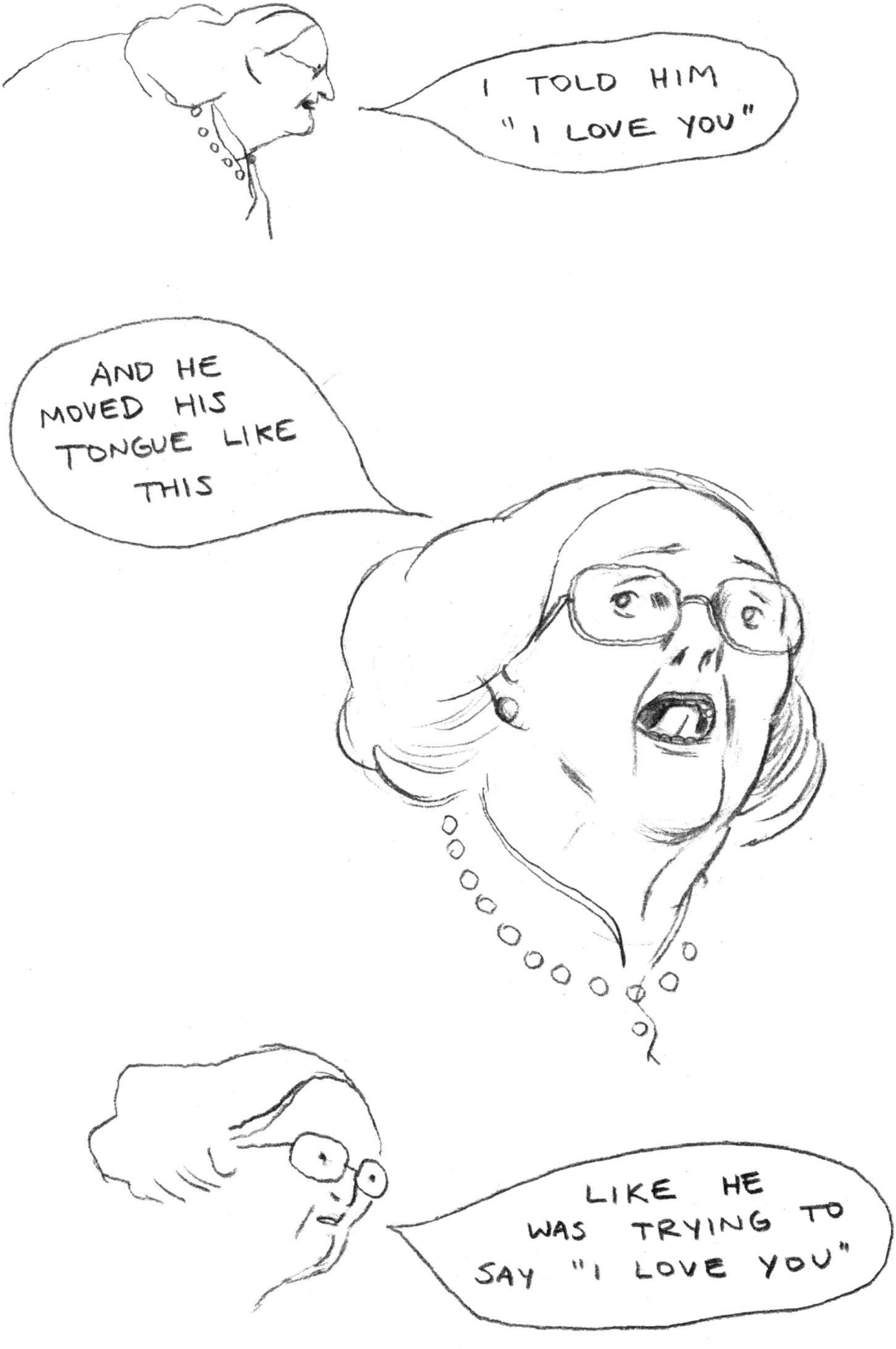
I TOLD HIM "I LOVE YOU"
AND HE MOVED HIS TONGUE LIKE THIS
LIKE HE WAS TRYING TO SAY "I LOVE YOU"

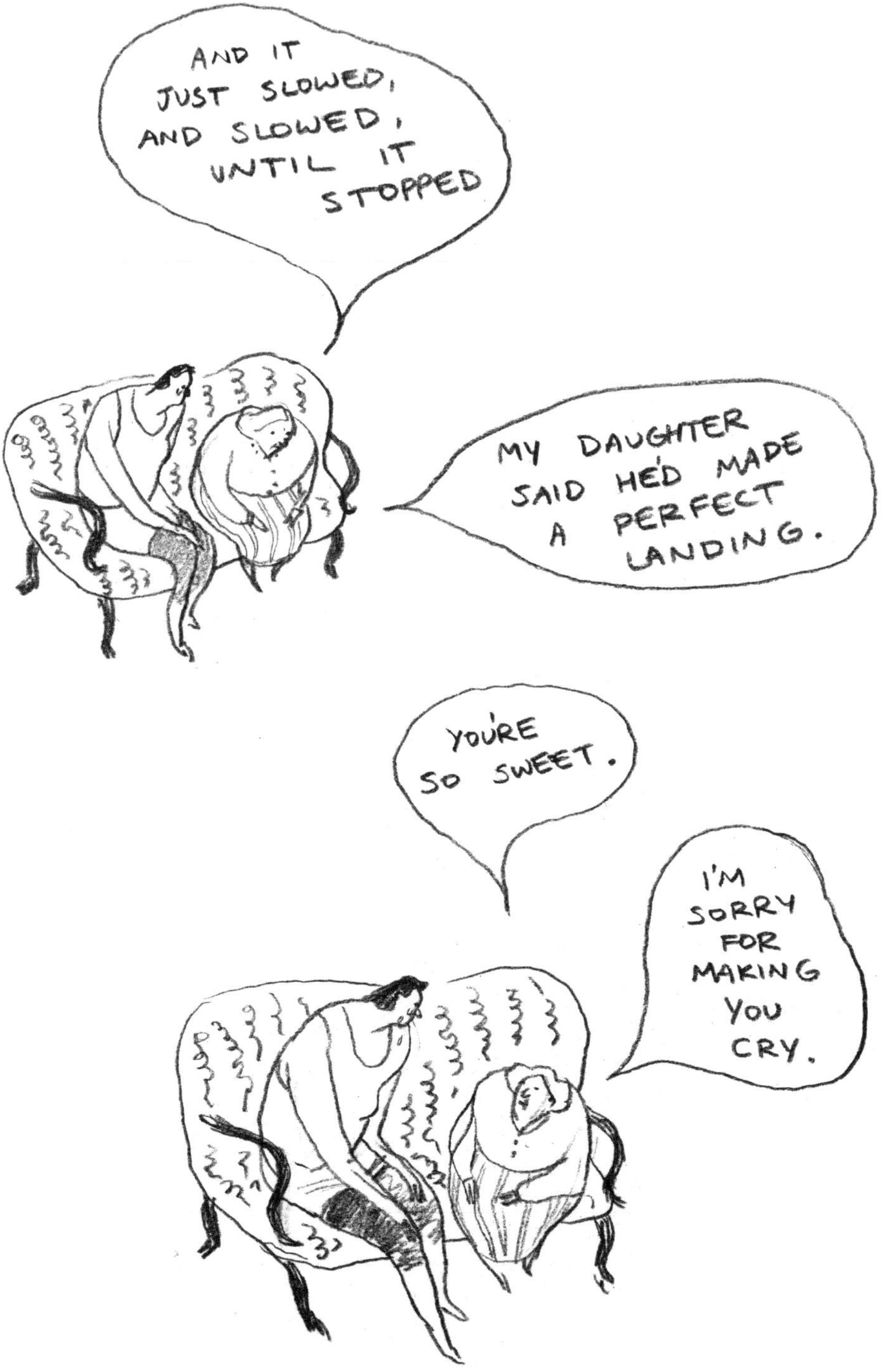
AND IT JUST SLOWED, AND SLOWED, UNTIL IT STOPPED
MY DAUGHTER SAID HE'D MADE A PERFECT LANDING.
YOU'RE SO SWEET.
I'M SORRY FOR MAKING YOU CRY.

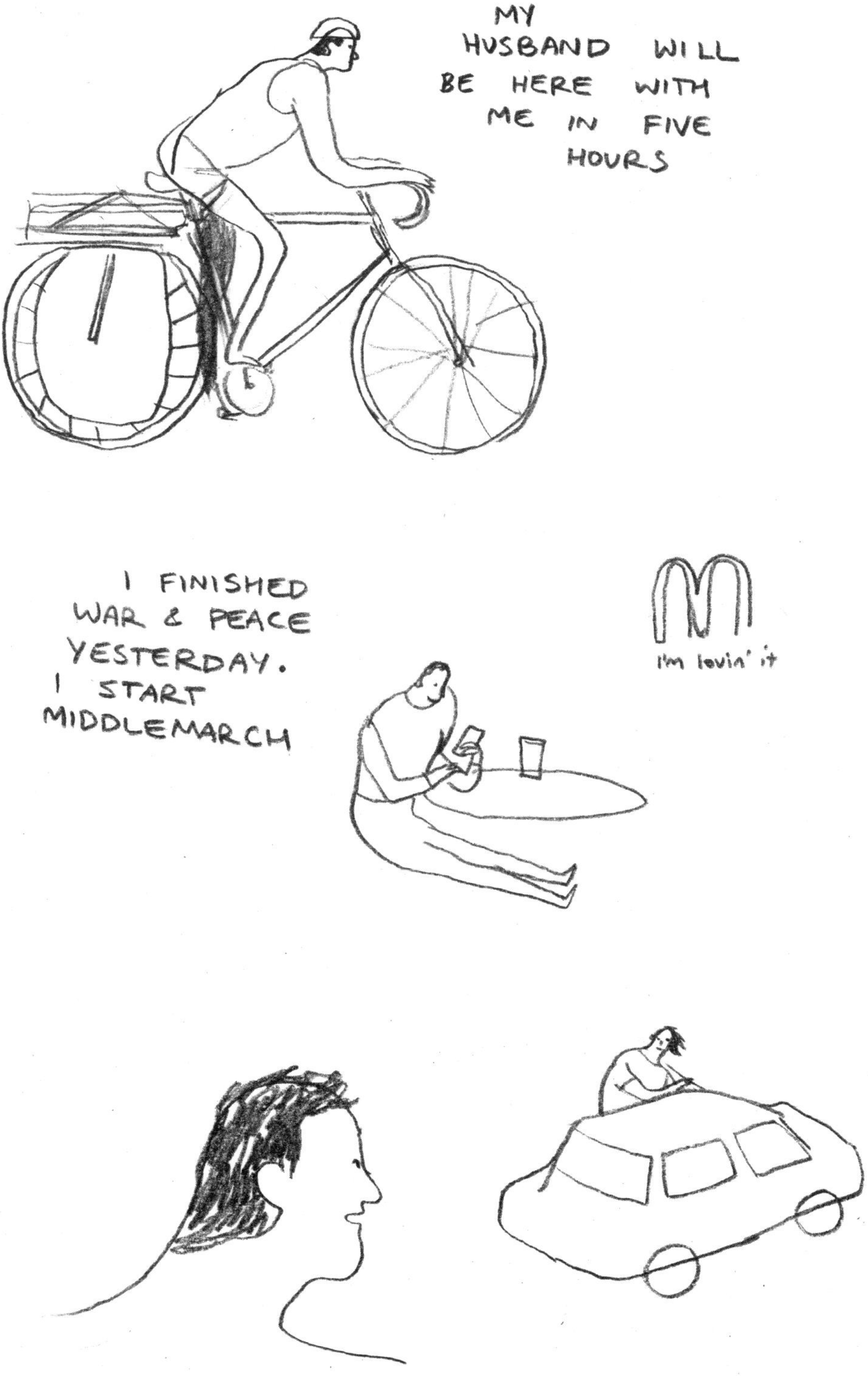
MY HUSBAND WILL BE HERE WITH ME IN FIVE HOURS
I FINISHED WAR & PEACE YESTERDAY. I START MIDDLEMARCH
I'm lovin' it

DAY 58 5/13

JACKSON, MS TO ATHENS, GA - 450 MILES

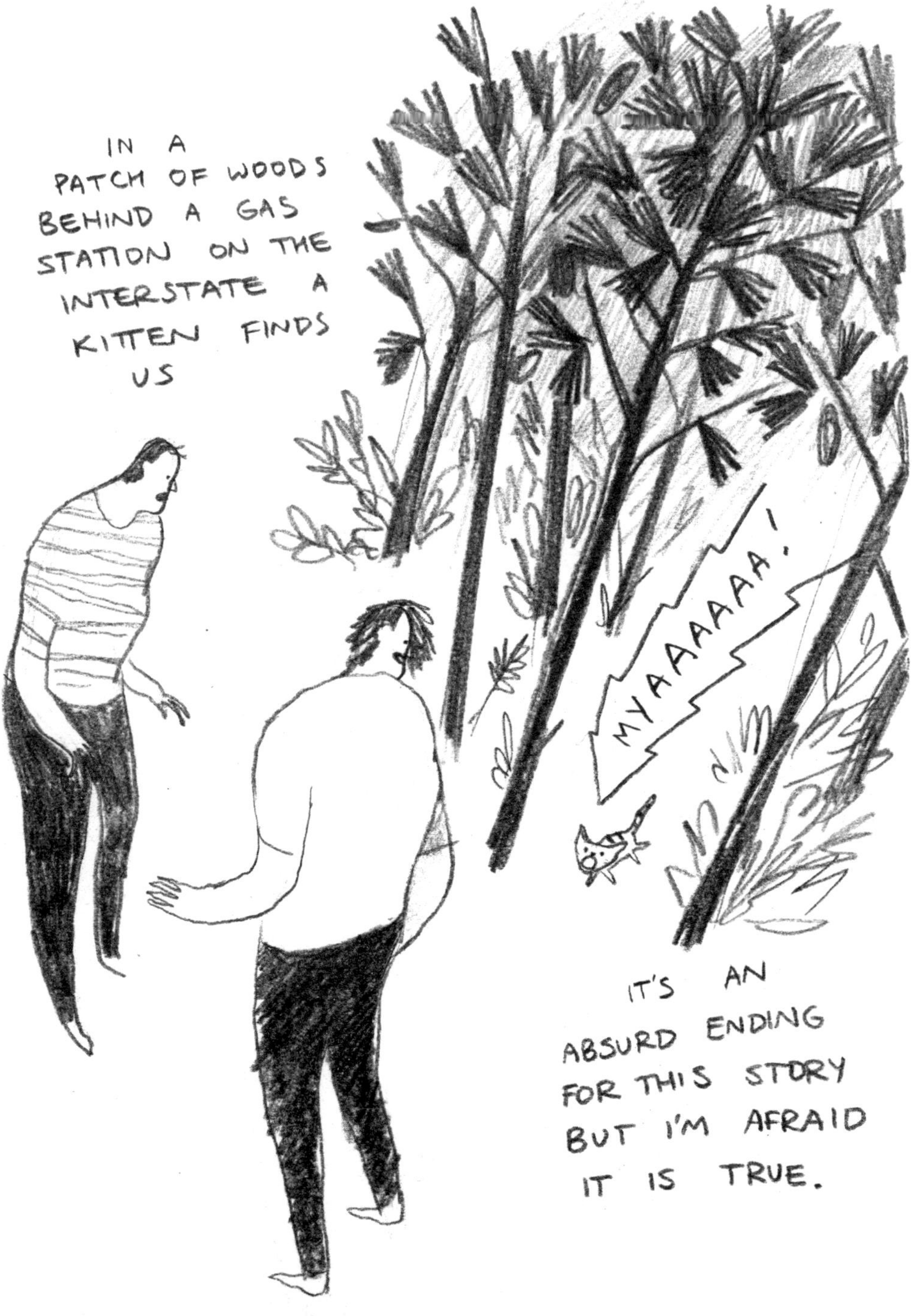
IN A PATCH OF WOODS BEHIND A GAS STATION ON THE INTERSTATE A KITTEN FINDS US
MYAAAAAA!
IT'S AN ABSURD ENDING FOR THIS STORY BUT I'M AFRAID IT IS TRUE.

THANK YOU

MY DAD,
WHO TAUGHT
ME TO RIDE
BIKES

KATE,
WHO BIKED
SOLO THROUGH
EUROPE

LAURA, WHO
BIKED SOLO
FROM GEORGIA TO
OREGON

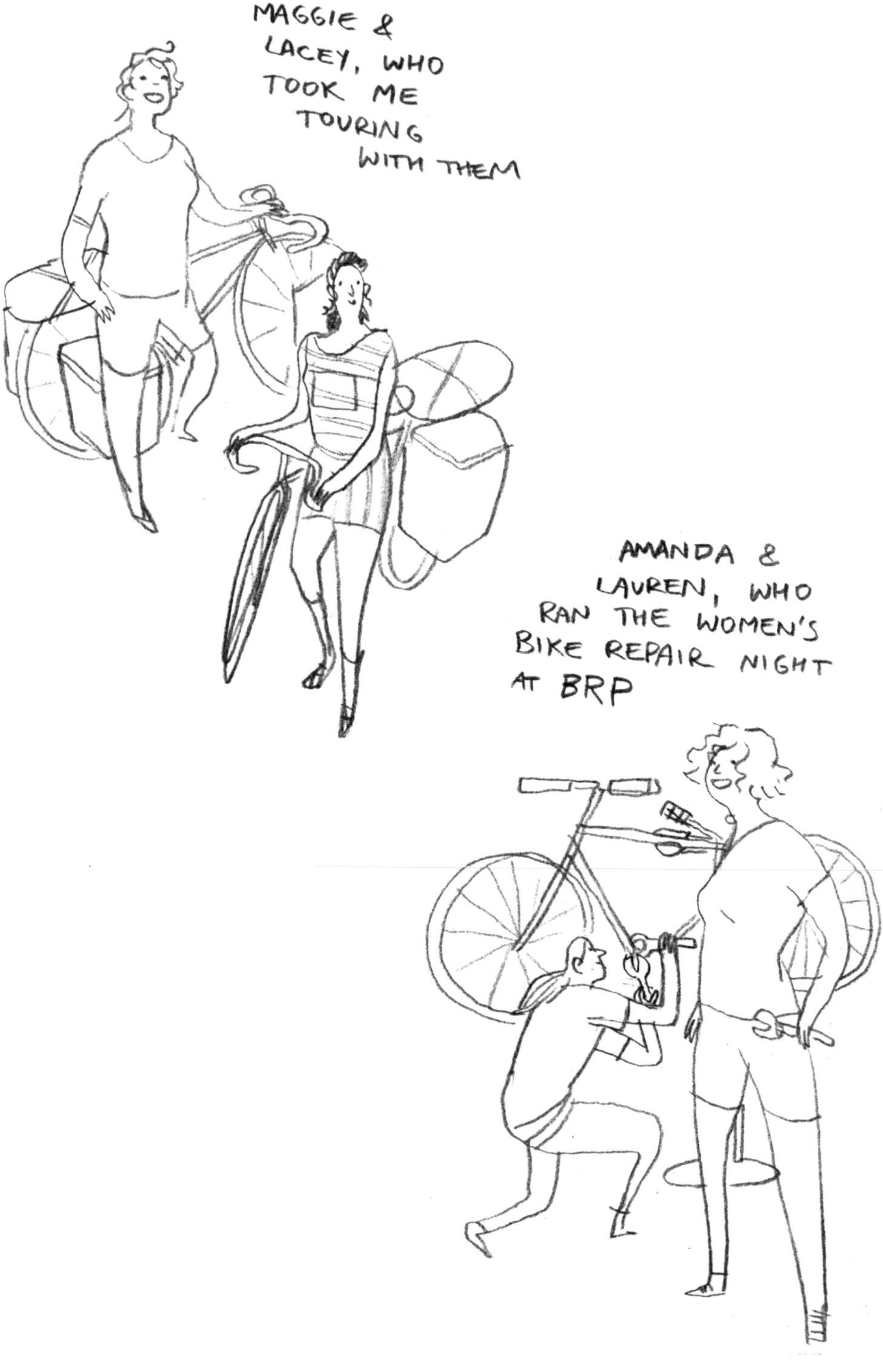
MAGGIE & LACEY, WHO TOOK ME TOURING WITH THEM
AMANDA & LAUREN, WHO RAN THE WOMEN'S BIKE REPAIR NIGHT AT BRP

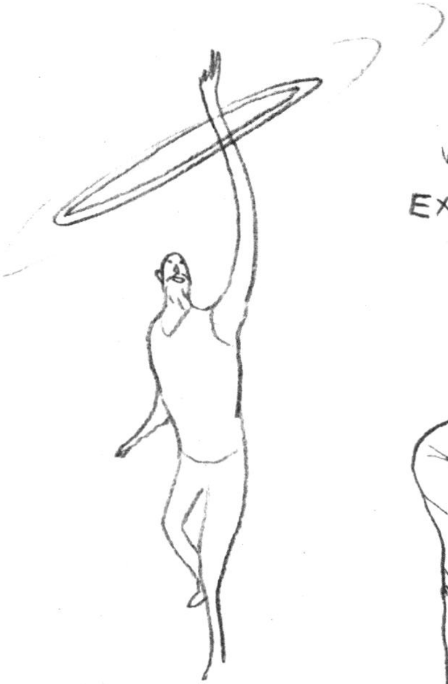

JOHN, AND
BRIAN AND GAIL,
WHO WERE SO
EXTRAORDINARILY GOOD
TO ME

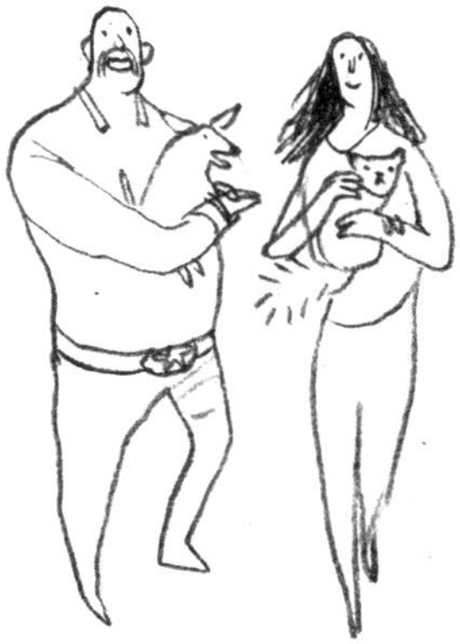

AND
EVERYONE
ELSE WHO
SHOWED ME
KINDNESS ON
THIS TRIP

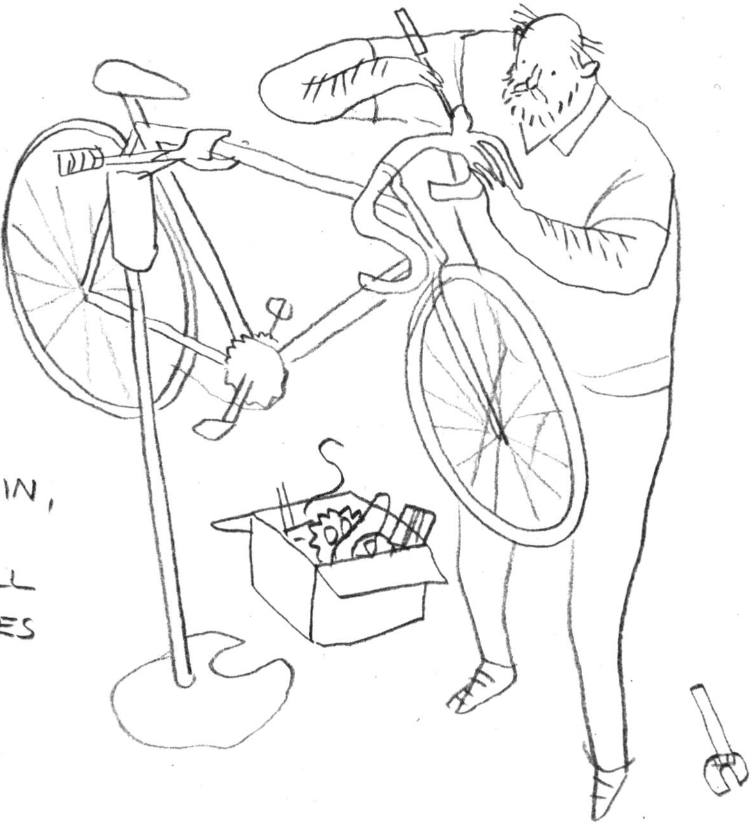

MY
DAD AGAIN,
WHO HAS
BUILT ALL
MY BIKES

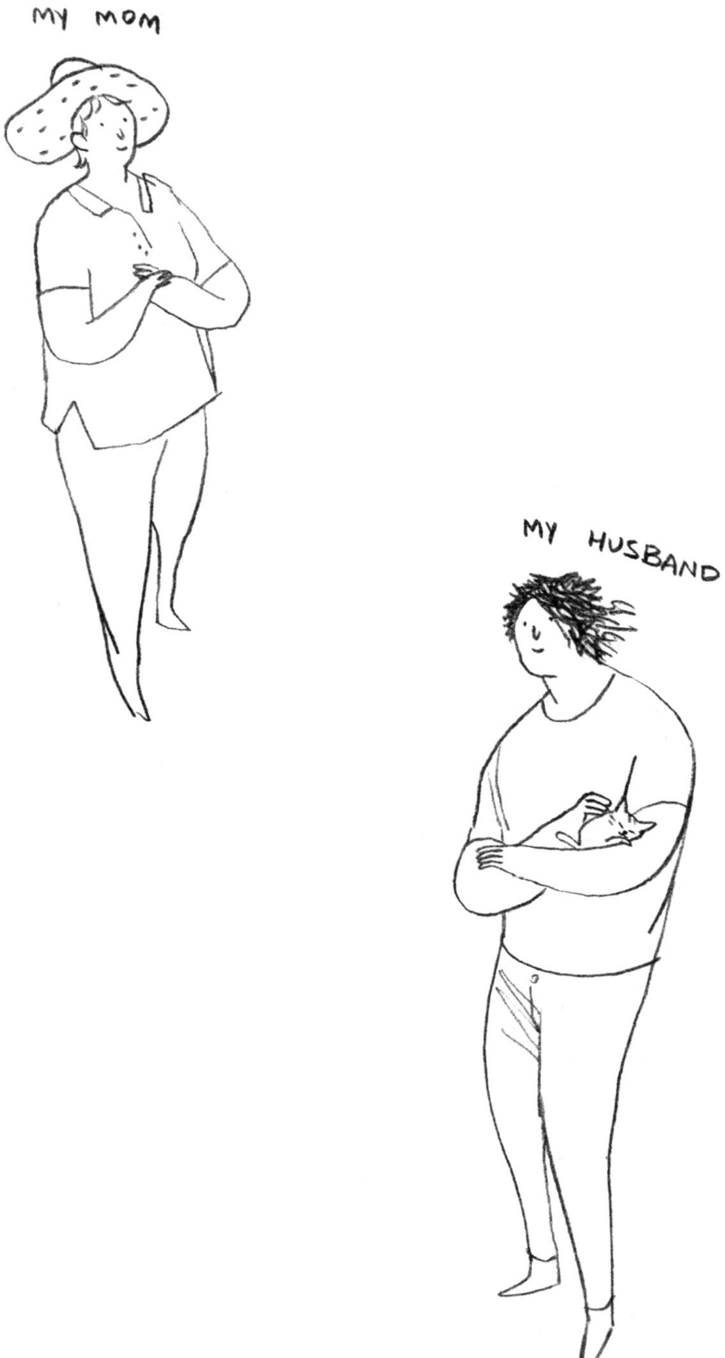
MY MOM
MY HUSBAND

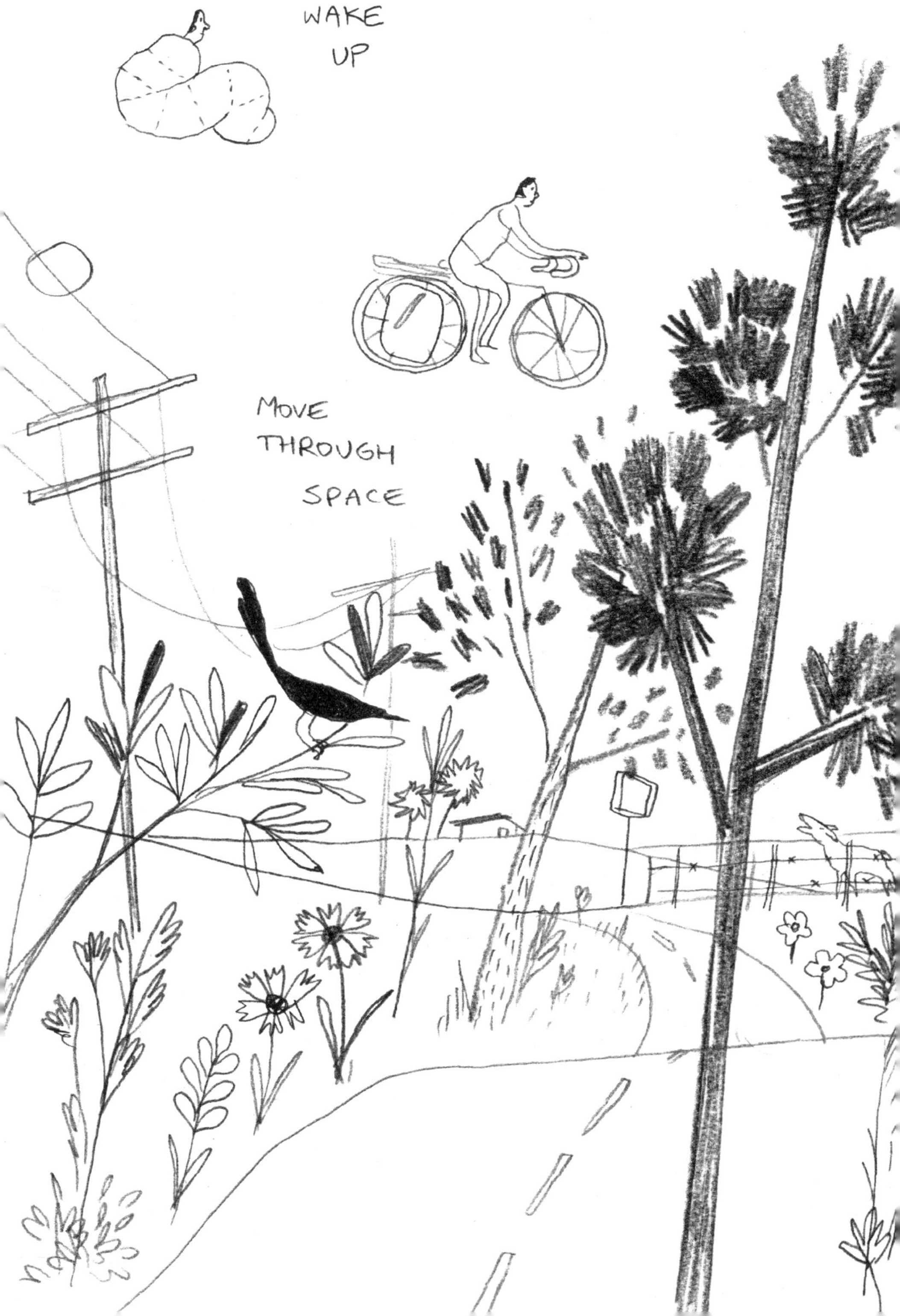
WAKE UP
MOVE THROUGH SPACE

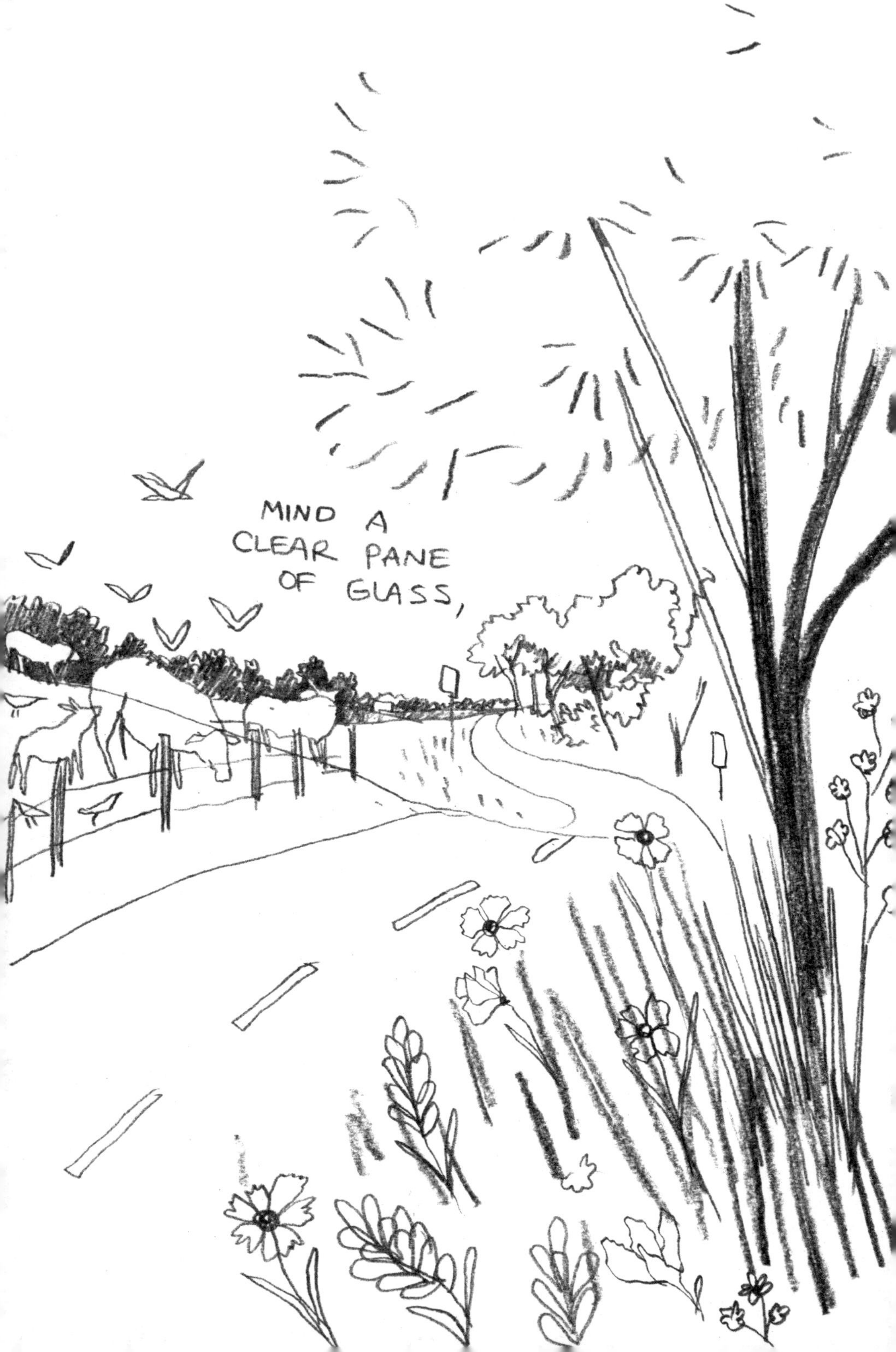
MIND A
CLEAR PANE
OF GLASS,

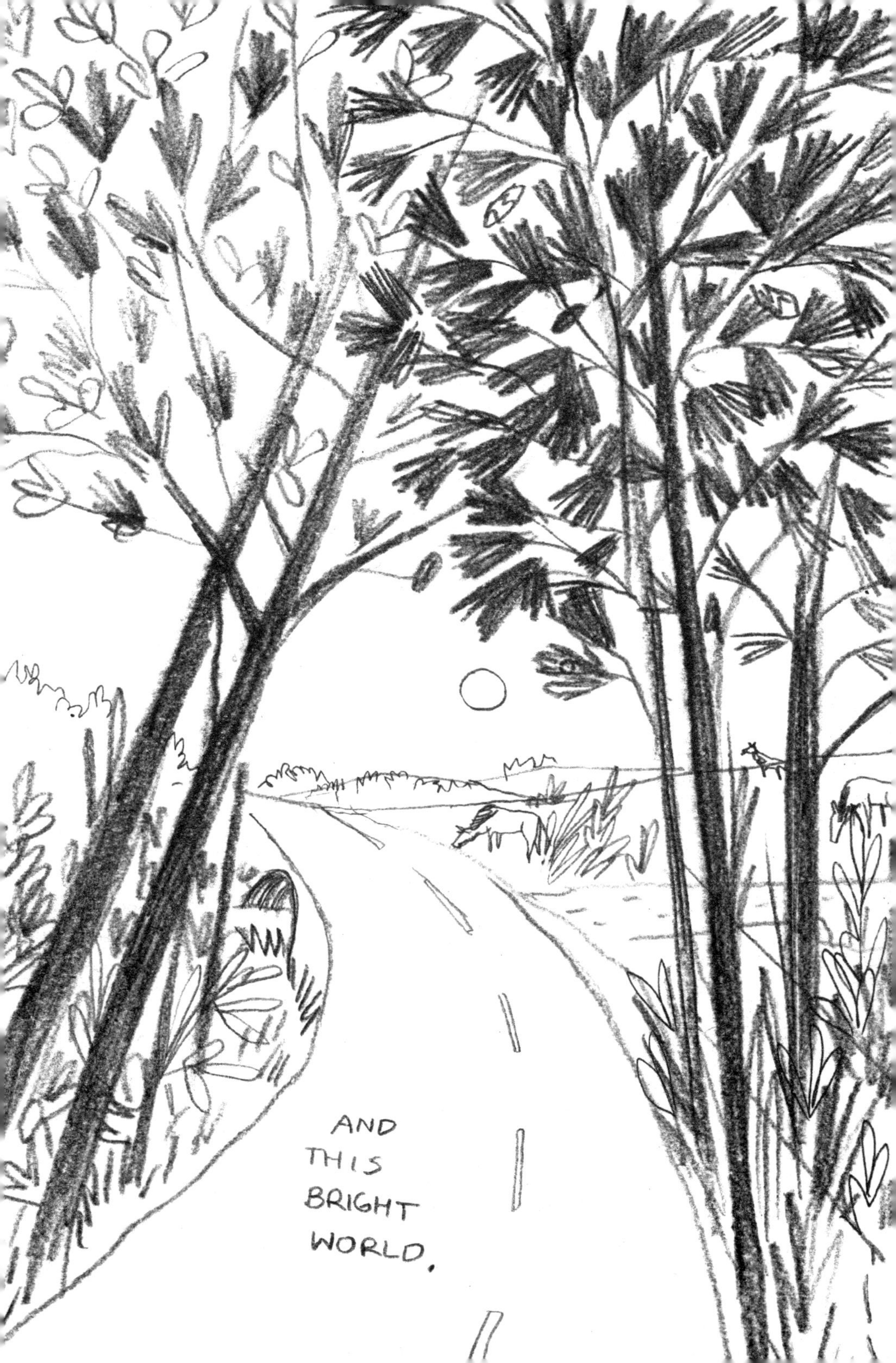
AND
THIS
BRIGHT
WORLD.

THE NATIONAL NETWORK FOR IMMIGRANT
AND REFUGEE RIGHTS & COALICIÓN DE
DERECHOS HUMANOS ARE TWO OF MANY
GROUPS ADVOCATING FOR IMMIGRANTS IN THE
UNITED STATES. YOU CAN GET INVOLVED
OR GIVE YOUR SUPPORT AT
NNIRR.ORG & DERECHOSHUMANOSAZ.ORG.

IF YOU ARE INTERESTED IN BIKE TOURING, YOU
CAN GET TONS OF TIPS FROM
CRAZYGUYONABIKE.COM & ADVENTURECYCLING.ORG.
ADVENTURE CYCLING SELLS WONDERFUL MAPS
THAT SHOW SAFE(ISH) ROUTES, ALONG WITH
INFO ABOUT CAMPGROUNDS, BIKE-FRIENDLY
R.V. PARKS, FOOD & WATER AVAILABILITY ETC.
FROM EL PASO TO BRACKETTVILLE & THEN FROM
AUSTIN TO DERIDDER I WAS ON THEIR
SOUTHERN TIER ROUTE.

GOING EXTREMELY LONG DISTANCES ON A BIKE
IS, GENERALLY, EASIER THAN WE TELL OURSELVES
IT WILL BE. BUT IT'S A BIG STRAIN ON YOUR
BODY. I'D DONE WEEK-LONG TOURS BEFORE &
BIKED 20-MILE DAYS ON THE REG, BUT THE
JUMP TO 50-MILE DAYS FOR MULTIPLE WEEKS
WAS TOO MUCH FOR ME. TRAIN BEFORE YOU GO,
AND IF YOU HAVE WEAK KNEES I HIGHLY
RECOMMEND STRENGTHENING EXERCISES!
LEARN FROM MY MISTAKES!

♡ELEANOR
JULY 2016